SENT OFF
AT GUNPOINT
THE WILLIE JOHNSTON STORY

SENT OFF
AT GUNPOINT
THE WILLIE JOHNSTON STORY

Tom Bullimore with Willie Johnston

Know The Score Books Limited
118 Alcester Road, Studley, Warwickshire, B80 7NT
Tel: 01527 454482   Fax: 01527 452183
info@knowthescorebooks.com
www.knowthescorebooks.com

A CIP catalogue record is available for this book from the British Library

ISBN: 978-1-84818-515-9

Printed and bound in Great Britain

by Athenaeum Press, Gateshead, Tyne & Wear

CONTENTS

FROM THE DICTIONARY OF
SCOTTISH SURNAMES

JOHNSTON: John, a 12th-century holder of Annandale lands under the Bruces, gave the name to his citadel or 'toun' from which his son took the surname de Johnston or Johnstone, the spelling indicating no real difference, though the 'e' is less frequent in the north than the south. A turbulent Border clan – hardly "the Gentle Johnstons" to their Maxwell and Douglas rivals – they were frequently appointed Wardens of the West March, hence their motto "Aye Ready".

Note: By coincidence the motto of Glasgow Rangers is "Aye Ready". It means: always ready.

ACKNOWLEDGEMENTS

Many people have helped in putting this exciting project together and I apologise if I have missed any names from the following list: Sir Alex Ferguson, John Greig MBE, Sandy Jardine, Alex McDonald, Colin Stein, Alex Smith, Alfie Conn and Gary Mackay. Johnny Giles, Ron Atkinson, Jim Smith and Tony Waiters. Len Cantello, Asa Hartford and Andy Cameron. Willie's mother, Cathy, who supplied her scrapbooks, which provided so much information. Willie's wife, Margaret, who remembered things Willie had long since forgot. Author and West Brom fan Simon Wright, Bobby Robertson, Jackie Watson and Bobby Grubb, Colin MacKenzie, who supplied playing statistics on Willie's career, and Rod Simpson, who spent many a late night sifting through all my material. Simon Lowe and his team at Know The Score Books, especially Ivan Ponting and Graham Hales deserve special mention. You all played your part in making the book possible – for that I give you my thanks.

Tom Bullimore
September 2008

PREFACE

It is now 30 years since the World Cup finals in Argentina. What took place there shocked a nation as the Scottish team fell at the first hurdle with a defeat at the hands of Peru and a draw against minnows Iran, leaving the previously buoyant Scots supporters desolate. But it was the events following the Peru game that would make more headlines than Argentina's victory in the World Cup final itself – Willie Johnston was sent home in disgrace after failing a drugs test. The press, who so often praised the darting winger's skills, turned against him and made life, for Willie and his family, a nightmare of such proportions that it almost drove him out of the game.

The 30th anniversary of the event brought several journalists to Willie's door seeking permission to write the unexpurgated story. Although Willie felt that the time was right to redress the situation, his mistrust of journalists would not allow him to take up any of their offers. Having been a friend of Willie's for a number of years, I discussed the issue with him on a number of occasions and eventually he proposed that I should take up the gauntlet and tell the true story, not only of Argentina but of his whole career.

It was a career that would see him win 22 caps for his nation, score two goals in a one-match European cup final (the only Scot ever to do so) and be red-carded 20 times.

Anyone meeting Willie for the first time would struggle to relate this mild-mannered, intriguing man with the fiery temper that has become legend in footballing circles.

This is Willie's own story, one that he tells in full for the first time. It is time to set the record straight.

Tom Bullimore
September 2008

FOREWORD
BY SIR ALEX FERGUSON

When I joined Rangers in 1967 Willie Johnston was a young, promising fledgling, full of energy, vitality and enthusiasm, blessed with lightning pace and a temper that was quicker than his feet. He was an absolutely likeable person with an endearing simplicity of life. Travel in those days was different, there were no motorway systems as today and, as I knew when I played at Dunfermline Athletic, it could be a long day back and forward from Glasgow. Such was the way of Willie's daily expedition to Ibrox Stadium and I always thought how refreshing it was to see Willie along with Billy Mathieson, Billy Lang, Billy McPhee and Davie Cairns, all aspiring young men from the Kingdom of Fife, commit themselves to their careers in football. I never knew them to miss that train that would bring them to Glasgow, but I'd bet they missed a few on their way back to Fife. Such is the way of a footballer once he mingles with his colleagues at the training ground.

Willie's rise was much quicker than his mates from Fife, simply because he was an extremely talented player. And even before I had the pleasure of playing with him he had already made his mark in the first team, playing in the 1966 Cup final against Celtic in a 1-0 win with the goal scored by the late Kai Johansen. Willie excelled that Wednesday night and posted his enormous potential in a way that caused Celtic's defence anxiety throughout the game. I was a spectator that evening, and being a Rangers fan, goodness me, I was excited that Rangers had this young talented lad.

When I joined Rangers I did so with enormous pride, being born only a mile from the stadium, and to play alongside a player of Willie's talent simply added to my pride. However, as in the way of all football careers, there are low points and when Willie broke his ankle playing against Berwick Rangers in that disastrous Scottish Cup tie which Rangers lost 0-1 it emphasised how fragile players can be. Fortunately he recovered in time to play in the Cup Winners Cup final against Bayern Munich, which Rangers also lost by the only goal. His career thereafter flourished as he became one of the most dangerous forwards in the game. His energy and courage were without question – you can't play for Rangers without these qualities – but add his ability to play on either wing or as a striker who could use both feet with equal power and accuracy, then you have a player of wonderful gifts.

Of course, it is difficult to talk about 'Bud' – as he was nicknamed after buying an overgrown fur coat reminiscent of the one Bud Flanagan wore on stage – without talking about his famous temper. I think I can talk about this aspect of his game with some first-hand experience as I was sent off eight times in my career. Sometimes losing your temper is justified if it's for the right reasons. On many occasions this applied to Willie when opponents gave him some rough treatment. Yet, as we know, those who retaliate get punished more severely than the aggressors. There were other times when that short fuse blew, and he faced the consequences of his actions more times than he would have liked. But I always believe that what you are you can't change, and there is no point in portraying his disciplinary record as a blip on an otherwise outstanding career. I played on the day he was sent off for the first time. It was against Hamilton Accies in a Scottish Cup tie. I could see the frustration in him build as he was fouled repeatedly, so I felt his discontent as much as anyone.

However, at the end of the day we are talking about a player who brought excitement to the game of football; a player, whose commitment was always total in a career lasting more than 20 years; a career that began with his great love, Rangers, before he moved to West Brom and then off to explore the other side of the world at Vancouver Whitecaps.

I think Willie has a fascinating story to tell. It's a story that will be colourful, honest and forthright, just as I would expect from Willie Johnston, and it is an honour to be asked to write the foreword.

Sir Alex Ferguson
September 2008

A SON OF FIFE

In January 1946 Emperor Hirohito of Japan announces he is not a god. In the same month, George W Bush, Donald Trump and Dolly Parton are born. In March, Britain agrees to India's right to independence, Sylvester Stallone and Cher are born. In July the United States drops an atom bomb on Bikini Atoll (the fourth atomic explosion). August sees George Orwell publish *Animal Farm*. On 19 December 1946 William McClure Johnston entered into this world, the midwife smacked his bottom – and he retaliated. A legend was born.

Although the first few years of his life were spent in Glasgow, the Johnston family moved to Cardenden, Fife, when Willie was just three years old. The 'Kingdom' of Fife is situated on the east coast of Scotland and is separated from the city of Dundee to the north by the River Tay, and Edinburgh to the south by the Firth of Forth. Fife is Scotland's third largest area with a resident population of just under 360,000. The historic town of St Andrews is located on Fife's east coast and is famous for its university and, of course, for being the home of golf. Fife probably takes its name from Fibh, a seventh-century Pictish warrior king. With the arrival of Willie, Fife was to become home to another warrior of a slightly different ilk.

Willie's father's move to Fife was very much a work-related one. Fife, at the time, was a county with a coal-mining heritage, and work was plentiful – if you were willing to venture down a shaft and risk your life in the darkest of places. His father took a job in Bowhill Colliery. The family became settled in Fife, and Willie, as he grew up, became very much a Fifer.

From a very early age his talent with a ball was evident, and his father encouraged him every step of the way. By the time Willie went to school the family had grown, with brothers Alan and Les, and sister Rosemary, expanding the Johnston clan. At school Willie was very much average academically – and he admits to having been just a bit of a rascal. He would avoid school at every opportunity, especially if he could earn a few bob collecting hips and haws (berries from wild rose bushes and the hawthorn tree) which were sold to local chemists for twopence (old money) per pound in weight. Then there was 'tattie howkin' (picking potatoes) in late October for seven shillings and sixpence a day (post decimalisation, that would be 37.5p). Or pinching the lead from derelict roofs, melting it down and selling it to the local ragman. These money-earning ventures did little for Willie's academic skills – but he didn't half enjoy himself.

Where he did excel, when he took the time to attend school, was on the sports field. He was a flying machine over 100 or 200 yards, good at the long jump and high jump; but he was exceptional at football. Willie would hone his skills in the same manner that the academic students would deal with algebra and geometry – by watching, learning and putting it all into practice.

He played for the school team and, later, the district schools and county schoolboys. He even played at adult amateur level before he was old enough to do so. Yet, he never achieved his first ambition – to represent Scotland at schoolboy level. How he was overlooked at this level remains a mystery, but perhaps it can be put down simply to the selection process at the time. There was a tendency to select the majority of boys who lived in the west of Scotland. At 14 he signed for the local youth team, Bowhill Strollers, who were run by Will Kerr. Will's passion for the game rubbed off on the young Willie. Mr Kerr was undoubtedly responsible for guiding and developing the talent that was there for all to see.

> *Willie remembers: I loved all sports at school; high jump, long jump and sprinting – but football was my real love. There was a gentleman from the village, Mr Kerr, who dedicated his life to helping youngsters develop their football skills. He ran Bowhill Strollers and Bowhill Colts. Often he used his own money to sponsor the teams and was totally dedicated to the development of any youngsters who wanted to take up the game. A number of his players would go on to achieve professional success and he convinced me that I could surpass them all – I needed no more encouragement than that. Mr Kerr knew his football and, by many in Fife, was considered the Alex Ferguson of his time.*

On leaving school Willie followed his father into the depths of the coal-mine, but he always remained focused on becoming a professional footballer.

Willie: Like many Fife boys I was destined to go down the pit on leaving school. As a 15-year-old I set out to attend Muircock Hall, near Dunfermline, on a 16-week course in mining. At the end of the course I was qualified to work underground. One week later I found myself as a miner in Bowhill Colliery. I will never forget the experience of my first trip underground. Only one thought dominated my mind and that was to get back to the surface as quickly as possible. I hated the pit and was resolved to get out of mining. I saw football as my tool to escape and threw my heart and soul into the game at every opportunity. Thankfully, the chance came along after five or six weeks. Several clubs were showing interest: Raith Rovers, Rangers and Manchester United. Having spent less than two months down a mine shaft, I said goodbye to mining for good and signed professionally for Glasgow Rangers.

In fact, Willie's blistering performances for Bowhill Strollers soon caught the attention of the local media, and scouts were on the scene to check out the youngster. Raith Rovers became the first professional club to make a move. They were so impressed with what they saw that they offered Willie reserve-team football at the age of 15. The Rovers were a top-flight team at the time and doing well. Willie decided to train with the Rovers, hold back on his decision on the offer and wait to see who else came along. For the first week or so all was quiet. Then, just like when waiting for a bus, four clubs came along together. Namely, Glasgow Rangers, Dunfermline, Manchester United and Leeds United. The manager of Dunfermline was Jock Stein and he was more than keen to lure the young Willie to East End Park. Willie then travelled through to Glasgow with his father. Scot Symon, the Rangers manager, put an offer on the table. Willie was honest with the Rangers boss and informed him that Manchester United had made an approach and wanted him to go to Old Trafford for a two-week stay. The stay would include a number of games behind closed doors. It was an opportunity Willie felt he could not turn down – especially as his dad was included in the all-expenses-paid trip. He left Ibrox with the promise to Scot Symon that he would not make a snap decision and sign for Manchester United, but would return home first to consider where his future lay.

The Manchester trip was a success. Willie played two trials behind closed doors and shone in both. Matt Busby duly offered a contract immediately. His dad, who was enjoying the all-expenses part of the trip, said: "You can do a lot worse than this, son!" But Willie would stick to his promise to return to Scotland to think things over. During his brief spell in

Manchester he felt homesick, missed his mum and couldn't understand the lingo! These thoughts would play a decisive part when Willie made his final decision. One evening, following his return to Fife, Willie and his father were invited to a Dunfermline European tie at East End Park by Andy Young. Andy had been involved with both Fife clubs Raith Rovers and Dunfermline, and acted as a scout for Leeds United. After the game Willie and his dad went back to Andy's house and were surprised to find a gentleman sitting in Andy's living room. The gentleman was Don Revie, manager of Leeds United. He wanted to take Willie to Elland Road. The offer to Willie was attractive – £40 a week, a house for his parents and a job for his father, but Willie again would not be drawn into a decision. Willie admits that to have such an array of prominent, influential managers (Jock Stein, Scot Symon, Matt Busby and Don Revie) all chasing his signature was quite daunting. However, he would not be rushed. Although he didn't know it at the time, the media would have a part to play in where his future lay.

One morning Willie travelled the short distance to Kirkcaldy to train with Raith Rovers. He was totally unaware of the headline that had appeared in a Scottish national newspaper that same morning: RANGERS LOSE RACE FOR STARLET. The story continued: "Manchester United have beaten Rangers in a race to sign a 15-year-old Scots soccer star. He is Billy Johnston of Cardenden, Fife, inside-forward of Bowhill Strollers, and he leaves next week to join the English club ..."

As Willie was getting stripped to join the Rovers players in training, one of the management team arrived in the dressing room, and on seeing Willie exclaimed: "What the f*** are you doing here?"

Willie was taken aback, and who wouldn't be? It was hardly the way to talk to a 15-year-old boy. He struggled to reply and eventually he answered: "I'm here to train."

"You've signed for Manchester United ... so pack your gear and f*** off!"

It was a somewhat upset and confused Willie who travelled back to Cardenden that evening. When his father asked him why he was home so early he had no option but to tell him the truth. Willie could tell by the look on his father's face that he was far from amused by the incident. Later that evening there was a knock on the door. Willie's father answered and found two officials from Raith Rovers standing on the doorstep. They were highly apologetic. "We realise the newspaper report was wrong ... we made a mistake ..."

"Oh, you're right you have ..." replied Willie's father and continued: "Now f*** off!" and slammed the door on them.

Willie: I had been down at Man United for a trial and had elected not to sign when offered a contract. I returned home to consider my two other options; Raith Rovers (my local team) and Rangers. I had been training with Raith and turned up as usual the night following my return from Manchester. I was met with a load of verbal abuse from the Raith management, which totally confused me. Apparently I had signed for Man United (unknown to me) and they were not amused. I was sent packing. I was only sixteen, confused and hurt by it all. I disappeared quickly from the ground that evening and my love for Raith disappeared with me.

A few days later Willie and his father travelled through to Glasgow to meet with Scot Symon. Willie had made his mind up – he had no desire to play down south. Matt Busby was disappointed but he probably got over it a week later when he signed another promising youngster for Manchester – a lad named George Best. Don Revie was also left disappointed and Raith Rovers had blown any chance they had of luring the youngster to Stark's Park. At Ibrox a deal was struck and Willie became a Rangers apprentice.

INTRODUCTION TO RANGERS
BY JOHN GREIG MBE

(John Greig played 755 times for Rangers, including a record 121 League Cup games and 64 games in the European Cup. He captained the club when they won the European Cup Winners' Cup, with Willie scoring two goals in the final, in 1972. He played 44 times for Scotland, 15 of them as captain. He won five Scottish League championship medals, six Scottish Cup winner's medals, four Scottish League Cup medals and was Scottish Footballer of the Year in 1966 and 1979. As manager he guided Rangers to win the Scottish Cup twice and the League Cup twice. His statue stands outside Ibrox Stadium as "the greatest Ranger of all time.")

Willie arrived at Glasgow Rangers as a 15-year-old and it soon became evident to all the established players, including myself, that there was something special in our midst. He was an outstanding talent and one of the best young players I had ever seen. He was two-footed and could strike a ball with either of them. He was also fast … oh, so fast. I soon got to know the young Willie Johnston better than most at Ibrox. He would travel through to Glasgow by train along with the other Fifers. Sandy Jardine and myself would link up with them at Edinburgh. I found him to be a quiet, unassuming young boy who would only come out of his shell when the conversation was about football.

When he broke into the first team he was still a young boy and it didn't surprise me that the Rangers fans took to him immediately. Players of his immense talent don't come along everyday. Before a game he would be very nervous, but once he was on the park he would fight with his granny! He had a bit of a temper, but this was always related to his desire to win – combined with the harsh treatment he would receive from opposing defenders.

A number of years later I would become manager of Rangers and would bring Willie back to the club from Vancouver Whitecaps. My reasoning was simple: he was still one of the best wingers in the world and I knew he would do a great job for me back at Ibrox where his career began. I wasn't disappointed; he turned on the style whenever required to do so.

I hold him in the highest regard as both a person and a player, and to this day I rate him as one of the greatest players ever to pull on the blue jersey of Rangers Football Club.

2

BEING A BOY IN BLUE

On signing for Rangers Willie was immediately farmed out to Lochore Welfare, a Fife junior team. Willie may have felt that he had walked a long road and found himself back at the beginning again. He may have been back in Fife – but he was now going to play at a level of football he had yet to encounter. For those not acquainted with the Scottish junior game this is not a league for youngsters, as the name might imply. Boys who play in this league have to become men very quickly. This is a league of mainly 20 to 35-year-olds, many of whom have not made it into the senior ranks or have retired from senior football and wish to continue playing. This is as tough as it comes and Willie was only 15 years old. But Scot Symon felt (knew!) that the boy would do well and he was not to be disappointed.

Although he was playing for Lochore, Willie was, in every sense of the word, a Rangers player and, naturally, some of his time was to be spent at Ibrox. Here he had his first taste of the regimented discipline that exists at that great club. The manager, Scot Symon, was God and the first-team players were addressed as Mr Caldow, Mr Shearer, Mr Baxter etc. Willie recalls the first time he met the master, Jim Baxter. He had taken the opportunity to walk up the Ibrox tunnel for the first time, and looked on in awe at the vastness of the stadium. A number of first-team players were knocking balls around and generally doing their own thing. The young Willie recognised the majority of them but his eyes were trained on one man in particular – Jim Baxter. Willie looked on in awe as Baxter demonstrated his skills. Eventually Baxter turned and approached Willie. "Are you the wee boy from Cardenden?" asked the great wing-half. "Yes," replied a hesitant Willie.

Baxter smiled, put his arm around Willie's shoulder, and led him on to the pitch. "Come on, I'll show you what football's all about, son." Baxter led Willie towards the closest goalmouth. While they walked, other first-team players ignored the pair and continued to knock balls about nonchalantly. Slim Jim reached the 18-yard line and placed a ball down. As he did so, players like Ronnie McKinnon, Bobby Shearer and Jimmy Millar drifted towards Willie and Baxter – they knew what was coming.

"What I want you to do," said Jim, "is take a shot and hit the bar."

"Hit the bar? I can score every time!" exclaimed Willie.

Baxter smiled: "We can all score every time!" he replied. "Now hit the bar."

Willie had a number of attempts and failed. Baxter then took over. He had three attempts with his left foot and on each occasion hit the bar. Baxter then turned to his onlooking team-mates and asked: "Any bets on my right foot?" Baxter, unknown to Willie, had already bet his colleagues on his left-foot accuracy, although now on his weaker foot (if he had one) there were no takers. Baxter then repeated the exercise with his right foot and hit two out of three. Willie knew he was standing in the presence of a genius – something that he believes to this day.

Willie would play junior football at the weekend and return to Ibrox during the week to train and carry out all the mundane tasks that all the apprentices had to do – domestic cleaning, painting, scrubbing and polishing first-team players' boots. At break times Willie enjoyed going to the recreation room where he would play table tennis. On one occasion he was playing a game against Billy Semple, another apprentice. The score between them was 19-19 when several first-team players entered the room including Jim Baxter, Jimmy Millar and Ralph Brand. The rule was quite simple – if first-team players entered the apprentices had to stop what they were doing and sit down. First-team players had priority and Ralph Brand told them to put the bats down. Willie turned towards Ralph and pleaded: "Oh, come on … it's 19-19. Let us finish the game!"

"Put the bats down!" demanded Brand.

Willie threw the bat on the table but held on to the table tennis ball. Ralph Brand asked for the ball but Willie dropped it and crushed it with his foot and made to exit. Jim Baxter got a hold of Willie. Jim had a liking for his fellow Fifer, and was well aware that he was a talented youngster, but he had to abide by the rules.

"Why did you do that?" asked Jim.

"Because I'm better than him!" exclaimed Willie.

"You've never played him at table tennis," said Slim Jim.

"I'm talking about football" replied Willie, before storming off.

Ralph Brand was a player of the highest order. He had been capped eight times for Scotland, had scored a total of 206 goals for Rangers in 317 games – a bit above apprentice level. What they had witnessed of Willie was his unmistakable self-beliefand a glimpse of the temperament yet to come.

Tragically Willie's dad died in a car crash while he was still an apprentice and it saddens him to this day that his father didn't get the chance to see him play for Rangers or Scotland.

Willie: My father was killed in a car crash shortly after I signed for Rangers. I have always carried a certain amount of guilt surrounding his death – I gave him the money to buy the car from my signing-on fee when I joined Rangers. To this day I have never taken driving lessons and have no desire to ever get behind a wheel. I won't even drive a golf cart when on the golf course. My father was a great influence on my football career and it hurts me that he never got to see me make my debut for Rangers or Scotland.

Not long after his father's death in February 1964, Willie was called up by Rangers to play in the reserves and was an immediate success. The media were hailing him as another Willie Henderson* while others were saying that he was one of Scot Symon's finest signings.

The young Colts were on fire and only needed a victory against Dunfermline reserves to secure the league title. They did not disappoint. The first goal came in the 48th minute when Jim Forrest finished off a move between Willie Johnston and Alex Willoughby. Alex headed home the second in 53 minutes. Bobby Watson added a third two minutes later. Then came the wonder goal – an angled left-footed 20-yard shot from Willie which smashed into the net to make it four. Dunfermline pulled one back before the end but the Colts were deservedly the champions and in the press Willie was being hailed as an inside-forward who was certain to gain international distinction. The 1963/64 season finished with Willie adding another medal to his collection when the Colts won the Second XI Cup.

*Willie Henderson was two years older than the young Willie Johnston. He broke into the first team at 16 years old and was already a Scottish international when only 17 years old. Although still a boy he had claimed the right-wing position as his own.

3

A STAR IS BORN

Willie's thoughts now turned to season 1964/65. At 16 years of age he wanted to retain his place in the reserves and perhaps win a few more medals. That was his desire, his dream. But most dreams seldom come to fruition.

The season was only a few weeks old when Willie had a shocker of a game for the reserves. He tried to redeem himself by training exceptionally hard, in a bid to impress. On the day before the next match, Willie studied the reserve team sheet, and his name was missing. His heart sank, and he had a feeling of nausea. The name Willie Johnston didn't appear on the third-team sheet either, and visions of Lochore Welfare bombarded his mind. His eyes took a quick glance at the first-team sheet, and he did a double take – his name occupied the outside-left berth. It turned out that regular outside-right Willie Henderson was injured. The regular outside-left, Davie Wilson, was switched to the right and Willie would make his debut for Rangers at on the left flank. He was about to play alongside Davie Wilson, Ralph Brand and the great Jim Baxter. One minute he had been feeling demoralised, the next minute he felt euphoric.

On the day of the match, manager Scot Symon took Willie aside for a long chat. His objective was simple, he wanted to make Willie as calm as possible. He emphasised the fact that the rookie should simply go out and enjoy the experience. Willie smiled, nodded and probably didn't take in a word that the manager had said. He was about to make his debut for the famous Glasgow Rangers, wearing a pair of boots that he borrowed from the injured Willie Henderson, because his own were falling apart.

As the young Willie ran out on to Ibrox Park to face St Johnstone, he felt no element of calmness at all. His nerves were jingling and his heart was thumping. At which point during the match the nervousness disappeared, he doesn't recall. And certainly the Ibrox faithful witnessed no signs of nerves from the youngster, as the left flank of Baxter, Brand and Johnston ripped the visitors apart. The game turned out to be an easy 3-1 victory for Rangers with scoring machine Jim Forrest collecting all three goals. Willie's contribution was impressive, and he recalls his only disappointment was that he did not pull on the light-blue jersey that day. Rangers had played in their change strip.

Two weeks later Hibs were the visitors to Ibrox. They had beaten the great Real Madrid in midweek and naturally felt that they could get a result in Glasgow. Rangers were carrying injuries and would be taking the park without the presence of Caldow, Wilson and Henderson. A great excuse, if one was needed at the close of play. Yet, on paper, it was far from a weak team that would face the Hibees. Rangers lined up: Ritchie, Shearer, Provan, Greig, McKinnon, Baxter, Watson, Millar, Forrest, Brand, Johnston.

Willie wasn't quite so nervous, but far from calm, as the game got under way. He found himself in the thick of the action from the kick-off and looked impressive. Then eight minutes into the game all his Christmases came at once – he scored with a beautiful header. The Ibrox fans went wild and knew they had another great player in the making at the club.

But the Hibs would not be outdone. Young Peter Cormack was also having a great game for his club and he equalised on 42 minutes. The second half saw the match start in the same fashion as the first. It was end-to-end stuff. Then in the 52nd minute up popped the young Willie to score again with another good header and put Rangers back in the driving seat. Ibrox erupted and hundreds of youths invaded the pitch from all angles, many of them reaching Willie to congratulate him. It took several minutes for normality to be restored and the pitch to be cleared of fans. Willie was clearly shaken by the ordeal, as were several more experienced Rangers players. When the game restarted Hibs were the team to take command of the game and ran out the eventual 2-4 winners. Despite the final result everyone at the club was talking about the young Willie Johnston. He had thrown down the gauntlet to all the left-sided players at Ibrox; none of them would be guaranteed a regular game when he was around.

Willie: After training on the Friday I checked the thirds and reserve teamsheets for the following day, and my name was on neither. If your name wasn't on any of these sheets then you had to report to Ibrox along with all other players on the day of the match. Jim Baxter was giving me a lift back to Fife after training on the Friday and asked me what I was doing the following day. I told him I had no desire to turn up to watch the first team and would probably watch my local junior team, Lochore Welfare, play on the Saturday. Baxter advised me that I should make the trip with him to Ibrox. On the way home Jim stopped at the Daily Record offices and disappeared for ten minutes. He never told me what he had been up to, but it became apparent when I looked at football headlines in the Record the following morning: 17-YEAR-OLD WILLIE JOHNSTON TO MAKE HIS DEBUT AT IBROX TODAY. Baxter knew I was to play and had never said a word.

In the dressing room prior to the match against St Johnstone I was so nervous that I was violently sick a number of times. All my team-mates that day worked hard to calm me down, Jim Baxter in particular became the major calming influence. Eventually I pulled myself together, thought of my father and knew that I had to go out and play well for him. Strangely I have limited memory of the match itself. I played down the left with Baxter, which was an honour in itself. I knew I had played well and created two of the three goals scored by us in a 3-1 victory. Pre-match nerves would become a thing of the past.

It was shortly after the game with Hibs that Willie was to experience a slight name-change. He turned up for a match sporting a long fur coat. John Greig was the first to spot him and exclaimed to the rest of the squad: "Look who's here ... Bud Flanagan!" Bud Flanagan was a member of The Crazy Gang, a well-known comic variety act who had been performing together since the 1930s. Bud Flanagan's trademark was a long fur coat down to his ankles and a stupid hat. Willie claims that he wasn't wearing the hat but could not deny the coat – although it wasn't quite to his ankles (on tall men like John Greig and Ron Mckinnon it would have probably been a blazer). The name Bud stuck and was to be with him for the rest of his playing career and beyond.

Willie: I liked the name Bud. it was different and having a nickname at football was a sign that you had made it. Many people even today refer to me as Bud – although, during my playing days the fans would occasionally call me by other names and some of them were far from complimentary.

Having now played in four first-team games Willie had the feeling of belonging. But he wasn't naive enough to think he had made it. Ibrox was full of good players, many of them far more experienced than the young Fifer. Consistency in performance was the key and Willie would strive to achieve it. In his next game it would be very important to keep that consistency going. Scot Symon informed Willie that he would play in the League Cup final.

Several firsts would come for Willie on the big day: his first cup-tie, his first final, his first game at Hampden and his first Old Firm outing. It would also be the last time he would ever experience pre-match nerves in his career.

The crowd numbered 91,423 that day. It was little wonder that he would have no more pre-match nerves – his nervous system probably disintegrated as he ran out on to the park. It was a match full of skill, flair and continual excitement. Jim Baxter gave an inspirational performance in a 2-1 victory. Young Willie delighted the crowd with a great display on the left wing, and who could blame him for smiling from ear to ear as he collected his first League Cup winner's medal – after all it was only his fifth senior game!

> Willie: Prior to the match Jim Baxter, who was captain on the day, took me aside and had a long conversation with me. He praised my style of play, ensured me that I would destroy their defence, told me to enjoy the day and treat the whole experience like a training session. By the time I went on the park I felt ten feet tall and had no fear of the opposition. With Baxter supplying the passes I repeatedly destroyed the Celtic full-back, Ian Young, and we eventually went on to lift the Cup. As I stepped up to receive my medal that day I had a tear in my eye and my thoughts turned to my father – he would have been so proud.

The team that had won the League Cup were on a bonus of £500 following the victory. To Willie £500 was a small fortune. The bonus would be paid out the following week at Ibrox. The prospect of so much money excited Willie, and he promised all his mates back in Cardenden a real good night out. The day of the payouts arrived and, as was the Ibrox custom, the players were individually summoned to Scot Symon's office, where they were handed a brown envelope containing the bonus. When it was Willie's turn he rushed up the stairs and stood outside the great man's door. A red light was visible above the door. Willie pressed the buzzer and when the light turned to green he entered. Scot Symon sat in his chair like a king (which, of course, he was). Willie was invited to sit. Scot Symon leaned forward and handed Willie a brown envelope. Willie took the envelope and thanked him.

"Willie, you have a great future here," said Symon, before leaning over his desk and gently patting Willie on the shoulders, then on the cheeks. Then he continued: "Stay away from Jim Baxter".

Willie thought he knew what was meant by the reference to Baxter. Slim Jim, despite the great player that he was, had several flaws. To put it mildly, away from the game he liked to enjoy a good time. Willie nodded that he had taken the manager's words on board. Scot Symon smiled, and Willie knew at this point that he was dismissed. He thanked Mr Symon and left. As he headed back down the stairway he hurriedly opened the envelope to find it contained only £50. At first he was shocked. Where was the other £450? At the bottom of the stairwell he approached Baxter. "Jim," said Willie, "there's been a mistake. There's only £50 in my envelope!"

"Don't let him away with it!" replied Jim. "Get back up those stairs and tell him you want the full bonus!" Willie turned and rushed back up the stairs. Outside the office, he hesitated momentarily before pushing the buzzer. The light turned to green and Willie entered. Scot Symon invited him to sit and Willie started to speak as he did so.

"There's been a mistake, Sir," said Willie. "there's only £50 in my envelope ... " "Willie ... Willie ... " said Symon, " ... you're a very talented young lad who will become a great player. But too much money can turn a boy's head. It's my job to make sure that doesn't happen and to keep your feet firmly on the ground." Symon then leaned over his desk, once more patted Willie on the shoulders, then the cheeks, and continued: "And stay away from Jim Baxter!"

Willie left the office both bewildered and deflated. The only thing he knew for certain was that he would have to avoid his mates in Cardenden – but he didn't avoid Jim Baxter. At the bottom of the stairwell he met Slim Jim and explained what had happened. Baxter put his arm around Willie's shoulder and said: "Never mind Willie ... your day will come. Come on – I'll take you with me to St Enoch's Hotel and we'll have a few drinks".

Jim Baxter had a reputation for being rebellious, and inviting Willie to do the same was all part of his make-up. Willie, at least on this occasion, was smart enough to have only two lagers that day. He sensed that, although away from Ibrox, all the customers in the hotel would recognise Jim and some might even recognise him. The one thing he didn't want was any negative reports getting back to the club and Scot Symon in particular. Of course, there was another reason why Willie only had two drinks that day – he was only 17 years old!

Willie: Jim Baxter on the park was a total genius, a one-off and undoubtedly world class. He could read a game better than any other player and could pass a ball and land it on a penny. But, like most players with genius, he had flaws. Outside football he had three loves – the ladies, gambling and alcohol. The latter would eventually take its toll on his body and his playing career would be cut short at the age of 29. Scotland will never see a player of his ilk again.

As if being called into the first team and winning a League Cup medal weren't enough firsts for a 17-year-old footballer, another two were to come his way. He would play his first European Cup tie and make his debut for Scotland's youth team.

In September 1964 Rangers had been drawn against Red Star Belgrade in the first round of the European Cup. Rangers won the first leg 3-1 at Ibrox but were beaten 4-2 in Belgrade, making the aggregate score 5-5. In those days away goals afforded no extra advantage so a play-off was arranged to take place at Arsenal's Highbury stadium. Willie hadn't been selected to play in either game. Symon had elected to go for experience. For the play-off, though, Willie found himself part of the squad. On the evening of the match he was informed that he had been selected to make his European debut. Prior to the match he followed Jim Baxter outside Highbury.

Willie was in awe of Baxter and admits that in his early days he tailed him everywhere like a collie dog. Baxter was Rangers superstar; he had been the fifth Beatle before the Beatles existed! He found Baxter standing on the steps of Highbury talking to Sean Connery, who had just finished making the film *Goldfinger*, and was now busy discussing golf with Slim Jim. Willie sidled close to Jim Baxter and stood in awe as they arranged to play golf together. Willie felt he was standing alongside two superstars and had thoughts that someday he might become a superstar himself. He stood and listened in amazement for several minutes. Eventually he tugged on Jim's arm and whispered: "Introduce me to Sean, Jim". Baxter ignored Willie and simply continued his conversation. Willie tugged again and repeated his request. Again Baxter ignored him. Frustrated, Willie tugged harder and repeated: "Introduce me to Sean, Jim!". Baxter turned his head slightly, smiled and said: "Willie, f*** off!" An embarrassed Willie "f***ed off" back into Highbury.

In the dressing room he soon put the Sean Connery encounter out of his mind. His first European game was upon him and nothing else entered his thoughts as he prepared for the big event. Rangers were victorious that evening, winning the play-off 3-1 with goals from Jim Forrest (two) and Ralph Brand. Willie had a fine European debut and took another step towards making the left-wing position his own.

Things were coming together nicely and he continued to find himself in the first team. In December Rangers played Rapid Vienna in the Prater Stadium in the second round, second leg, of the European Cup. Willie had missed the first leg at Ibrox, which Rangers had won 1-0, through injury, but he would play in the return. Rangers won 0-2 with goals from Jim Forrest and Davie Wilson. Willie had played well, but the victory was marred when, tragically, Jim Baxter broke his leg. Although Jim was to make a full recovery, despite later playing a masterful part in the famous 3-2 win over England at Wembley in 1967, he would never be quite the same player again.

Back in the hotel that evening Rangers held a banquet to celebrate reaching the European quarter-finals, but there was a dampener on the evening – Slim Jim was missing. He was still in the local hospital having his leg set in a plaster. As the evening was drawing to a close, word was filtered from Rangers player to Rangers player. The word was that Jim Baxter, plastercast and all, was back in his room having a party. When Willie heard the news, he and his room-mate, Roger Hynd, slipped away and headed for Baxter's room. The boss, Scot Symon, met them at the top of the stairs. The two of them stopped in their tracks as Symon announced: "Bed ... both of you!"

"But we're going to visit Jim ... " pleaded Willie.

"Bed!" shouted Mr Symon.

Somewhat disappointed and with some reluctance, both headed for their bedroom. You didn't argue with Scot Symon.

In the confines of his room as the evening went on, Willie found it impossible to settle. Eventually curiosity got the better of him and he sneaked out and headed for Jim Baxter's room. As he opened the door and peeked his head into the room, he saw four or five senior Rangers players passing alcohol around. Slim Jim was lying back in bed, enjoying the banter with his fellow players and the attention of a young lady of the night. Willie entered, kept quiet, and enjoyed a couple of drinks when they were offered. He listened to the banter (mainly provided by Baxter) and throughout his stay in the room he kept thinking to himself: "Jim Baxter can't be beaten ... not even with a broken leg!"

Willie: Baxter had been having an inspirational match and basically was taking the mickey out of any player who came near him. During the game he nutmegged the same player on three occasions and this was enough for the hatchet men to come looking for him. Eventually he was brought down with a horrendous tackle which saw him being carried off with a broken leg. Back at the hotel that evening, and despite knowing he would be out for some time, Jim was in high spirits and even a broken leg couldn't stop him from having a great time – and he knew how to party!

In 1965 Rangers were drawn in the European Cup quarter-final against Italian giants Internazionale of Milan. Prior to the match Rangers had the little matter of dealing with Hearts in the League. Willie doesn't recall much of the match, which is hardly surprising. He does remember putting Rangers in front with a header after two minutes but from then on in it becomes a blur. He had stitches applied above his left eye at half-time, the result of an elbow in the face from his frustrated opponent, and stitches above his right eye at full-time, thanks to the attention of the same defender. As he boarded the plane for the Milan match he looked like a boxer returning from a battle, as opposed to a footballer on his way to one. Defenders were now becoming wary of the talented youngster and over the coming seasons a great deal of punishment would come his way.

Against Milan over the two legs, Rangers were beaten 3-2 on aggregate with Jim Forrest scoring both goals. The European dream was over and it was of little consolation that Inter went on to win the trophy.

Willie: There is nothing nice that I can say about Italian defenders – the majority could only be classed as animals. Like the Argentinians, they were trained in the art of dirty tactics and they would use every means possible to hurt or enrage an opponent. This only served to inspire me when I played against them and I would take great pleasure in making look like fools.

That season the League title was won by Kilmarnock, who were guided by former Rangers hero Willie Waddell. Later, of course, he would become Rangers manager. The campaign finished for Willie with two youth caps for Scotland in the Junior World Cup in Germany. Several of that team, including Willie, would go on to win full Scotland Caps – goalkeeper Thomson Allan and defender Frank Munro among them.

The following season would be the beginning of a transitional period for Rangers and Willie would make another exciting first in his still young career.

4

SCOTLAND CALLS

During the close season Willie became engaged to his girlfriend, Margaret Kennedy. Margaret, like Willie, hailed from the Fife village of Cardenden. They had met at a local dance and had talked of marriage if, and when, Willie broke into the first team. The breakthrough had come much sooner than they had expected and they agreed to wait another year before entering into marriage.

Season 1965/66 would be one of changes at Ibrox. Famous names were disappearing, none more exalted than Jim Baxter, who was sold to Sunderland. Baxter and Willie had become good friends, despite Scot Symon. Baxter was an icon at Rangers and being an icon would often mean that he could get away with anything short of murder. The pair would travel together by train from Fife to Ibrox, and to their destinations on match days. Baxter would take charge of expenses and would claim for meals both to and from each game, and even had the audacity to charge the club ten bob (50p in new money) for a tip for the waiter on both journeys. His claims were always unchallenged and young Willie shared the proceeds.

Willie also recalls that during the close season, the players' holidays, wages were slashed, sometimes by half. He remembers an instance when one player challenged Scot Symon on this issue. The player (who shall remain nameless) took the trip up the marble staircase to Symon's office and in anger said to his boss: "Why have my wages been cut and Jim Baxter's are three times mine?"

Scot Symon smiled and replied: "It's simple son … Baxter's a better player than you." This was followed by the player's retort: "Not during the close season he's not!" Fair point – but there was no beating Scot Symon and the player left the office with his tail between his legs. Yes, Ibrox would

SENT OFF AT GUNPOINT

mourn the departure of Jim Baxter and Willie would miss him perhaps more than most.

Rangers started the 1965/66 season well enough, qualifying from their section in the League Cup, brushing aside Airdrie in the quarter-finals and Kilmarnock in the semi-finals. They were now in the final against none other than Celtic. The media was now beginning to rant about Willie and his exceptional skills. Headlines abounded: WONDER-BOY WILLIE! ... TAKE A BOW, JOHNSTON! ... HE'S GOT THE MAGIC TOUCH! ... WHIZ KID ON THE WING!

They were just some of the banners that hit the press following match day. But it was not only the press who were heaping praise on the youngster. His former team-mate Jim Baxter wrote the following in a newspaper column shortly after joining Sunderland:

"I'm wondering if this could be the pay-off year for the youngster I rate the best outside-left in Scottish football. I know that most of you will reckon that the man I'd pick for my ideal team would be Davie Wilson. After all, Davie and I played in a lot of great teams with both Rangers and Scotland, but now I don't even rate Davie as the best left-winger at Ibrox.

"The man I'd hand that honour to is young Willie Johnston. This kid, who lived not far away from me back home in Fife, is the greatest prospect I've ever seen in years.

The boy has everything. He has wonderful ball control, great passing ability and tremendous confidence. He showed all of them in our European Cup games against Red Star and Rapid Vienna last season; in these matches he played with all the skill of a veteran. Eventually I expect young Willie to move to inside-forward, where his football brain can develop fully. But right now I can't think of a better player for that left-wing spot."

Great praise, indeed, especially when it is heaped upon a youngster by one of the greatest players, not only in Scotland but in the world! So perhaps it came as no surprise, with such lavish plaudits being spoken and written about him, that Willie was to notch up another first in his young career. He found himself named in the 18-strong Scotland squad for the vital World Cup qualifier against Poland at Hampden Park. Victory would put the Scottish team well on the way to reaching the finals in England. In his mind Willie gave himself little chance of playing, and who can blame him? He was still only 18-years-old.

Before naming the team that would play against Poland, Jock Stein (the stand-in manager) had a problem to ponder. His concern was the poor form of his own Celtic player John Hughes. Hughes had played badly in the previous Saturday's game against Hearts. But Stein had only one alternative and that was to field young Willie. This match would be a battle and not a place for the faint of heart. John Hughes was highly experienced, a giant of 6ft 2in and weighing over 13 stone. Willie was still a boy and had never been capped, he stood 5ft 7in and weighed little more than ten stone! A dilemma, indeed. Jock Stein had already declared himself an admirer of the classy Rangers winger when he had tried to sign him for Dunfermline. The day prior to the match, Jock took John Hughes and Willie aside and had a chat with both individually – Willie doesn't recall the exact content of the conversation, but will never forget its outcome – before naming the following team: Brown (Spurs), Hamilton (Dundee), McCreadie (Chelsea), Crerand (Man Utd), McNeill (Celtic), Greig (Rangers), Henderson (Rangers), Bremner (Leeds Utd), Gilzean (Spurs), Law (Man Utd), Johnston (Rangers).

Willie would, at 18, join his team-mate Willie Henderson and Denis Law in becoming one of the youngest players ever to play a full international for Scotland.

Willie: Jock Stein was an inspirational manager with great presence and technical ability – he is right up there alongside Sir Alex Ferguson and Bill Shankly. Every good orchestra needs an exceptional conductor, and Jock Stein was the best conductor in Scottish Football. When I made my debut for Scotland, Jock Stein was the manager. Jock had agreed to stand in while the SFA looked for a full-time boss to take up the post. He was more than happy with his role at Celtic and had no desire, at that time, to become Scotland's national manager.

Even so he spent a great deal of time with me and his advice on how I should approach the game served to relax me and undoubtedly played a big part on how I performed that day. Although we lost the game I sensed I had played well and the reaction of the fans towards me confirmed that. The newspapers the following day agreed with the fans and a great deal of praise was heaped upon me. Despite the result I will never forget my international debut, especially as it was the first time I played alongside my hero, Denis Law.

Willie wasn't in the least bit nervous about making his Scotland debut in front of the 107,000 who turned up for the match that evening, but he was anxious at the prospect of playing shoulder to shoulder with Denis Law. Although Willie had a good match that evening, at times making the Polish right-back wish he hadn't visited Hampden Park, the result was a disaster. At half-time Scotland led through a Billy McNeill goal and looked comfortable. The second half turned out to be an entirely different proposition. Poland flooded the midfield and struck twice in the last five minutes to snatch victory. The players were gutted and Scotland's World Cup finals dream was all but over. However, the press the following day, despite the result, agreed wholeheartedly on one thing – Willie Johnston was a resounding success in a Scotland jersey.

Willie: Denis Law is six or seven years older than me and as a schoolboy I worshipped him. It was never in my wildest dreams that a few years later I would line up alongside him as I won my first cap for my country. Throughout the years I have listened to many an argument among fans on just who is the greatest Scottish player of all time. For me there is only one name that fits the bill – Denis Law. He is a true living legend, the striker who had everything. He had flair, bravery and was the ultimate goal-scorer. So many of his strikes were spectacular. He was the King!

Back at Ibrox for training following his first cap, Willie was summoned to Scot Symon's office. Expecting to be complimented on his debut for his country, Willie was surprised to find himself getting a dressing-down, and that Symon would make no mention of his performance.

"Willie ... Willie ... Willie," said Symon with a shake of his head, before continuing. "When they play the national anthem you do not stand with your arms folded! They should be straight by your side as you stand to attention. Now get back to training!"

Willie turned to leave when Symon spoke again: "And Willie ... stay away from Jim Baxter!" Willie stopped in his tracks, thought about it, and then decided to ignore his manager's final comment – Baxter was no longer at Ibrox, he was in Sunderland.

Two more caps would come Willie's way before the League Cup final. The first was against Wales, on 24 November 1965 at Hampden Park. Scotland won the match convincingly 4-1 with goals from Bobby Murdoch (two), Willie Henderson and John Greig. His next cap was the one he would really savour – it was at Hampden against the 'Auld Enemy' – England.

The date was 2 April 1966 ... only months before England would be crowned world champions. The Scotland team that day was: Ferguson (Kilmarnock), Greig (Rangers), Gemmell (Celtic), Murdoch (Celtic), McKinnon (Rangers), Baxter (Sunderland), Johnstone (Celtic), Law (Man Utd), Wallace (Celtic), Bremner (Leeds), Johnston (Rangers).

England played the front combination of Hurst and Hunt for the first time, and a deadly combination it was. Bobby Charlton, Geoff Hurst and Roger Hunt (two) were England's scorers in a 3-4 victory. Jimmy Johnstone replied twice for Scotland and Willie laid on a cross for Denis Law to score with a header. George Cohen, who had a difficult day against Willie, brought the young Ranger down inside the box for what was a blatant penalty – but the referee waved play on and England emerged winners.

Willie: On the day England would field nine of the 11 players who would go on to win the World Cup that year. It would be the first time that the strike partnership of Hurst and Hunt would play together. Despite the abundance of talent in the English team that day, we certainly had no fear of them. After all, we had a few good players ourselves – Jim Baxter, Jimmy Johnstone, Billy Bremner and Denis Law. During the game I had been giving George Cohen a torrid time and knew for certain that I wouldn't be on his next Christmas card list. As the game was drawing to a close I again made my way into their penalty area. Cohen panicked and lunged at the ball, missed and took me instead. It was a clear penalty, every player on the park knew it, over 100,000 fans knew it, the referee … well, he was obviously a good mate of Alf Ramsey!

In December 1965, Scotland would travel to Naples to take on the mighty Italy in the last of the World Cup qualifiers. Although part of the squad, Willie would not play in the game in which Scotland lost 3-0 and the World Cup dream was finally over. Willie recalls that after the game he and several other players went walkabout in the back streets of Naples. At one point they found themselves in a grubby little shop where an unscrupulous looking character produced an array of rings. Then he declared, convincingly, that the stones set in each were top-quality diamonds. His asking price for each ring indicated otherwise, but to prove his point the shopkeeper produced a piece of glass and proceeded to draw the diamonds across the glass. On each occasion the stone cut into glass and the shopkeeper snapped the glass in two. Willie thought of his girlfriend, Margaret, whom he would marry the following June, and paid the asking price. Back in the hotel the players sat around a glass table enjoying a coffee when they were joined by striker Alan Gilzean. Willie produced the ring and handed it to Gilzean, who smiled and announced: "You've been done, Willie." Willie grabbed the ring and snapped: "Watch this then!" Then he

SENT OFF AT GUNPOINT

scratched the ring heavily across the glass coffee table. The stone in the ring disintegrated to dust – Willie had indeed been done and was too embarrassed to seek out the salesman to demand his money back.

The next day the players boarded their coach and last aboard was Gilzean, carrying the largest transistor radio – about the size of an average suitcase – any of them had ever seen. "Can you get Radio Scotland on that?" shouted one of the players. "You can get anything on this, son!" replied Alan as he sat down. He then pulled out the aerial, which almost touched the roof of the coach, before turning the radio on. Nothing! Not even a peep! Eventually he opened the back of the radio to check the batteries only to find that inside there was absolutely nothing at all. Willie smiled and shouted: "Alan, you've been done, son!"

Back at Ibrox Willie's mind turned to the League Cup final clash with Celtic. Unfortunately, the encounter turned out to be another Hampden nightmare. By half-time Celtic led 2-0 through two penalty kicks converted by John Hughes. John Greig pulled one back late in the second half but it was to be Celtic's day. That season Rangers weren't faring any better in the League. Celtic would eventually win the title and Rangers' only saving grace would be victory in the Scottish Cup. Rangers had beaten Airdrie (5-1) and Ross County (2-0) to reach the quarter-finals where they defeated St Johnstone 1-0. The semi-final saw them drawn against Aberdeen. After a 0-0 draw, Rangers won the replay with goals by Jim Forrest and George McLean. Their opponents in the final would be, yes you've guessed it … Celtic.

> *Willie: Unfortunately when Celtic and Rangers are mentioned in the same breath, religion raises its head. This was something I could never understand. I was brought up in a small Fife village where, like in all Fife villages, religion was never an issue and it is such a pity that such a great derby is clouded with such bigotry between the rival fans. On the park, between the players, no such bigotry exists – but winning … now that's a different matter.*

The final was played in front of a crowd of 126,552 at Hampden Park and finished in 0-0 draw. The midweek replay, on 26 April 1966, attracted a crowd of 98,020 and the teams lined up as follows. Rangers: Ritchie, Johansen, Provan, Greig, McKinnon, Watson, Henderson, McLean, Millar, Johnston, Wilson. Celtic: Simpson, Craig, Gemmell, Murdoch, McNeill, Clark, Johnstone, McBride, Chalmers, Auld, Hughes.

The replay was a hard-fought affair and after 70 minutes neither side had managed to break the deadlock. Then Willie's deflected shot bounced in the direction of Kai Johansen. The Dane connected perfectly and the ball flew past Ronnie Simpson into the Celtic net. The goal was to prove the winner, and the Rangers players congratulated each other at the final whistle. Bobby Watson threw an arm around Willie as they were leaving the field and said: "Great result, Bud!" To which Willie replied: "Better than you think, Bobby … the win bonus has just paid off my mortgage."

The bonus that night was £500 each and Willie would receive the full amount this time around. It is worth noting how the structure of Scottish teams has changed since that period in our football history – of the 22 players on the park that evening all but one was a Scot.

Rangers had won the Scottish Cup, but there was no hiding the fact that their greatest rivals, Celtic, had won both the League Cup and the Scottish League (their first in that magnificent run of nine triumphs in a row). The Rangers fans expected more, as did the club's board of directors. The following season would be a time of change at Ibrox.

THE END OF THE SCOT SYMON ERA

Season 1966/67 would be one of numerous lows and no highs for the Rangers team. The season was no more than three months old and already Rangers had found themselves beaten three times by their greatest rivals, Celtic. In August Celtic destroyed them 0-4 at Ibrox in the Glasgow Cup. The following month they went down 2-0 in the League at Parkhead. Then in October Celtic, for the second year in succession, defeated them in the League Cup final at Hampden, emerging as 1-0 victors. To Rangers fans the start to this season was nothing short of disastrous ... but worse was still to come.

Away from the domestic scene there was a modicum of relief from the Celtic menace in the shape of the European Cup Winners' Cup. The first round saw Rangers drawn against the Irish side, Glentoran. The first leg was played on 27 September at the Oval in Belfast. Glentoran were managed by former Celtic player John Colrain and he had them playing as a solid unit that evening as they held Rangers to 1-1 draw. The second leg, in early October, was a much more comfortable affair for Rangers and they ran out 4-0 winners. Willie was to claim his first European goal that evening and the others were added by George McLean, Dave Smith and Denis Setterington.

The second round saw them drawn against the Cup holders, Borussia Dortmund. Willie and his team-mates were well aware that a formidable task lay in front of them. Dortmund had beaten Liverpool at Hampden the previous May to lift the trophy and several of their team had played in the World Cup final against England just a few months earlier. The first leg was to be played at Ibrox. Although Rangers were by far the better team on the evening they would have to travel to Germany with a slim 2-1 lead, Kai

Johansen and Alex Smith having supplied the goals. The second leg at the Rote Erde Stadium was a battle royal and no place for shirkers. Bobby Watson was stretchered off five minutes from half-time as the result of an horrendous tackle. The injury to Watson served to bolster the remainder of the team and they fought like lions to come away with a 0-0 draw, a result that was good enough to dispose of the holders and take Rangers into the next round, where they would meet the crack Spanish side, Real Zaragoza.

However, before the next round of the Cup Winners' Cup there was the little matter of a Scottish Cup tie against another Rangers – Berwick Rangers. This Rangers hail from the English border town of Berwick-upon-Tweed and in 1955 they became the only English club to participate in the Scottish League. This clash with the Glasgow giants would go down as the most memorable day in their history. The date was 27 January 1967, a date imprinted in the mind of every Glasgow Rangers player who took to the field that day – and none more so than Willie Johnston. He, like the others, cringes when the humiliating defeat is mentioned but it is also the day he was stretchered off the park with a broken ankle. Willie rarely tries to analyse what went wrong that day, other than complimenting the Berwick part-timers on the way they approached the game and the passion they put into it. He does, however, recall his foolishness in going into a tackle with Jock Wallace, the Berwick goalkeeper who was later to become Rangers boss, for a loose ball. Wallace won and Willie was off to hospital while Berwick achieved the giant-killing act with a 1-0 victory.

> *Willie: The result against Berwick was perhaps the worst in Rangers history and I was unfortunate to be part of the team that day. We didn't play well, myself included, and during the game I broke my ankle and I was carried off. That incident probably helped me escape the wrath of the manager – but others were not so fortunate and, for several, their Rangers careers were over.*

Indeed. At Ibrox there was an inquest and heads rolled, notably those of strikers Jim Forrest and George McLean, who were dropped and soon transferred by the club. Scot Symon remained as manager but his stay of execution was not a lengthy one. With the League Cup and Scottish Cup now gone, Rangers were left to chase Celtic in the League and they also hoped to continue their quest to reach the Cup Winners' Cup final. Willie, because of his broken ankle, would play little part in the remainder of the season and had to content himself with sitting in the stand as the team tried to close the gap on Celtic.

Rangers brushed aside Real Zaragoza on a snowswept Ibrox Park with an impressive display of attacking football. Dave Smith opened the scoring after ten minutes and Alex Willoughby scored a second midway through the second half. The second leg was a completely different affair, however, and Rangers found themselves under intense pressure, finally conceding when Laporta scored from a free-kick and closed the overall gap to one. Four minutes from the end John Greig was adjudged to have handled the ball in the penalty area. Santos levelled the tie from the spot and the game went into extra time. Thirty minutes later the teams were still locked at 2-2 on aggregate. The result would be decided in the most ridiculous manner ever used in professional football – on the toss of coin. The captain, John Greig, called tails and seconds later Rangers were in the semi-final of the Cup Winners' Cup.

Their last-four opponents were the Bulgarian outfit Slavia Sofia, while the other semi-final featured Bayern Munich against Standard Liege. The Scots had to travel to Bulgaria for their first leg. Willie had been making fine progress since the plaster had been removed from his broken ankle and it was hoped he would make his return in the game although he still had a slight limp. However, the state of pitch put paid to any chance he had of playing in the match. In some areas there was scarcely a blade of grass, and in places where it did grow, it appeared in ugly, awkward clumps. The Rangers outside-right, Willie Henderson, commented as he strolled round the pitch: "I've played on better pitches when I was at school."

Slavia Sofia turned out to be the poorest team Rangers had met in the competition, and the condition of the pitch failed to assist them. Davie Wilson scored the only goal of the game and gave the visitors a great advantage to take back to Glasgow for the return leg. In that leg Scot Symon made several changes to the team – Willie returned to replace Davie Wilson and Roger Hynd replaced Alex Willoughby at centre-forward. Willie Henderson scored the only goal of the game and Rangers were in the Cup Winners' Cup final for only the second time in history.

Celtic had also reached the European Cup final making it only the second occasion on which two teams from the same city had reached the two major European finals. Celtic would play in Lisbon against the mighty Inter Milan in the week prior to Rangers meeting Bayern Munich in Nuremberg. Willie doesn't believe that Celtic's success against Inter put any more pressure on Rangers but he does believe that the home advantage of playing in their own country was a huge boost for Bayern. The teams lined up as follows:

Rangers: Martin, Johansen, Provan, Jardine, McKinnon, Greig, Henderson, Alex Smith, Hynd, Dave Smith, Johnston.

Bayern Munich: Maier, Nowak, Kupferschmidt, Roth, Beckenbauer, Olk, Nafziger, Ohlhauser, Muller, Koulmann, Brenniger.

Some 70,000 fans were party to a massive tactical battle. The Germans didn't use Beckenbauer as the midfield play-maker as Rangers had expected. Instead he controlled the defence – and very effectively. Although Rangers, on occasions, outplayed Bayern, the Germans had anticipated Scot Symon's theory that his team would win the game down the flanks. This resulted in Willie Henderson and Willie Johnston being shadowed all over the park. Bayern scored in extra-time through Roth and the dream of Glasgow's European double was over.

Celtic had returned home the previous week to a reception at the airport that would have been worthy of the Beatles, but when Rangers landed they were met by two old men and a dog. Just to rub salt into the wound Celtic had also won the League title and Rangers finished the 1966/67 season without a single honour.

Willie: It's hard to express what my feelinsg were when Celtic won the European Cup in '67 and we lost in the other European final. The best way I can put it is that at the time Celtic fans would often say to me, when I met them in the street: "The 25th of May 1967 must give you night-mares, Willie." My reply would always be the same: "No, it was the happiest day of my life!" They would walk away confused – Celtic may have won the European Cup that day, but on that same day my daughter was born. We may have lost our final but one thing Scotland did prove, at that time, to the rest of Europe was that we were a force to be reckoned with.

At the start of the next season there were several new faces already in place at Ibrox. Alex Penman had arrived from Dundee, Orjan Persson from Dundee United, Eric Sorensen from Morton and striker Alex Ferguson (later to become Sir Alex) signed for a Scottish transfer record fee of £65,000 from Dunfermline. However, a poor start to the campaign sealed the fate of Scot Symon and he was sacked. Willie was saddened by Symon's departure and will never forget the breaks he gave him as a young boy, opportunities which led to him becoming a professional footballer. Willie reflects that Scot Symon was old-school and that things may have been different if he had succumbed to internal pressure and aligned his style of management with the modern game. Nevertheless, a new manager would be arriving at the club and it wouldn't all be wine and roses for Willie.

THE REIGN OF 'THE BOY DAVID'

Dave White had an undistinguished career as a player, being an old fashioned half-back who spent all his active days at Clyde. He was later appointed manager of the Bully Wee (as Clyde are nicknamed) and after a year was brought to Ibrox as assistant to Scot Symon. White was still a young man and the aim was that Symon would slowly groom him so that in time he would take over the reins. But only five weeks after White's arrival, Symon was sacked and the newcomer was cast into the deep end to sink or swim. Sadly, he would sink.

He would have the misfortune to be the only Rangers manager, until he was joined by Paul Le Guen, never to win a major trophy. During his time at Ibrox he would often face a hard time from the press who, because of his youth, had dubbed him 'The Boy David'.

Prior to Dave White being appointed the new manager, Willie had been working extremely hard to strengthen his ankle, which had been broken during the ill-fated Berwick Rangers Scottish Cup tie. Part of his routine was to run the two miles of sand dunes between Kinghorn and Burntisland – in heavy pit boots.

Willie: During the close season I would always train with a sprint coach and race against sprinters. When I trained alone I would often do so wearing pit boots. The result of wearing those heavy boots was probably more psychological than anything else. It made me believe that when I put on spikes or football boots they were as light as ballet shoes in comparison – not that I've ever worn ballet shoes! – and therefore that I was getting faster and faster.

Willie now felt that the time was right to switch from outside-left to inside-left. In addition to his solo sessions during the close season he trained three nights a week at Raith Rovers. He was now as fit as he ever was – it would all now be down to the new boss. Willie recalls that White was very much a tracksuited manager who spent a great deal of time with the players on the training ground. He had an abundance of ideas and wanted them put into practice. One those ideas was to see Orjan Persson take over the left-wing role, leaving Willie floundering in the reserves – a situation that would see him lose his Scottish jersey to Celtic's Bobby Lennox.

Orjan Persson had been an immensely popular player at Dundee United. He'd played 101 matches for the club, scoring 17 goals. Dundee United fans were disappointed when he left to join Rangers in May 1967. Willie shared their disappointment. The big Swedish winger was playing for Rangers' first team and things looked precarious for Willie.

Rangers had been drawn against Celtic, Aberdeen and Dundee United in their League Cup section – the games didn't go well and they failed to qualify. White knew he had to get his side motoring for the League campaign and Willie was drafted back into the side as an inside-forward (always his favourite position) alongside striker Alex Ferguson. Willie enjoyed playing alongside Fergie and believed that their contrasting styles often created havoc with the opposition defence. Sections of the press would dub them 'the new Ibrox double act'. They menaced defences with their net-finding touch.

Willie would score 11 goals in 11 games and the press wanted to know why? What was the secret behind Willie Johnston's sudden emergence as a forward of deadly striking power? To Willie there was no secret – he had simply moved from the wing to his favourite position of inside-forward. He was now doing what came naturally to him. Before coming to Ibrox he hadn't ever played on the wing before. He found the wing frustrating as for long periods he found himself out of the game. Willie was a worker who loved total involvement. It had become a strain playing wide and he had lost a lot of his enthusiasm. Now, playing alongside Alex, he had never enjoyed his football so much. Willie would run like a deer and burst into spaces other players were barely aware of. Although Alex was not as quick on his feet he had lightning reflexes in front of goal and less than midway through the season they had scored 25 goals between them.

Willie: For a short time Alex was my striking partner at Rangers and we worked well together, scoring a large number of goals between us. Alex was an awkward type of player who would often use his arms, and elbows, to keep defenders at bay. Of course, his achievements as a manager have now greatly surpassed those of his playing career.

Unfortunately, Alex would play only 41 times for Rangers, but during those games he would net 21 goals. In fact, when Ferguson finally left, the reasoning behind his departure was somewhat mysterious. Some believe he was allowed to go because of the arrival of Colin Stein, while others reckoned there was an element of discrimination against him because he had married a Catholic. Alex himself puts it down to a mistake he made in a Cup final that led to a goal against Rangers. Whatever the reason he would move on and join Falkirk.

It was around this time that journalist and former Rangers player Willie Waddell wrote in his newspaper column, 'Willie Waddell's View', about the most promising players in Scotland. He singled out for special praise Aberdeen's inside-forward Jimmy Smith, Dundee wing-half Steve Murray, Hearts full-back Arthur Mann, Kilmarnock striker Eddie Morrison and Hibs striker Colin Stein, who was destined to join Rangers in October.

Jimmy Smith would go on to play for Newcastle and win four caps for Scotland before a knee injury forced him out of the game. Steve Murray would become a record signing for Aberdeen in 1970, take over the captaincy following the departure of Martin Buchan to Manchester United and win one Scottish cap. The classy Arthur Mann would never be capped, and he would move from Hearts, for a record fee for a full-back at the time, to Manchester City. When his playing career ended he would have a short time as manager of West Bromwich Albion. Eddie Morrison would go on to be remembered fondly by Kilmarnock supporters as a prolific marksman who gave his all for the jersey. Although he would never win a full cap, nobody would deny he was a quality player. He would later manage Kilmarnock from 1984 to 1988. Colin Stein … well, we'll talk about him later.

Willie Waddell was obviously not a bad judge of a good footballer (of course, he wasn't a bad one himself). After dealing with that gifted quintet, he turned the spotlight in his column on one player in particular – Willie Johnston. He wrote: "Willie is the most exciting youngster in Scotland. Recently there has emerged a fresh, dynamic player with all the features we look for in star material. He is now the ideal image of the modern inside-forward. He has found his niche as a striker. As such his future is unlimited."

Nice words, indeed. Waddell, of course, would take over the role of Rangers manager in the not-too-distant future and Johnston would endeavour to prove that Willie Waddell had been right about him.

Meanwhile, Dave White had got it right in the League and victory followed victory as the campaign progressed with the team unbeaten. In November Willie was reinstated to the international scene when he was called up to face Wales at Hampden. The game was a European Championship match and although Bobby Lennox retained his position on the left wing, Willie played at inside-left. The Scotland team that day was: Clark, Craig, McCreadie, Greig, McKinnon, Baxter, J Johnstone, Bremner, Gilzean, W Johnston, Lennox. Scotland ran out 3-2 winners with Gilzean (two) and McKinnon supplying the goals. Willie had an excellent game and he was delighted to be back wearing the Scotland strip.

Meanwhile, back on the Ibrox front, Rangers were drawn against Dynamo Dresden in the Fairs Cup, and they won 3-2 on aggregate. There seemed to be no avoiding the Germans – when the draw for the next round was made, Rangers' opponents were Cologne. Willie recalls that the first leg took place at Ibrox on a blustery winter's evening and the visitors found themselves played off the park as Rangers brushed them aside 3-0. Alex Ferguson scored twice and Willie Henderson provided the third. They lost the return 3-1 on German soil but went through 4-3 on aggregate. Everything was going well. White's men were still undefeated in the League and were given a bye in the Fairs Cup third round, which saw them into the last eight of the competition.

Now a battle of Britain loomed because Rangers' quarter-final opponents were Don Revie's Leeds United, the first encounter scheduled for Ibrox on 26 March. When the big day arrived, Rangers still had not lost in the League. Celtic had been knocked out of the Scottish Cup by Dunfermline, while Rangers had progressed at the expense of Hamilton. Willie and his team-mates could perhaps be forgiven for believing that the Celtic hoodoo was about to be dislodged – only time would tell.

For now there was the little matter of Leeds United. The Leeds squad included a plethora of international players, including Gary Sprake (the Welsh goalkeeper); Johnny Giles (Republic of Ireland), and Jackie Charlton, Paul Reaney, Terry Cooper, Norman Hunter and Paul Madeley (all England). They had a few Scottish stars up their sleeves as well, namely Billy Bremner, Peter Lorimer and Eddie Gray. It was a formidable force to say the least. On the other hand, Rangers were not short of a few internationals themselves, in the shape of Orjan Persson, John Greig, Ron McKinnon, Willie Henderson and Willie Johnston. Still, Leeds would win the encounter if it came down to the number of internationals, boasting 11 against Rangers' five.

A full house turned up at Ibrox that night to watch the first leg. Throughout the game Rangers threw all they had at Leeds but Don Revie's defence stood firm.

Willie: When I played against Leeds at Rangers the game was described as "The Battle of Britain" – and a real battle it was. They would beat us over the two legs. I would describe them as a strong, fearsome team who didn't take prisoners.

When at West Brom under the leadership of Johnny Giles, he would tell us before going on the park: "There's only one thing to remember when playing this lot – retaliate first!" Trying to play dirty against Leeds was always a mistake. The dirtier you played, the more brutal they became. There wasn't a club in the country that liked facing Revie's men.

Rangers had several chances to score but failed to do so and they had to settle for a 0-0 draw. The second leg at Elland Road was always going to be an uphill affair. Leeds took the lead through Johnny Giles and Peter Lorimer rubbed salt into the wound when he scored the second.

Another dream was over – Leeds would go on to win the trophy, while Rangers were left to turn their attentions to the League championship and the Scottish Cup. In the knockout competition, with Celtic already eliminated, who could blame Rangers for believing that silverware would be heading to Ibrox in Dave White's first season in charge? Then along came Hearts in the quarter-final at Ibrox. The visitors held out to draw 1-1 and in the replay at Tynecastle Donald Ford nipped in to score the only goal of the game to take the Jambos into the semi-final. Hearts would eventually lose the final to Celtic's conquerors, Dunfermline.

Rangers' good form in the League continued, but Celtic were hot on their tails, and as the season drew to a close White's men slipped up at Cappielow, where they could only manage a draw against Morton. The initiative now switched to Celtic, and Rangers knew they had to beat Aberdeen at Ibrox in the final game of the season, and hope that Celtic would fall again to Dunfermline at East End Park. It was the 30 April 1968. Rangers lost 3-2 to Aberdeen while Celtic beat Dunfermline 2-1 to retain the title by two points. Willie's dream of his first League medal was over for at least another season.

The 1968/69 campaign would be one of mixed emotions for the Fifer. Rangers would once more find the home front dominated by Celtic, while Willie, on a personal level, would achieve a record that still stands to this day. He would also find himself taking the dreaded early bath for the first time, but certainly not the last, in his career.

Rangers kicked off their season against Celtic at Ibrox in the League Cup, and Willie Wallace hit a brace for the visitors as they ran out winners. Rangers then met Morton in the League Cup and they got off to a flyer. Willie scored after 90 seconds, but despite tremendous pressure Rangers couldn't extend their lead and the game finished 1-0. Willie was voted Man of the Match, but there were concerns in the camp – they had wasted chances and against stronger opposition they might not have been lucky enough to come away with a victory.

A fortnight later Willie Wallace scored the only goal at Parkhead against Rangers and the League Cup campaign was over. Dave White would explore the transfer market that season in an attempt to strengthen the squad. Alex McDonald was bought from St Johnstone for £50,000 (a lot of money at the time) and Colin Stein came from Hibs for a record transfer fee between Scottish clubs of £100,000. Willie and Colin would become good friends – a relationship that exists to this day. The two signings would prove to be excellent buys. But White made a mistake later in the term by bringing Jim Baxter back to Ibrox when he was released from Nottingham Forest. Baxter was a shadow of his former self. The good life had taken its toll and in less than a seaon his career was over. Willie recalls this period with sadness. Baxter was not only a fellow Fifer and his friend, he had also been one of the greatest players in the world.

Rangers had qualified for the European Fairs Cup and were drawn in the second round against Vojvodina of the former Yugoslavia. The first leg was at Ibrox and Rangers won the match comfortably, 2-0, with Sandy Jardine and John Greig hitting the back of the net. The second leg in Novi Sad should not have been a problem for the Ibrox outfit and that was the way it was going until the Russian referee saw red and sent off Trivic of Vojvodina for taking a swing at John Greig. The official then turned to Greig and to everyone's amazement sent him off, too. Vojvodina scored and then fought for an equaliser, but Rangers' makeshift defence stood firm and they went through with an aggregate score of 2-1.

In the third round Rangers were drawn against Irish part-timers Dundalk. The first leg at Ibrox went very much according to plan with a 6-1 victory making the return leg a formality. Rangers added another three goals in Ireland to win 9-1 on aggregate.

On paper, it seemed that the next opponents would be a different kettle of fish. Rangers found themselves up against DWS Amsterdam. Feyenoord and Ajax had proven that football teams in Holland were a force to be reckoned with and Rangers would need to treat DWS with respect – at least that's what the Dutch thought. Rangers travelled to Holland for the first leg and did what no one expected them to do – they attacked. The wing combination of Willie Johnston and Willie Henderson tore the Dutch side apart and it was fitting that both players scored in a 2-0 victory. The return leg at Ibrox did not prove daunting and Rangers ran out 4-1 winners on aggregate, a victory that took them to the quarter-finals.

That season, in a League match against Falkirk, Willie would experience his first ever second booking in a game and be given his marching orders. The sending-off was for retaliation following an horrendous tackle. Willie was no newcomer to being on the receiving end of terrible challenges, but the early bath was something new – and, sadly, something he would become accustomed to throughout the remainder of his career. Perhaps it's worth pointing out to younger readers that in those days skilful, tricky players who were willing to take on defenders did not receive the same protection afforded to the modern player – and to this day Willie has pains in his legs to prove it.

> Willie: Falkirk's John Lambie was my opposing player that day and I had been giving him a torrid time. As the game went on his tackles became fiercer and fiercer. Unlike today, players weren't protected against wild tackles and eventually he went one bad tackle too far. I lost the plot and retaliated and was duly sent off. Retaliation would be one part of my game that I could never control and it would haunt me throughout my career. If I was playing today I'm sure my disciplinary record would not be as bad … or then again, maybe it would be!

Nevertheless, retaliation is, and never will be, acceptable. The outcome of the incident was a 21-day suspension. Following his return to the domestic scene Willie set about proving just how talented a player he was by setting another remarkable new record. In September 1968 Rangers defeated Celtic 4-2 in the League and Willie scored two. In March 1969 Rangers destroyed Aberdeen in the Scottish Cup semi-final 6-1 with goals from Andy Penman (two), Willie Henderson and a hat-trick from Willie. The following month Rangers played in the Glasgow Cup and again Willie scored three. Amazingly all three games took place at Celtic Park – giving Willie the distinction of being the only visiting player to score eight goals in three games over a season at that venue, surely a record that will never be beaten.

Back in Europe, Rangers' opponents in the quarter-final of the Fairs Cup were the crack Spanish outfit, Atletico Bilbao. The first leg was at Ibrox and despite John Greig missing a penalty the team was in sparkling form with goals from Alex Ferguson, Andy Penman, Orjan Persson and new boy Colin Stein. Rangers enthralled the fans with a 4-1 victory. However, if the Rangers players thought that the return leg in Spain would be a formality they had another think coming. Willie, in particular, would find out why.

The Spaniards intimidated Rangers with every trick in the book, the worst of which was their continual spitting. Every Rangers player became aware that dampness on the back of the neck was unlikely to be sweat. Eventually Willie was soaked from head to toe. This, coupled with some harsh some tackles that had come his way, prompted him to lose his temper and he was again shown to the tunnel for retaliation. Despite the antics of the Spaniards, Rangers went through with an aggregate score of 4-3. Their opponents in the semi-final would be Newcastle United.

Willie missed the first leg at Ibrox through suspension following his sending-off in Spain. The Magpies from Newcastle defended well throughout the match and held Rangers to a 0-0 draw, turning the tie in their favour as they approached the second leg at St James' Park.

Prior to the trip to Newcastle, Rangers were at Hampden for the Scottish Cup final against Celtic. The League had already gone the way of Celtic and Rangers again had to settle for second spot. Any thoughts White's side had of adding a trophy to their bare cupboard vanished by half-time as Celtic took an interval lead of 3-0. More than 130,000 fans looked on as Celtic added a fourth in the second half. Willie recalls that he had a bruising battle with big Tommy Gemmell, that day but it was Celtic's George Connelly who stole the show. If the Rangers players and fans thought at this point that their season couldn't get any worse, they were wrong – it did!

Rangers felt that they could get something out of the European game at Newcastle. But it was not to be. The visitors' fate was not decided by Geordies, but by two Anglo-Scots, namely Jim Scott and Jackie Sinclair. They scored the goals as Rangers slumped to a 2-0 defeat. As if losing wasn't enough, the behaviour of a section of the Rangers fans turned the whole evening sour. Newcastle Brown ale bottles rained down on the park and this was followed by a pitch invasion. Order was only restored when the police released their dogs into the fray. Willie has great admiration for Rangers fans – but that small section did nothing for themselves, or indeed for Scottish football as a whole. Rangers' miserable season was over.

Willie: Rangers fans can be the best in the world when the club is playing well. They expect the team to win everything and when they turn against players who are going through a bad patch they can be brutal. I was no different from most players and certainly had my fair share of bad games. When verbal abuse was directed at me I did the thing I was best at – I retaliated and gave verbal abuse back.

Before season 1969/70 began, Rangers headed for the United States for three friendlies involving European competition. In New York they were to encounter the Italian side Fiorentina – and there was nothing friendly about it. It was as if the men from Florence had been in contact with Spanish club Atletico Bilbao and had been given lessons in the art of spitting. On top of this disgusting habit they had mastered the dubious practice of nipping – they nipped bums, faces, arms, in fact any part of a Rangers player they could get a hold of. They were also outrageous in their tackling and, inevitably, the player to take the brunt of this tactic was the player who had run their defence ragged – Willie Johnston.

Eventually the referee had to take action and he sent off one of the Italian hitmen. However, the Fiorentina coach must have been communicating with the Mafia and Willie was duly chopped to the ground. Willie, in good Fife dialect, pleaded with the ref for protection. The ref gave him the best protection available – and ordered him off! Willie continued to remonstrate with the official, but the fellow would not relent and pointed to the tunnel again. Willie refused to go – did he ever learn? – and stood his ground. Eventually, the official summoned a New York policeman into the affair and as the cop came on to the pitch, he drew his revolver and pointed it at Willie. Willie turned grey, then white, and thought: "To hell with it – an early bath sounds pretty good."

Willie: I had been sent off, again for retaliation, but this time I refused to go. Eventually the ref summoned a New York policeman to the scene and he immediately pulled his gun from his holster and aimed it at me. I could feel the blood drain from my face and knew that I was going off. I had to go anyway … I needed to visit the men's room.

It was Willie's third dismissal, but the first time he had been sent off at gunpoint! At least the authorities back home understood the situation and he received nothing more than a stiff warning.

Season 1969/70 started off well enough with a 2-1 League Cup victory over Celtic, but from that point it began to plummet. Rangers stumbled in their next match when they drew with Raith Rovers, and then lost another to give Celtic the advantage in the section, which the Bhoys took to the full.

Rangers' League Cup campaign was over for another season. Celtic, on the other hand, progressed and eventually lifted the trophy. In the League Rangers fared no better. Defeats in games against teams such as Airdrie meant that less than halfway through the title race Rangers were languishing in sixth place.

In Europe, they were drawn against the Romanian side Steaua Bucharest. The first leg was at Ibrox. Jim Baxter, who was spending his second spell at the club, had an excellent game but the Man of the Match was Willie Johnston, who scored both goals in a 2-0 victory. In the return the Rangers defence was solid and they stuck it out for a 0-0 draw, taking the club through to the next round. There their opponents would again be from behind the Iron Curtain, this time in the shape of Polish club Gornik Zabrze. The first leg was in Poland. Rangers were 2-1 down with only minutes remaining – Orjan Persson had scored for Rangers and the belief was that if they could hold out then all would not be lost in the return leg. Willie recalls that Gornik were awarded a free-kick some 20 yards from the Rangers goal. In the wall Willie Henderson screamed at Johnston: "What time is on the clock, Bud?" The stadium clock was one of the largest Willie had ever seen and he believed you could almost read the time on it from the other end of Poland. Willie Henderson couldn't – without his glasses he was almost as blind as a bat.

"Never mind the bloody time, they're about to take the kick," Bud screamed back.

Yet as Lubanski started his run-up Henderson turned his head to squint at the clock and as he did so the ball screamed past him into the net. Now Rangers would have to come back from a two-goal deficit at Ibrox.

After the match the players returned to their hotel and everybody was feeling down. In the bar (where else?) a number of the players including Willie Henderson, Willie Johnston, John Greig, Alex Ferguson and Ron McKinnon were having a few drinks and discussing the tactics that had been used a few hours earlier. During the conversation Alex Ferguson made what he felt was a relevant criticism of the tactics employed by manager Dave White. Willie Henderson took a long puff of his equally long cigar, blew out the smoke, looked Fergie in the face and said: "What the f*** do you know about football?"

Of course, in later years Alex would show the whole world exactly what he knew about football. Willie Henderson and Willie Johnston remain good friends to this day and every time they meet Bud reminds his chum of his *faux pas* on that night in Gornik by shaking hands with Menderson and saying: "What the f*** do you know about football?"

On the international front Willie won three caps during 1969/70, two against Northern Ireland and one against Denmark. Scotland drew the first game against the Ulstermen, won the second, and defeated Denmark. Although Willie didn't know it at the time, his cap against Denmark would be his last for seven years.

Willie: I recall Tommy Docherty becoming manager of Scotland and could only think, for whatever reason, he didn't fancy me as part of his squad. Then, of course, there was the situation with the SFA and their views on my disciplinary record. I strongly believe that they influenced every Scottish manager and strongly advised each and every one of them to exclude me from the international set-up. Later Willie Ormond and Ally MacLeod would defy them and bring me in to play for my country. For me the relationship between myself and the SFA has been a love-hate relationship – they don't love me and I hate them.

Back at Ibrox the eagerly awaited second leg against Gornik had arrived. A crowd of 63,000 turned up to cheer the Rangers on that night, but cheers turned to jeers as Lubanski and company tore Rangers apart and inflicted the same 3-1 scoreline as in the first leg. An aggregate of 6-2 and Rangers were out – and on the next day so was manager Dave White. Willie believes that White's downfall was something the young manager had no control over – his inexperience in top level management.

Willie: Dave White was a very likeable person and technically a very good coach, but he was very young to manage a team of Rangers' stature. I have always believed that if he had been fortunate enough to have had two or three seasons as assistant manager at the club before his promotion, then he could have gone on to achieve great things.

There had been suggestions that Dave did not command the respect of the older Rangers players in his squad but Willie dismisses this as utter nonsense and is convinced that White was in the right place at the wrong time. Who would be the new boss? The answer was quick to come when the sports correspondent and former Rangers player and Kilmarnock manager Willie Waddell was given the post. A new era was about to begin.

THE WILLIE WADDELL ERA

As a player, prior to being appointed as Rangers manager, Willie Waddell had enjoyed a long and lasting love affair with the club. He had joined as a boy in 1939 and made 339 appearances, winning four League medals and two Scottish Cup gongs. He was also capped for Scotland 17 times during his 16 years at the club.

Waddell was a gifted, powerful, fast right-winger and as such was already a great admirer of the talents of Willie Johnston. When Waddell retired from playing he took over as manager of Kilmarnock and guided the club to their only championship in the season 1964/65. Now, on his return to Ibrox, he would transform Rangers, returning them to their former glories and beyond.

Willie Waddell was quick to show all the playing staff that he was, indeed, the boss. Discipline was a major factor in his plan to bring the club out of the doldrums. He outlawed long hair and moustaches. He wanted to create the perfect image for all that represented Glasgow Rangers both on and off the park. There would be no prima donnas here – all players would be treated equally, irrespective of their previous standing within the club. The feeling of pride soon returned to Ibrox.

Willie: When Willie came to Rangers as manager we were a struggling team much in need of a boost. Willie gave us exactly that. He was a brilliant manager and he set about turning the club around. He could be quite ruthless and, as he set about his task, several big-name players would find themselves making quick exits from the club, while a number of new faces would appear. You did things Willie's way or you could kiss goodbye to your stay at Ibrox.

Rangers went on a 12-game unbeaten run in the League following the arrival of the new boss. Yet despite this Celtic would once again be crowned champions. Celtic would also dispose of Rangers in the third round of the Scottish Cup, but the gap between the two clubs was closing dramatically. Jock Wallace, the mastermind behind

Rangers' embarrassing defeat at the hands of Berwick, arrived as the new fitness coach. Players went – Baxter was freed, Johansen also departed. New players were brought in – goalkeeper Peter McCloy was bought from Motherwell, and defender Tom Forsyth and winger Tommy McLean were also purchased. The door opened for some youngsters to make their mark. These included Sandy Jardine, Alfie Conn and Colin Jackson as Rangers prepared for the season ahead.

Willie: You didn't mess with Jock Wallace. He was the sergeant major of Scottish football. He gained the nickname of the 'Sandman' because of his training methods on the sand dunes. He believed that fitness was the key to a successful team. He was also a great motivator, but most definitely technically unaware – perhaps Jock and Davie White would have made a good management team.

Willie recalls two early (inevitable?) run-ins that he had with Willie Waddell. The first was during a break from the domestic scene in which they were to travel to Israel and play the national team in a midweek friendly. Rangers had played Motherwell on the Saturday and had beaten them 6-0. Willie had dominated the game and scored a hat-trick. The following morning they left for Tel Aviv. Rather than travel home to Fife and then come back to Glasgow the next day, Willie, along with Graham Fyfe and Billy Mathieson, booked into a Glasgow hotel for the evening. A taxi was to collect them the following morning at 7.30 and take them to Ibrox where they would join the rest of the squad and take the coach to the airport. Willie didn't spend the night in the hotel. Instead he elected to spend the evening at a party in Drumchapel, a not completely salubrious part of Glasgow. In the morning when he surfaced, slightly under the weather, he knew he had missed the taxi to Ibrox. Thankfully, Billy Mathieson had collected Willie's baggage from the hotel room and had taken it with him in the taxi to Ibrox. By the time the coach was prepared to leave for the airport there was still no sign of him. Mr Waddell was not impressed and summoned Billy Mathieson. "Where's Bud?" he asked.

Billy, in an attempt to protect Willie, replied. "I dropped him off in the town. He wanted to buy a pair of swimming trunks."

"At 7.30 on a Sunday morning?" screamed Waddell. Mathieson cringed and said no more.

Willie eventually appeared at the airport and faced the wrath of Waddell before boarding the plane. He was made to sit with the management team away from the remainder of his team-mates. Waddell summoned the stewardess and told her to give all the players two bottles of beer. Willie's smile quickly disintegrated as Waddell pointed at him and added: "But he gets orange juice – nothing else!"

"Come on, Boss," Willie pleaded. "Two bottles of beer and I'll be fine for the game on Wednesday."

"You're not playing on Wednesday," snapped Waddell. "You're dropped!"

"You can't drop me, Boss ... I just scored a hat-trick on Saturday!" replied Willie.

"You're dropped ... enjoy your orange juice," Waddell shouted.

Willie: Rangers did put the whole team up in a Glasgow hotel the night prior to flying to Tel Aviv, but I sneaked out to a party and spent the night there. Billy Mathieson tried to protect me by telling Willie Waddell that I had simply gone off to buy a pair of swimming trunks – on reflection it was perhaps the worst excuse the boss had heard in all his time as a manager.

Willie did play on the Wednesday and had a great game as Rangers absolutely destroyed the Israeli national team. As a reward for their performance Mr Waddell allowed the team to go out on the town. Willie, along with a number of the squad, ended up in the plush Hilton Hotel. They were drinking bottles of lager and after sinking seven or eight each the group was approached by the head waiter. They were all well aware that by this point no beer had been paid for.

"Are you staying at the hotel?" asked the waiter.

Willie Henderson saw an opportunity and interjected: "Yes, of course!"

"That's fine, Sir. Name and room number?"

"Maurice Levante, room 202"

"Thank you, Sir." said the waiter and turned to walk away.

Willie Henderson shouted after him: "And add ten per cent for the service!"

The players quickly finished their drinks and scurried out of the hotel. As they walked down the steps Bud asked Willie Henderson: "Who the hell is Maurice Levante?" "I've no idea," replied Henderson and smiled. "I heard his name and room number announced on the Tannoy system as we came in."

A good evening was had by all – with the exception of Mr Levante, of course. Back at their own hotel, the players had a meal and retired for the evening. Bud invariably roomed with Willie Henderson and this trip was no exception. Henderson was a joker and often caught Bud out. During the night Bud was shaken awake by Willie.

"Bud, I'm thirsty … are you?"

"Willie, go to bloody sleep!" replied Bud.

"Bud, I've got a great plan," insisted Willie H.

Bud sat up in bed. "What are you going on about?" he asked.

"I'm thirsty!"

"Don't drink the water," exclaimed Bud.

Willie H had no intention of drinking the water. "Look out the window and tell me what you see?"

Willie shook his head in an attempt to become fully awake and looked out of the window. "I see orange groves," he replied.

"Exactly! Now my plan is simple. We'll go out there, you climb the tree, shake the branches and I'll collect the fallen oranges – we'll bring them back to the hotel, squeeze them and have a nice refreshing drink each."

Bud was too tired, but Willie H persisted and finally he gave in. The two of them sneaked out the hotel. Bud climbed the trees and shook the branches while the short-sighted Willie Henderson collected up the fallen oranges (the ones he could see). Back at the hotel they enjoyed fresh orange juice before going back to bed.

In the morning, after breakfast, the squad boarded the coach to head to the airport for the return trip to Glasgow. As the coach slipped up the hotel driveway Bud's eyes were drawn to a large sign that sat on the perimeter of the orange grove. It's huge letters read: DO NOT CLIMB THE ORANGE TREES! BEWARE OF SNAKES! Bud turned to look at Willie Henderson who was seated behind him. Henderson smiled at him and said: "Got you!"

Thankfully, Willie Waddell knew nothing about the Maurice Levante ruse, nor the orange grove adventures.

A further incident occurred during the pre-season break when Rangers travelled to Sweden, where they spent 12 days in a training camp. All the players knew that coach Jock Wallace, in preparation for the forthcoming season, would push them to the limits – thankfully there were no sand dunes!

Several days prior to the end of their stay in the training camp Jock announced that the boss was allowing them a night out in Gothenburg

SENT OFF AT GUNPOINT

58

following all their efforts. The deal was simple – they would board the coach at 7pm to be driven to Gothenburg and dropped off in the square, then they all had to be back in the square for midnight to be transported back to the camp. Simple? Not exactly. Willie Henderson and Willie Johnston missed the bus and returned to a bar. Eventually they got a taxi back to the camp at two in the morning. For the first time the players had single rooms and Willie Johnston was wakened in the morning by a loud knocking on the door. The knocking was followed by the unmistakable voice of Jock Wallace: "The boss wants you in his room in five minutes. Don't be late!"

Willie jumped out of his bed, threw on his tracksuit, looked in the mirror – and cringed. Not a pretty sight. Quickly, he splashed some water over his face and headed for Willie Waddell's room. When he arrived outside the room he was surprised to find Gerry Neef and Ron McKinnon standing outside. He was less surprised to find Willie Henderson also standing there; after all, he was his partner in crime. Gerry Neef was panic-stricken. He had never been on the mat before and could not shut up as he tried to explain to his fellow players that he had done nothing wrong. They tried to calm him and told him to accept whatever punishment came his way. Gerry was called in first and the three outside cowered slightly as they heard a raised voice (not Gerry's) from within the room. Eventually Neef emerged. Willie Henderson asked: "What was the shouting about?"

"He fined me £40," replied Gerry and continued: "He went crazy when I asked to pay it at 50p a week!"

Ron McKinnon was next and he was out again in 30 seconds – fined £40. Following Ron was Willie Henderson who re-emerged one minute later.

"What happened?" asked a distressed Bud.

"Fined £40 and I'm being sent home today," replied Willie H. Then he added: "You're being sent home with me."

Being sent home when you weren't in the public eye wouldn't distress most people. But being sent home when you were a footballer was disastrous. The media would put arms and legs on the story.

Bud's wife would also put arms and legs on those stories and the shit would hit the fan! Before he could quiz Henderson further, Jock Wallace ordered him into the room and Willie immediately went on the defensive, pleading: "Boss, you can't send me home. We were at the square 15 minutes before the bus was due. It must have been early. You can't send me home!"

Waddell replied: "You were to get the coach at midnight. It waited till 12.45am. Don't try and pull the wool over my eyes!"

Willie hesitated momentarily: "You can't send me home for 45 minutes," he pleaded. Waddell shook his head: "Who mentioned sending you home? I've sent no one home – fined £40." Outside the room Willie Henderson stood with a big smile on his face. Done again!

Season 1970/71 saw Rangers win their first trophy since 1966. The League Cup made its way to Ibrox and the victory was made much sweeter because Celtic were their opponents in the final. The margin was only 1-0 and Rangers' goal was scored by a lanky 16-year-old from Dundee, name of Derek Johnstone. It was Derek's debut, and his first Old Firm match, his first cup final and his first goal in senior football – quite a day.

However, young Derek was not the only player to be in the spotlight that day. Willie got in on the act as well. He had been giving the Celtic defence a torrid time during the match and on one occasion when he took the ball wide left to draw the defence with him there were no takers. No Celtic player wanted to go near Willie Johnston and be taken to the cleaners. Willie wasn't about to take it to them so he sat down on the ball and waited. That was all the encouragement the Celtic players needed and they moved towards Willie. He beat a few Celtic men before passing the ball to one of his colleagues. The Rangers fans chanted Willie's name while the Celtic fans screamed for his head.

Willie: Many people think that I sat on the ball through devilment, but that isn't true. Celtic defender Jim Craig and been backing off me repeatedly throughout the game and I had grown tired of it. I sat on the ball to lure him towards me and had no idea the fuss it would cause after the match. Would I do it again if the match was played over? Of course I would and that would be devilment!

Following the game some of the press slated Willie, claiming it was gamesmanship and that he had brought the game into disrepute. Willie felt hurt by the comments in the press and wondered what all the fuss was about. It was a bit of fun to entertain the fans. Well, some of them, at least!

The following week, upon arriving for training, he was informed by the Ibrox doorman that he was wanted immediately in the manager's office. Willie climbed the staircase towards Willie Waddell's office and with each step he wondered what he had done. He soon found out.

When Willie entered the office, Mr Waddell was seated at his desk but all he could see of his boss was from his eyes upward and Willie cringed. Piled high in front of the manager were stacks of mail.

"Do you have any idea what all this is?" screamed Waddell.

Willie gave a little smile: "Fan mail?" he replied.

"Don't get smart with me, Bud! These are complaints about your antics on Saturday."

Waddell ranted on for a while, fined Willie a week's wages and threw him out of the office. Willie couldn't help smiling to himself as he made his way back down the staircase. It may have cost him a week's wages, but he guessed that the combined price for posting all those letters was certainly more than £40. What's more, he knew that each and every complainer who put pen to paper would be a Celtic supporter!

Sadly, the event of winning the League Cup was greatly overshadowed by the tragedy that struck the club in January 1971 – the Ibrox disaster. Several weeks prior to the game Rangers played Hibs and Willie was put through the mill by defender Jim Blair. Blair obviously thought that the object of the game was to take Willie's legs away from him rather than the ball. Eventually Johnston retaliated and he took the lonely walk up the tunnel again. The suspension Willie received would keep him out of the line-up that faced Celtic on 2 January 1971. These were the teams:

Rangers: Neef, Jardine, Mathieson, Greig, McKinnon, Jackson, Henderson, Conn, Johnstone, Smith, Stein.
Celtic: Williams, Craig, Gemmell, Brogan, Connelly, Hay, Johnstone, Hood, Wallace, Callaghan, Lennox.

The game was played in front of an all-ticket crowd of 80,000. The match was an even affair and looked destined to finish in a 0-0 draw. That was until the 89 minute when Jimmy Johnstone scored for Celtic. Rangers centred the ball, went up the park and Colin Stein hit a 90th-minute equaliser and the referee immediately blew his whistle for full-time. Just after this moment the steel barriers of stairway 13 gave way and a total of 66 people were suffocated to death and many more were injured. Initially it was thought that Stein's dramatic equaliser caused fans who were leaving the ground to turn back and meet up with jubilant supporters coming in the opposite direction, a theory that still haunts Colin Stein. But the inquiry which followed the disaster found this theory to be untrue.

The crowd had remained to the end and all were heading in the same direction when the tragedy happened on stairway 13. Although Willie didn't take part in the game he still has dark memories of the events that transpired at Ibrox, and of the youngsters' funerals he attended.

Following the disaster Mr Waddell made sure that every funeral was attended by a Rangers players. Waddell would then set about turning Ibrox into one of the safest grounds in the world. The football season was over following the disaster – nobody cared about the results anymore.

Willie: The Ibrox disaster and the funerals that followed were without doubt the lowest point of my career. It was a horrible period in the club's history and attending those funerals of the young victims was soul-destroying. The disaster brought Rangers and Celtic fans together in mourning, yet it is sad that it takes such a tragedy to unite two sets of fans.

An Ibrox disaster fund was opened and money poured in from people from all walks of life. Star players offered their services to take part in a benefit match and the Old Firm came together to help the victims of the tragedy when Scotland played a Rangers and Celtic Select XI in front of an 81,405 crowd at Hampden. Willie played for the Rangers/Celtic Select that day in a team that included such guests as Bobby Charlton and George Best. The match finished with a 2-1 victory for the Scotland XI .

On the domestic front Willie had a visit to make in front of the SFA's disciplinary committee. To say he was apprehensive about the confrontation would be an understatement. The former Rangers player Willie Woodburn had been banned from the game *sine die* (without limit) for lesser offences than Willie had already accrued. The result was a 42-day ban, which seemed like a long sentence, but at least he was still in the game.

Making his return from suspension, he took part in a good Scottish Cup run that saw the Rangers reach their second cup final of the season. Again fate would play its part. In all his six previous final appearances for Rangers the opponents had been Celtic – and this final would be no exception. On 8 May 1971 the two teams met and the final finished all square at 1-1. Young Derek Johnstone scored the goal that saw the clubs go to a replay. As was becoming par for the course, Rangers lost 2-1. This season of mixed emotions was over – but no one at Ibrox realised what excitement awaited them away from the domestic scene during the subsequent term.

The League Cup of 1971/72 saw Rangers drawn once more in the same section as Celtic. The Gers started the campaign well with a 4-0 victory against Ayr United at Ibrox. This was followed by a 2-0 win over Morton. They then travelled to Ayr where they repeated the result from their last encounter with a 0-4 triumph. That same day Celtic slipped up by losing 1-0 to Morton. Things were looking good – at least, that was until Celtic came to Ibrox. Rangers were destroyed 0-3 and failed to qualify from the section. Celtic would eventually meet Partick Thistle in the final, and it would be of little consolation that Partick lifted the trophy.

In the Scottish Cup Rangers entered the fray in the third round but could only manage a 2-2 draw against Falkirk. In the replay at Ibrox Rangers ran out comfortable 2-0 winners. St Mirren were their opponents in the fourth round. The match was played in Paisley and Rangers brushed the Buddies aside 1-4.

In the quarter-finals Rangers again faltered away from home to Motherwell and could only manage a 2-2 draw. The replay at Ibrox went much more their way as the Ibrox men came out as 4-2 winners. Hibernian were their semi-final opposition and all at Ibrox felt they were only 90 minutes away from a return trip to Hampden for the final – or so they thought. Again Rangers slipped up and the game finished 1-1. This time the replay didn't go their way and Hibs snatched a 2-0 victory to put them in the final, where they lost to Celtic.

In the League championship race they would not fare any better as Celtic stormed away and were the eventual winners. Rangers finished the campaign 16 points behind their greatest rivals and the situation was made no better when Aberdeen managed to complete the season sandwiched between the Old Firm pair.

In Europe … well, that was a different story.

8

THE ROAD TO BARCELONA

Willie Waddell knew he had a momentous task on his hands in trying to lead Rangers out of the dark shadows that had enveloped the club on the day of the Ibrox disaster in which 66 fans had lost their lives. The side had lost four out of their first five games in the League – it wasn't going to plan. Although nothing could make up for the loss of those lives, and the clock could not be turned back, life had to go on.

Willie Waddell saw success in Europe as the way to lift the players, the fans and all connected with the club. Europe would be the stage on which to put the past firmly in the past. Waddell had added new players and had experimented with positions and line-ups as he sought the style that would suit his squad. Sandy Jardine would move to full-back and Dave Smith was switched from midfield to sweeper. The youngsters Derek Johnstone, Derek Parlane and Alfie Conn would be allowed to play a more active role.

Stade Rennes from France were Rangers' first-round opponents in the European Cup Winners' Cup. They were certainly not a household name, but any team coming from that footballing nation was worthy of great attention. Waddell would rather have avoided the Frenchmen. Rennes were riding high in the French League, lying in second position. Rangers, on the other hand, were struggling in the Scottish League and sitting close to the bottom of the table. They travelled to the picturesque town of Rennes for the first leg in September 1971.

The home side turned out to be a creative team, playing some clever, slick football and causing the visitors some concern. Rangers played as a solid unit. Colin Stein and Willie Johnston constantly stretched the French defence and Rangers came away from the match with a respectable 1-1 draw. Willie was the Rangers goal hero, scoring for the fifth time in

European competition. Rangers felt that the second leg in Scotland would not be a foregone conclusion. Rennes had already shown their footballing credentials and could not be underestimated. The French team arrived at Ibrox knowing that they needed a victory or a scoring draw to keep their hopes alive. The atmosphere in the ground was tense, but eventually Alex McDonald scored and the tension eased. Rangers ran out 1-0 winners and the second round beckoned.

The draw contained many household names, such as Chelsea, Liverpool, Barcelona, Sporting Lisbon and Torino, and Rangers were pitted against Sporting Lisbon. They were happy enough with the draw considering they could have faced the holders Chelsea or found themselves travelling into Eastern Europe. But when all was said and done, the seemingly easier tie against Sporting Lisbon nearly turned into a nightmare.

Prior to the European encounter Rangers had played Hearts at Tynecastle where they suffered yet another defeat in the League. Hearts won the game 2-1. Willie scored the Gers' goal, but an accident near the end of the game ruled him out of the first leg at Ibrox against the men from Lisbon. Willie had gone on one of his devastating runs up the wing and as he neared the corner flag he crossed the ball into the centre, but his momentum was such that he couldn't stop his run and he soared over the small wall behind the Hearts goal. Did the Hearts fans in the area catch Willie, saving him from harm? No, they did not! They parted like the Red Sea and Willie took a heavy blow to the head. Although he finished the match and seemed okay, that wasn't the case the next day. Willie and his family were having a day out at Leuchars Air Show that Sunday when Willie suddenly collapsed. An ambulance was called and he was rushed to hospital where he was found to be suffering from severe concussion.

Willie: I was going too fast for my own good but was determined to cross the ball before it went out of play. When I fell into the crowd I couldn't blame them for moving out of my way and letting me hit the ground with a thud. But I got my own back a few seasons later when I joined Hearts as a player. They had to put up with me, and my antics for a few seasons.

With Willie sidelined, a full house watched Rangers beat Sporting Lisbon 3-2 with goals from Colin Stein (two) and Willie Henderson. As the scoreline indicates this was a cracking match but it also served as a warning as to how tough the return leg in Lisbon would be. In the second leg Willie returned, but only to the bench as there was still some doubt about his recovery. The game itself had many twists and turns and one of the biggest blunders made by a referee in a first-class football match. When the whistle was blown at the end of 90 minutes, the score was the reverse of that at Ibrox – 3-2 to Sporting Lisbon. Extra-time was played and Sporting Lisbon drew the first blood when they took a 4-2 lead. Colin Stein had scored both Rangers goals to match his brace at Ibrox. Willie Henderson had also scored at Ibrox and it was perhaps fitting that he should score in Lisbon and the game was to finish 6-6 on aggregate. Rangers had won on the away-goals rule – or that's what they thought.

Unfortunately, this theory was not held by Laurens van Raavens, the Dutch referee. The whistler decided that away goals didn't count double in extra-time and the tie would be decided on penalty kicks. Nobody knew exactly what was happening, as Willie Waddell desperately tried to sort out the situation. He didn't succeed. Penalty kicks would go ahead. Spanish fans poured over the barriers to crowd around the touchlines. Rangers amazingly failed to score from four of their spot kicks and the Portuguese fans carried their goalkeeper Damas off the field in triumph. The Rangers players sat in the dressing room, a broken team. Over an hour elapsed before the UEFA representative at the game spelled out the rules to the referee and representatives from both clubs. "Rangers are through. It is a mistake by the referee. Our rules are quite clear. Away goals count double and penalties should not have been taken in this case."

Rangers, now ecstatic at finding themselves in the next round, celebrated. However, a cloud was to be cast over the celebrations when it was discovered that Ron McKinnon, who had been stretchered off during the match, had suffered a broken leg. Exploits in Europe were now over for the winter.

Willie: There was total silence in the dressing room, every player was gutted, some sat with their heads in their hands. Then a reporter came in and said: "Cheer up lads, the ref's made a blunder. You've won the game on the away-goals rule, the match should have never went to penalties."

The swing of emotions was slow to begin with, but as the reality of the situation sunk in celebrations began. The players shouted and hollered, they hugged each other, and the party was about to begin.

On the home front, Willie would finally come back into the fray following his bout of concussion. He came on as a substitute in a League match against St Johnstone with 18 minutes to go and proceeded to show the opposition's defence exactly how good a player he was. Through his trickery and skilful passing, Rangers were awarded three penalty kicks in the 18-minute period. Willie was to take all three and score on each occasion. Although it was unknown to him at the time, he had just set a world record for the fastest hat-trick of penalties in the history of the game.

The next League game was against Dundee and Rangers slipped up again, going down 3-2. Willie continued his goal run by scoring twice. He would then add another goal to his tally in the next game, which was a 2-1 victory over Morton at Cappielow.

The quarter-final of the Cup Winners' Cup would see Rangers paired with a team that was currently challenging for the Italian First Division championship – Torino. The Italians were formidable opponents who were at that time *Serie A* leaders, but would miss out on that season's title by just one point. The first leg was played in the Stadio Communale in Turin. Willie gave Rangers the lead on 25 minutes after a magnificent overlapping run and cross from Willie Mathieson. In the second half Torino attacked with a ferocity never encountered by a visiting team in Italy. But Waddell had set out to play the Italians at their own game. His strategy was one normally adopted by the Italians – bolt the back door! Derek Johnstone was asked to operate as centre-half alongside Colin Jackson, while the classy Smith dropped in behind this duo as sweeper. Torino did manage to break Rangers down once but this meant that the tie finished 1-1 and Rangers would go back to Ibrox feeling that a victory had been achieved on Italian soil. That night Willie had found himself the victim of some underhand tactics from the player given the task of marking him. He couldn't resist passing a comment as they went down the tunnel together at full time: "You won't kick me like that at Ibrox, son!" The Italian replied in broken English: "John .. ston … in Glasgow I breaka' your leg, okay!"

> Willie: *The threat was made to me in the tunnel, but his mistake was that he made it in front of big Jock Wallace. Wallace glared and him then barked: "You can go and piss off – or I'll show you just who is going to end up with a broken body!" The Italian defender disappeared quickly with his tail between his legs.*

There would be no leg-breaking in Glasgow. The Italians had underestimated Rangers and had failed to recognise that their form in Europe at the time was gloriously different from what they produced on the home front. Torino would face 75,000 fans and a Rangers team that would give no quarter. New signing Tommy McLean, who was challenging the great Willie Henderson for the right-wing position, picked up the ball inside his own half and took off on a run. He passed the Italian left-back Fosati, before sending over a brilliant cross. Willie Johnston rose for the cross along with the Italian goalkeeper Castellini at the near post, but the ball beat them both (Willie claims he dummied it). It dropped to Alex McDonald, who chested it into the net. The goal gave Rangers their first two-legged victory against an Italian side, but it had undoubtedly been earned by their brilliant performance in Turin. Rangers were now in the semi-final and all they prayed for was to avoid the favourites Bayern Munich, a team which contained half the German international side. Luck was not be on the side of the Ibrox team – Bayern Munich it would be.

Bayern were the favourites to win the Cup Winners' Cup and Rangers had felt that they would meet them face to face at some point during the competition. The clubs had been drawn together on two other occasions – once in a Cup Winners' Cup final and once in the Fairs Cities Cup first round. Rangers had lost on both occasions. Would it be third time lucky for the Ibrox side?

Munich were described in the press at that time as "West Germany's greatest ever club side" and there were few people in the game who would argue with that observation. They had two world-class players: Franz Beckenbauer, an elegant and classy sweeper, and Gerd Muller, the most lethal striker in Europe. The class didn't stop there. They had a talented goalkeeper in the shape of Sepp Maier, who was ranked alongside Gordon Banks and Dino Zoff as one of the best goalkeepers in the world. There was the 21-year-old Paul Breitner, a free-roaming left-back who was just as likely to score from right midfield as he was to stop an attacker in his own penalty area. Then there was Uli Hoeness, an inside-forward whose counter-attacking skills could be lethal. This was an outfit with immense talent.

The first leg would be played in Munich at the Grunwald Stadium. As the players came out on to the pitch that night Willie recalls the deafening sound of the German trumpets, but through it all he and his team-mates could still hear the unmistakable sound of Rangers fans singing: "There's not a team like the Glasgow Rangers … no, not one!" It would take more than trumpets to drown out the Scots.

The West Germans scored first that night through Paul Breitner but the Rangers team refused to buckle and were to equalise at the start of the second half. Colin Stein sent a rocket of a ball across Bayern's goalmouth and Zobel, the Germans' inside-forward, headed the ball into his own net as he tried to clear. It was another well-earned draw away from home. After the game, Bayern coach Udo Lattek complained that

Rangers had played tough-guy football and claimed that his team would still win at Ibrox. Some 80,000 fans, jam-packed into Ibrox on the night of the second leg, thought differently. However, Rangers did have concerns prior to the match. John Greig had been ruled out through injury and Willie Waddell made somewhat of a shock team selection that saw him give Greig's job the job to youngster Derek Parlane. The virtually unknown rookie was presented with the task of marking Bayern's powerful midfielder, Franz Roth.

Rangers started the game in the best possible manner as Sandy Jardine opened the scoring in just 45 seconds. The young Parlane had a magnificent match, dealing with Roth so effectively that the experienced midfielder was virtually a passenger in the German side. Then, just before half-time, Parlane got on to a Willie Johnston corner and crashed the ball into the net to score on his European debut. Bayern hardly looked like making any inroads on Rangers first half dominance and the game finished 2-0. Rangers were through to the final with a 3-1 aggregate win!

That victory meant that the Ibrox side had fought their way to the final by winning every home game. They lost only one away game, against Sporting Lisbon, 4-3 after extra-time. The German coach had little to say after the match, but as he left Ibrox, Bayern's captain Franz Beckenbauer said: "Rangers were magnificent. They will go on to win the cup. I have no doubts about that." High praise, indeed.

Willie: This was a star-studded team with more than its share of German internationals. Three in particular stood out a mile. Goalkeeper Sepp Maier was a daunting sight as you bore down on him. He knew no fear and had great positional sense. Gerd Muller was the supreme opportunistic goal-scorer. Although he didn't have the finesse of Denis Law, he was so dangerous and difficult to deal with anywhere within the 18-yard box. Franz Beckenbauer was a truly world-class player with extraordinary vision. He was the world's first ever attacking sweeper, who lurked deep in defence then suddenly surged forward and became an attacking midfielder. What a player!

It should have been a night of celebration at Ibrox, but not for one of the players. He had played his part in getting the club to the Cup Winners' Cup final and had been on the bench against Bayern. Immediately after the match Willie Henderson was summoned to Willie Waddell's office where he was given news that struck him like a bombshell. "You are no longer in my future plans and I'm giving you a free transfer," said Waddell.

Willie H was Rangers through and through and had seen himself finishing his career at Ibrox. That was not to be and he would join Sheffield Wednesday at the end of the season. Henderson made his career debut in 1960 at the age of 16. During his time with Rangers he won the Scottish League twice, the Scottish Cup four times and the League Cup twice. He was also part of the Rangers team that got to the finals of the 1960/61 and 1966/67 Cup Winners' Cup competitions. He made his debut for Scotland on 20 October 1962, against Wales in a 3-2 victory for Scotland, with Willie scoring the winning goal. He also scored in his second game for Scotland in a 5-1 victory over Northern Ireland. He went on to gain a further 27 caps and score three more goals, a total of 29 caps and five goals. His last game for Scotland was on 21 April 1971 in a 2-0 defeat by Portugal.

The official Rangers website states that Willie Henderson left Rangers under a cloud, but the reality is that it was a clash of personalities. Namely between the two Willies – Henderson and Waddell. Waddell would be the only winner and Wee Willie did not feature in the squad that would play in the Cup Winners' Cup final.

Willie: When Willie was told he would no longer be part of Willie Waddell's plans I was gutted for him. He deserved to be part of the team that went on to win the European Cup Winners' Cup and his departure was Rangers' loss. I have no doubt that it was a personality clash between him and the manager that brought about the end of his Rangers career. As I've said previously, Willie Waddell could be ruthless and even the talent of Willie Henderson couldn't escape him.

Dynamo Moscow were the winners of the other semi-final clash and would be Rangers' final opponents on 24 May 1972. They were the first Soviet side to reach a European final. The match would be played at the Camp Nou in Barcelona. Dynamo were no strangers to Rangers. The most famous Russian team had come to Britain just after the Second World War and played a memorable tour, which included a game against Rangers at Ibrox.

Dynamo's manager Konstantin Beskov had played in that game and had fond memories of the encounter, which finished 2-2. During the game, which the Russians had dominated, they tried, and got away with, adding to their numbers by bringing on a substitute without taking a player off. That would not happen in Barcelona.

Rangers had one more League game to play prior to the European Cup Winners' Cup final and that was against Ayr United at Ibrox. The home side won 4-2 and finished third in the table. In the dressing room after the game conversation turned to the forthcoming final and the financial implications of that match. The players were much in demand by the media to give their views on the achievement of reaching the final and on how they thought they would fare against the Russians. TV channels and newspapers were more than happy to pay for these services, especially for interviews with captain John Greig and strikers Colin Stein and Willie Johnston. Payment was normally in the region of £100 an interview. The players had agreed that this money should be pooled and split up equally between all the players who had played a part in the cup run once the final was over. They set up a committee to take charge of the monies involved. At this point there had been no word from the management on what level of bonus would be paid to the players who took part in the final and there was some trepidation in the dressing room about approaching Willie Waddell to discuss the matter. Colin Stein and Bud (along with a few others) felt that the matter should be resolved there and then. In the dressing room there was a phone which was directly linked to the manager's office.

No one had ever used it. No one dared. Willie pointed to the phone and said to John Greig: "You're the captain, Greigy. Tell him we want a meeting!"

"You must be joking! I'm not lifting that phone," replied Greig.

"Then I'll do it," said Willie and walked over to snatch up the phone.

It was immediately answered by Waddell: "Yes" he snapped.

"The boys want a meeting, Boss." said Willie.

"A f***ing meeting!" screamed Waddell.

Willie immediately replaced the receiver before Waddell could ask to whom he was speaking. The players all looked towards Willie and finally someone asked: "Is he coming?"

"I don't think he's in a good mood," replied Willie, before continuing to get dressed. A few moments later the dressing room door crashed open with such ferocity that had someone been standing behind it they would have been hospitalised. Waddell stormed into the room.

"What's this about a meeting?" he bawled.

Willie stood up and started to speak: "Well, Boss, we want to discuss ..." Waddell cut him short: "Bud, sit on your arse. You'll get your turn." Willie sat down. Waddell now turned towards the seated Tommy McLean and asked: "What's this all about, Tommy?"

Tommy was the new boy on the block and rather quietly spoken – he wouldn't want to upset his new boss and struggled to get the words out.

"Well … Boss … the boys were wondering … wondering … about the … bon … bonus for Barcelona."

"Bonus!" screeched Waddell. "What about the bloody bonus?"

Willie stood up. "We were thinking along the terms of £2,000, Boss" he said. Waddell glared at Willie and screamed: "£2,000 … £2,000 … is that between you?"

Willie replied: "Each, Boss. A win bonus only, absolutely nothing if we get beaten."

Waddell slapped his brow with his left hand and shouted: "£2,000 each?"

"Yes," replied Willie.

Waddell then turned on his heels and walked towards the dressing room door muttering under his breath as he went: "£2,000 each … £2,000 each!" He almost took the hinges from the door as he exited. The subject of the bonus would not be discussed again – at least until after the final.

The Cup Winners' Cup final in 1972 was Rangers' 83rd competitive European tie and they became the first team to have made three final appearances in the competition. The men who took the park that day were: McCloy, Jardine, Mathieson, Greig, D Johnstone, Smith, McLean, Conn, Stein, McDonald, W Johnston.

It would be fitting at this stage to tell something of the background of each of those players:

PETER McCLOY: The goalkeeper joined Rangers from Motherwell in 1970 in a swap deal that took Bobby Watson and Brian Heron to Fir Park. He earned his first medal with the club when he kept a clean sheet in the 1970 League Cup final. One of his major assets was his ability to start attacks from the back, a skill he would use to great effect in the final against Dynamo. He would go on to play 535 games for Rangers and in that time he would win four League Cup medals, four Scottish Cup gongs and one League championship medal. He would also win four Scottish caps during his time at Ibrox, which spanned from 1970 to 1984.

SANDY JARDINE: Joined Rangers as a 15-year-old in 1964. He was to play in various positions, including wing-half, inside -orward and even as a striker before the arrival of Willie Waddell. He would develop into a truly world-class full-back who would go on to play 674 times for Rangers, win three League championship medals and four medals in each of the Scottish and League Cups. He would also win 38 caps for Scotland during his Ibrox career from 1964 to 1982. Jardine would then join Hearts as a player/assistant manager, later serving as manager. Amazingly, during 1985/86 he would win Scotland's Player of the Year award at the ripe old age of 37.

WILLIE MATHIESON: Joined Rangers in 1960 but it wasn't until 1965 that he made his first-team debut at left-back. It was often claimed he had only one foot – his left, and he himself would admit that his right foot was purely for standing on. During the Waddell era he was given more freedom to go forward and support the front men and this was an opportunity he relished. He would go on to play 250 times for Rangers between 1965 and1975. In 2007 he was inducted into the Rangers Hall of Fame, an honour that he always wanted and one greatly appreciated by the former no-nonsense defender.

JOHN GREIG: Despite his boyhood allegiance to home-town team Heart of Midlothian, he was to spend his entire career in Glasgow with Rangers. He would become one of Rangers' most celebrated captains and was a determined, forceful player who did not take prisoners. Greig made 857 appearances for Rangers (including a club record 496 League outings), winning three domestic trebles. He played for Scotland on 44 occasions, 15 of them as captain, between 1964 and 1971.

Perhaps his finest moment in Dark Blue was scoring his late winner in Scotland's 1-0 victory against Italy at Hampden Park in 1965. Greig's playing career ended in 1978, when he was appointed manager of Rangers, replacing Jock Wallace.

DEREK JOHNSTONE: One of the youngsters in the Ibrox squad at that time and had made his first European appearance against Torino in Turin. He was likened to the famous Welshman, John Charles, because he could play anywhere, with central defence and striker being his strongest positions. Later in his career he would play in defence, midfield, and attack for Scotland. His 132 League goals for Rangers stood as a post-war club record until Ally McCoist surpassed it. He would go on to win 14 Scottish caps.

DAVE SMITH: Scotland's football writers' Player of the Year in 1972. He joined Rangers from Aberdeen in 1966 for a fee of £50,000. Smith was an elegant left-sided midfielder who would become a classy sweeper. Amazingly he would only gain two Scottish Caps, which is perhaps a reflection on the depth of talent available in the country during his era. Smith would be inducted into the Rangers Hall of Fame in 2007.

TOMMY McLEAN: Arrived at Ibrox from Kilmarnock in 1971 for £65,000. A very clever and perceptive player with the ability to supply the strikers with pinpoint accurate crosses. He would take over from Willie Henderson as first choice on the right wing and would play 452 times for Rangers in a career that spanned from 1971 to 1982. He would also gain nine Scottish caps.

ALFIE CONN: Joined Rangers as a boy (Alfie is the son of the famous footballer Alfie Conn senior, who was one of the "Terrible Trio" of Heart of Midlothian in the 1950s). Conn had great dribbling skills and a box of tricks with which to beat defenders. He was a creative dead-ball artist with a devastating shot. He left Rangers in 1974 when he was sold to Spurs for £150,000. Later he would become one of only a handful of players to have represented both Celtic and Rangers. Alfie would also follow in his father's footsteps by signing for the Tynecastle club in 1980, following a short spell playing indoor football in the United States with Pittsburgh Spirit. He retired in 1983, having won two caps for Scotland.

COLIN STEIN: Began his career with Armadale Thistle, and went on to play for Hibernian. He was the subject of the first £100,000 transfer between Scottish clubs when he joined Rangers. Colin was a prolific goal-scorer with bags of talent and he began his Ibrox career by scoring a hat-trick on his debut. Later he would go on to join Coventry City but would return to Ibrox in 1975 until he retired in 1977. He is the last player to score a hat-trick while representing Scotland at international level. He won a total of 21 caps, scoring ten goals.

ALEX McDONALD: Started his career with St Johnstone but was snapped up by Rangers in November 1968 for £50,000. He quickly became a fans favourite at Ibrox as he demonstrated his passion for the blue jersey. During his time at Rangers he played 503 games and scored 94 times. He won three Leaguechampionship, four Scottish Cup and four League Cup medals. He joined Hearts for £30,000 in 1980, becoming their player/manager in 1981. He took them to within eight minutes of winning the Scottish Premiership title in 1985/86. Alex was capped once by Scotland, against Switzerland in 1976.

WILLIE JOHNSTON: Had been at the club since he was boy and perhaps hit his finest form to date in the semi-finals against Bayern Munich. After the first leg a poll of European journalists voted him one of the best three players (and the only Scot) playing in the two major European tournaments. At this point he had been capped nine times for Scotland, but there were more to come – a lot more.

* * * * *

The final was upon them and droves of Rangers fans headed for sun-soaked Barcelona using every mode of transport available. The team itself arrived at their luxury Spanish headquarters and confidence was running high. History would be in the making.

Despite this confidence there were concerns in the camp. John Greig was nursing an injury, as was Colin Jackson, while centre-half Ron McKinnon had been out for some time with a leg break. To have all three players missing in the final would give the Light Blues a massive headache when it came to selecting their defence. Jackson was finally ruled out and his place went to the youngster Derek Johnstone. Greig, on the other hand, would have played on crutches if necessary, and he had every intention of leading the team out on to the pitch at the Camp Nou. As the teams took the field a crowd of nearly 25,000 looked on, and judging by the noise the bulk of them were Rangers supporters.

Spanish referee Jose Maria Ortiz blew for the kick-off and three seconds later blew again for an infringement as Willie handled the ball. After a nervous first few minutes Rangers began to take control and dictate the play. Tommy McLean nearly opened the scoring with a cracking shot and traffic started to go one way – towards Dynamo's goalmouth. In the 23rd minute the classy Dave Smith found Colin Stein with a 30-yard pass and Colin duly ran on to open the scoring. The Rangers fans went wild. It was all Rangers now, and Smith again supplied a superb cross, Willie rose for the ball and headed home goal number two in the 40th minute. Rangers were looking more than comfortable and went in at half-time with a 2-0 lead.

They could perhaps be forgiven for thinking that the second half might go all their own way, and in the 49th minute that seemed to be the case. Goalkeeper Peter McCloy sent one of his renowned long clearances deep inside the Dynamo half. The ball caught the two central defenders sleeping and Willie nipped in between them, gathered the ball and slotted it beyond the keeper into the net.

Dynamo would now have to commit themselves to all-out attack – and that's exactly what they did. In the 60th minute Eshtrekov pulled one back for the men from Moscow and they followed this up with wave after wave of attacks on the Rangers goal. Rangers defended bravely, but they were beaten again in the 87th minute when Makovikov pulled another one back for Dynamo. The last three minutes would be hectic. With two minutes to go the referee blew for an infringement. Jubilant Rangers fans thought he had blown for full-time and invaded the pitch. It took several minutes to calm the situation and the match was restarted. Another few minutes elapsed before the ref blew again and the match was all over. Rangers had won the Cup Winners' Cup – the first Scottish club to do so.

For Willie it was a game in which he'd set another record (which stands to this day) as the only man to have scored two goals in a European final for a Scottish club. But the drama wasn't over and Rangers supporters invaded the pitch again to celebrate with their heroes. Willie recalls that the players had other ideas and all sprinted for the tunnel. He was a flying machine, the fastest player at Ibrox and he was somewhat surprised to find that Colin Stein had beaten him down the tunnel. "Colin had never moved as fast, prior to that day, or since," claims Willie.

The players were ushered into the dressing room where the celebrations began – they were totally unaware of the events that were developing on the pitch. Later the players would understand the emotions of the Rangers supporters as they celebrated their first ever European trophy win – but they could not condone the actions of a minority who involved themselves in a pitched battle with the Spanish police. The violence would mean that the cup and medals were presented in a small room instead of on the playing surface of the vast stadium. The triumph would now be overshadowed by the fans' behaviour and Rangers would be handed a two-year ban from European competition. Later, due to the efforts of Willie Waddell, this was reduced to a one-year ban. The Light Blues would not get the chance to defend their title. Yet still, it would be their finest hour – or 90 minutes, to be more precise.

Back at their hotel headquarters, the squad could think of nothing other than celebrating their success. Willie Waddell allowed wives and girlfriends to join the celebrations for two hours before ejecting them and allowing the squad to continue with the festivities. The journey back to Glasgow the next day was relatively quiet and alcohol-free, the alcohol being replaced by *Aspirin*.

In Glasgow the team was met by pouring rain and thousands of fans. Hangovers were forgotten as the squad joined the supporters in the celebrations. Thousands more fans had packed into Ibrox as the team entered on the back of a lorry with the trophy held high. "Follow, Follow" rang out around the ground and Willie recalls it as being a fitting and emotional way to round off what had been a great campaign.

Willie: Winning the Cup Winners' Cup was beyond doubt the highlight of my career. Dynamo were no mugs and the team as a whole played exceptionally well that evening – but it was to be our night. Colin Stein opened the scoring with a magnificent goal, then I followed with the second and third (I always had to try and outdo Steiny). My first was created by Dave Smith. When he broke out of defence down the right I knew exactly what he would do. I made my run into the penalty area, Dave did exactly as I expected; he checked the ball to his stronger left foot and delivered a beautiful cross into the area. I met the cross with my head and scored one of the best headed goals of my career.

There is often speculation as to whether my second goal was offside – it definitely wasn't. Our keeper, Peter McCloy, had gathered the ball and I anticipated that he would launch one of his famous clearances up the park. The Dynamo defence were all lurking at the halfway line while I began my run up our side of the line from left to right. Peter launched the ball, I gathered it and broke away, leaving the defenders in my wake. I saw the keeper advancing and picked a spot to his left and struck it home. Dynamo tried, and nearly did, pull the game back but our passion for victory drove us on and we held out to win the cup. When the final whistle blew my heart was thumping, it was such an emotional experience that it's difficult to explain my feelings. This time when we arrived back in Glasgow we arrived as champions and the reception was unbelievable. The Rangers fans had at last experienced European glory and they let the whole of Glasgow (and Scotland) know about it. I awoke the next morning with one of the worst hangovers I've ever experienced ... but boy, was it worth it!

It was now the close season, but the players would get together one more time to attend the wedding of goalkeeper Peter McCloy. Before heading for the wedding Willie made a phone call to Ibrox and spoke to one of the girls in the office. His question was a simple one: "Have we been paid any bonus?"

"£2,000 has been in your bank account today Willie" she replied.

Willie punched the air and screamed: "Ya beauty!"

At the wedding Willie made it an even happier occasion when he passed the news of the bonus to his fellow players. During the reception manager Willie Waddell made an appearance, congratulated the bride and groom, had a few drinks and made to leave.

However, before doing so he joined the congregation of the Cup winning team and said: "You'll be glad to know that £2,000 bonus has been paid to you all, and you can thank Bud for that." The players all smiled at Bud as Waddell continued: "If it hadn't been for him I was going to pay you £3,000!"

Smiles turned to glowers. Willie Waddell would never be beaten.

9

OUT OF THE BLUE

During the close season of 1972 Rangers were still in the news, never more so than on the day Willie Waddell announced that he would no longer be manager. He had been in control for less than two years so why would he make the decision to step upstairs and become general manager? Did he feel that he could do no more in terms of taking the team to the next level? Did he already know that some players would be leaving the club and that a certain amount of rebuilding would have to be done? Perhaps he simply felt that to follow the club's greatest triumph – that of winning the European Cup Winners' Cup – was a tall order that could not be achieved. Who knows? He'd made his decision, and the new manager would be coach Jock Wallace, but the presence of Willie Waddell would never be far away.

Jock Wallace had played a large part in the success in Barcelona and the manager's position was not new to him. After all, he had masterminded the downfall of the Gers in the Scottish Cup when with Berwick Rangers. As a player he played in goal for Blackpool, Workington, Airdrie, West Brom, Bedford Town, Hereford United and, of course, Berwick Rangers. When at Hereford, he held the distinction of being the only player ever to play in the English FA Cup, the Welsh Cup and the Scottish Cup in the same season. In 1968 he became assistant manager at Hearts before joining the coaching staff at Ibrox in 1970. The players already knew him as a hard man, who had completed his National Service with the Kings Own Scottish Borderers. He had fought in the jungles of Malaya and had served in Northern Ireland – you didn't mess with Jock. On taking the manager's post he invited each and every one of the first team players individually into his office and asked them one simple question: "Do you want to play for Glasgow Rangers?"

Willie's answer to this was equally simple: "Yes."

"Good," Replied Wallace.

"But …" added Willie, "I want more money!"

"More f***ing money?" howled Wallace.

The tone and the aggression in Wallace's voice would have frightened many players into submission – but not Willie. Willie had never shirked a tackle and he wasn't about to shirk an argument. Bud knew that Willie Henderson, by that time with Sheffield Wednesday, had been on £100 a week. Colin Stein was on £100 a week, and he knew, from playing internationals, that the Anglo-Scots were on even more. Willie was an international, an influential player at the club and had scored two of the goals in the European final – but he was being paid £60 a week and felt he deserved to be treated better.

"I want £80 a week and a £10,000 signing-on fee," demanded Willie.

"Listen, Bud," said Wallace. "You've just won a European medal and this team can go on and win a lot more medals."

"You can't eat f***ing medals!" Willie informed him. "My brother is earning more money than me working in a factory in Kirkcaldy!" he shouted. Wallace frowned and dismissed Willie from the office. Although big Jock didn't say anything at the time, Willie knew that Wallace would now take their conversation to another level – Willie Waddell. Johnston suspected that there would be little joy coming his way from the general manager. Waddell was a man who, since arriving at Ibrox, went around turning out lights at every opportunity to save on the electricity bill. He was the man who every Monday would cut up a lump of carbolic soap into thin slices, issue a slice to each player and say: "Remember that's to last you all week!" He was hardly likely to agree to a £10,000 signing-on fee. An offer did come back – £65 a week and a six-year contract. Willie turned it down.

The 1972/73 season was barely under way when events in a game against Partick Thistle would play their part in deciding the future of Willie Johnston. The date sticks in Willie's mind – 9 September 1972. Willie had been having a rough time against Thistle defender Alex Forsyth, who would go on to play for Manchester United and Scotland, but the Rangers man kept at it and the tackles got harder. Eventually Willie threw a punch. It didn't connect, but the intention was there and he took another lonely walk down the tunnel. Willie felt he was a marked man, and not only on his legs. Referees seemed to be less tolerant of him because of his bad-boy image and appeared blind to the treatment he was receiving from opposing players during nearly every match he played in. As he took that walk he was well aware that big trouble was coming his way.

Willie was such a regular at the SFA headquarters that he felt he should be on their Christmas card list and invited to staff dances. They even knew how many sugars he took in his tea when he arrived to face the Scottish Inquisition. This trip would see him receive the biggest punishment ever given to player (outside life suspensions) in the history of the game. Banned for 63 days!

The committee also made it quite clear what would happen to him if he should ever appear before them again. Staff dances were definitely not mentioned.

WILLIE'S DISCIPLINARY RECORD TO THIS POINT:

June 1966: For receiving three cautions; seven days.

July 1968: For receiving three cautions; seven days.

January 1969: Sent off v Falkirk; 21-day ban.

April 1969: Sent off v Bilbao in the Fairs Cup; censured and banned for one match.

June 1969: Sent off v Fiorentina (at gunpoint) during Rangers US tour; warned.

December 1969: Sent off v Clyde; 21 days.

December 1970: Sent off v Hibs; 42 days.

September 1972: Sent off v Partick Thistle; 63 days

On all of these occasions Willie was disciplined for retaliation.

Willie knew his playing days in Scotland were all but over. Something dramatic would have to happen soon – and it did! Jock Wallace had previously lost the plot with Willie following his sending-off against Partick for what he called Willie's "lack of self control". A fortnight after the Partick match on 23 September 1972, Willie turned out for Rangers against Falkirk in a League match. Although he didn't know it at the time this would his last appearance for Rangers. After the game Willie was called into Willie Waddell's office; Jock Wallace was also present. Waddell informed Willie that negotiations had already been started with West Bromwich Albion and a fee agreed. A bitter argument ensued which could possibly be heard on Glasgow Green. Finally, although he would be heartbroken at leaving Ibrox, Willie agreed to join West Brom. The fee was £138,000, a record between Scottish and English clubs. As he was leaving the office Waddell declared: "You will not be receiving one brass f***ing farthing from the deal."

Willie turned and replied: "I don't want a brass farthing. You can stick it all up your arse." Then he left.

Willie: When Don Howe arrived at Ibrox to complete my transfer to Albion I passed him on the stairwell and was flabbergasted that he didn't recognise me. I later found out that it had been the Albion chairman who wanted me at the club and not Don Howe. This started alarm bells ringing in my head – had I made a mistake in joining a club I knew little about and with a manager who didn't really want to buy me? Little did I know that I would fall in love with the club and fans and go on to play the best football of my career.

Willie would now move out of the blue of Rangers and into the light blue of West Brom. He recalls that a few years later, when it was announced that he was to be reinstated into the national side, the first person to phone and congratulate him was Willie Waddell. The bitterness would be over.

INTRODUCTION TO WEST BROM BY JOHNNY GILES

(59 caps for the Republic of Ireland. Manager of West Brom and Republic of Ireland)

When the author of the book asked me to write an introduction relating to Willie Johnston's time at West Brom, I answered without hesitation – no problem. Prior to arriving at the Albion as player/manager in 1974 I had played against the Baggies on a few occasions, when Willie was part of the team. I'd paid him little attention; I seldom paid attention to any of the opposition. They were opponents, no more. I would be totally focused on my own game and those of my club-mates. So when I arrived at West Brom, I knew little of the flying winger from north of the border. I had listened to others and formed a preconceived impression of the man. I'd heard he was a free spirit, who could be volatile and liked a drink.

When I took the hot seat at the West Brom things were far from well, as far as results had been going, and the club was languishing in the Second Division. I expected to find a team whose spirits were shattered, but this was not the case. Their spirits were high, in the dressing room there was great camaraderie, and nobody contributed more to this than Willie Johnston. He was a character, motivator and a winner. As far as the drinking claims went – well, he liked a beer with the lads, but Willie could get drunk on a packet of wine gums. He was not what I expected – I was pleasantly surprised. Here was a dedicated professional, who was extremely fit and could often be found doing extra training when he had no need to do so. I could make no complaints about Willie in any way. Yes, he liked to do his own thing, he entertained, but he was a flying machine who could cross the ball with such great accuracy, games could be turned around or even won through his contribution. He was a valuable player during my reign at the club and beyond.

Willie's one failing was his impatience, and I had to work hard with him on this aspect of his game. He was desperate to get back in the Scottish international set-up, and his impatience came through in his attitude. He wanted to be involved in every move and would often try too hard to impress. If the ball wasn't coming to him every time the team went forward, he would drift from his left wing to the right in search of action. We would have many a discussion, in the dressing room, on the subject. I would explain that the Scottish call-up would come – not simply because he was playing well, but because the team was playing well.

He got the message, results started coming and Willie received that Scottish call-up. No one deserved it more. He was the best left-winger in the country at the time. People have often asked me about the incident which transpired after I had left West Brom – namely the saga in Argentina. My answer's always the same. Many players were taking tablets during this time. It was part of the game. If Willie had taken a pill for the first time in his life in Argentina, there would be only one certainty – if anybody was going to get caught, it would be Willie Johnston. That would be his luck. Often clubs would give players pills purely to have a psychological affect. A placebo. It is my belief that stimulants do not work in football as they do in athletics. Footballers use speed over short runs, completely different from on an athletics field. When it came to speed, Willie would certainly have no need to enhance his performance. He was already one of the fastest and most highly talented players in the world.

10

A NEW ERA BEGINS

The transfer to West Brom was a long drawn-out affair. Don Howe, the West Brom manager, made four trips to Ibrox in order to get the player he so sorely wanted. Amazingly, he had never seen Willie play. To everybody involved in football, the signing of Willie Johnston seemed so unlike Don Howe. Howe was a fanatical tactician who put together teams which were, at times, robot-like as they followed their master's instructions. Willie was an individualist, a crowd pleaser and undisciplined.

What were Don Howe's thoughts at this time? West Brom were languishing near the foot of the table – did he think that he had to break from his own traditions to save their skins, (and probably his own) by throwing a wing wizard into the fray? Who knows? Whatever the reason, Willie's arrival would not change the course of events. West Brom would be relegated.

The fact that Don Howe had not seen Willie play was remarkable in itself, but he would at least have had some knowledge of the player. After all Willie was a Scottish international and had scored two goals for Rangers in the European Cup Winners' Cup final only months before.

The West Brom fans probably felt that they were a bit in the dark about the newcomer. Scottish football was not regularly viewed on English TV and Willie had not played in the last few Scotland internationals. It was without doubt that the media would do what they could to fill in the missing blanks, and Willie had been concerned that the majority of those blanks would be about his disciplinary record rather than his ability. In retrospect, Willie knew very little of West Brom and probably felt, as he took the journey south several weeks before his 26th birthday, that he was being pushed down a dark, dismal road by unseen hands.

Willie arrived in Birmingham in early December 1972. His last journey south, other than those made with Rangers, was as a boy, when he came down to Manchester for trials with United. He'd become homesick then and he hoped that leaving his wife and young family back in Scotland would not produce the same result. Perhaps he thought the financial advantage of the transfer deal would help ease his mind. His signing-on fee was £10,000, quite a sum in those days, and his wages were now almost three times what they had been with the mighty Glasgow Rangers. Although he would stay in a hotel initially, he knew he could look for a nice house without any financial fears and quickly bring his family to what would be their home city for the next few years. On his first night in the hotel he had a visitor, the West Brom midfielder Len Cantello, who had arrived to introduce himself and welcome Willie to the club. The gesture was much appreciated by Willie and the two of them went for a few drinks together.

Although the Baggies were struggling at the foot of the League table, the club was not short of big-name players such as Jeff Astle, Tony Brown, John Osborne and Asa Hartford. Jeff Astle was a striker who would go on to play 361 games for West Bromwich Albion, scoring 174 goals. He was one of the most iconic players in the history of the club. He also won five caps for England. Sadly, Jeff died in 2002, but to this day he is well-loved and remembered among the fans of the club, to whom he was affectionately known as the King of the Hawthorns.

Tony Brown, another prolific goal-scorer who in season 1970/71 topped the First Division charts with 28 strikes, was rewarded with his only full England cap in 1971, when played in a goalless draw against Wales at Wembley. Brown would spend 17 years at the Hawthorns during which the 'Bomber' (as the fans called him) broke both the appearance and goal-scoring records for the Baggies, netting 218 goals in 574 League games. Anyone who had seen Willie play could imagine how Astle and Brown could benefit from the arrival of such a wing wizard.

John Osborne was one of the best goalkeepers in the League and only the abundance of talent available in that position at the time prevented him from being capped for England. Osborne was a member of Albion's winning team in the 1968 FA Cup final. Asa Hartford, a Scot born in Clydebank, was a classy act in midfield. He would go on to make 275 appearances for the club and score 26 goals. During the year prior to Willie's arrival at the club, Asa had been in the process of joining Leeds United when, during the medical examination, it was discovered that he had a heart condition. That put paid to the high-profile transfer and Asa would spent a few more seasons at West Brom before finally moving to Manchester City.

Added to this list of players, there was Len Cantello, an industrious, clever midfielder, and John Wile, a no-nonsense central defender, who was unlucky never to be capped. Later Wile would go on to skipper the club for almost a decade. Waiting in the wings at the club there was a youngster just itching to take the world by storm – Bryan Robson. With players such as these the fans could be excused for thinking they would avoid the drop that season.

Eight days after his arrival, Willie made his debut at the Hawthorns. The opponents that day were Liverpool. The men from Merseyside were cruising to another championship triumph in Bill Shankly's penultimate season as manager, despite competition from Arsenal, Leeds United, Ipswich Town and Wolverhampton Wanderers. The attraction that day was not the champions elect, but Willie Johnston. The reception he received from the crowd as he ran on to the park was phenomenal and any doubts he carried at the back of his mind about coming to the club disintegrated that day.

In the Liverpool team there were players such as skipper Tommy Smith, Scotsman Peter Cormack, Kevin Keegan and the classy wing pair of Peter Thompson and Ian Callaghan. But it was the wing play of Willie Johnston that stirred the fans that day as he gave them a taste of what was to come. The game finished in a disappointing 1-1 draw, but there was nothing disappointing about the player making his debut. Willie Johnston had arrived in style.

Shortly after his arrival, Willie got his first taste of playing in the FA Cup. It's an experience he finds hard to describe. Back home he was used to the knockout competitions being dominated, except on the odd occasion, by the Old Firm of Celtic and Rangers. In England it wasn't that straightforward. Yes, the FA Cup was invariably won by a major team, but that team could never be predicted with any manner of certainty. In England very few winners have had the opportunity to defend their title in the final the following season.

West Brom's record in the Cup was something other clubs envied: 18 appearances in the semi-finals, ten appearances in the final, winners five times. A good run in the FA Cup could put a silver lining on a bad season for a club. Willie so much wanted to be part of such a run. His FA Cup baptism was against Nottingham Forest, a club he would grow to love facing. It was a cracking tie that went to a third game, in which Willie was immense and Albion ran out 3-1 winners. He would have many classic confrontations with the Forest defence, but in the first game he certainly made a huge impact.

In the next round Albion were drawn against Swindon Town and enjoyed a comfortable 2-0 victory at the Hawthorns. In the fifth round the draw was not so favourable, pairing them with Leeds United at Elland Road. Leeds were perhaps at their peak at this time. They had won the European Fairs Cup in 1971, the FA Cup in 1972 and would go on to take the First Division title in 1974. Willie, of course, had experienced playing against Leeds while he was still at Rangers and had no doubts regarding their pedigree. Leeds won the tie 2-0 and went on to reach the final where, despite being favourites, they lost to Sunderland in an epic match.

Willie found two major differences on arriving at the Hawthorns from Rangers. The first was the language barrier – he struggled with all the different dialects. He recalls arriving for training each day and invariably bumping into Jeff Astle. They would exchange greetings, yet for months neither understood a single word said by the other. The second difference (and the most important one) was the position he found himself playing within the team set-up. At Rangers he had moved inside from the wing, a move that proved overwhelmingly successful and turned him into a goal-scoring machine. Don Howe would play Willie wide all the time, although within a set pattern of play. In other words Willie would be restricted from being creative, which had become his hallmark. The Scot believes that Don Howe would have made a great British general, but was far from convinced that his battlefield tactics would win the day on the football park. They stifled individuality and bored the fans. Willie isn't convinced that had he been allowed to use his creative freedom, he would have saved the club from relegation – after all, a football team is about 11 players, not one – but perhaps the club would not have finished the season at the absolute bottom of the pile. Perhaps.

Relegation left Willie feeling despondent. He had come south with two things in mind: to prove that he was one of the best players in the UK and to ultimately win his place back in the international set-up. Playing in the Second Division would hardly be the ideal place to achieve either.

West Brom had spent 25 consecutive seasons in the First Division. The fans were gutted, the players were gutted. They now had to regroup and get back to the top flight as quickly as possible and Willie was committed to that end. He already felt part of the club. He had bought Bobby Gould's house – Gould had been transferred to Bristol City prior to Willie's arrival – and his family had settled into the area. Everybody at the club had made him and his family feel very welcome and he wanted to repay them by helping to bring success. He was certain that relegation would not see West Bromwich Albion disappear into obscurity. They were too big and ambitious a club for that to happen.

11

THE SECOND DIVISION

Willie knew from his experience in the English First Division that it
was one of the toughest leagues, if not the toughest, in the world. At
that time, the difference between the English and Scottish First Divisions
was not in the fitness of the players, but in the tactical awareness of the
English. Scottish managers were far less attentive in this department
compared with their counterparts south of the border. Willie would now
taste life in the English Second Division. His thoughts, shared by his team-
mates, were that they would bounce straight back up into the top flight. But
there were some big-name clubs who thought the same, and some of them
would attempt to thwart West Brom. Among the teams battling to gain
promotion that season were Sunderland, Aston Villa, Nottingham Forest,
Middlesbrough, Fulham and Bolton Wanderers. Getting into Division One
would hardly be a walk in the park.

Don Howe would continue with his brand of tactics at the start of
season 1973/74. Willie would often feel as if he was handcuffed to a short
leash and couldn't do what God had given him the gift to do – destroy
defences. Yet, occasionally, he would slip his cuffs and do his own thing.
The fans loved it and Don Howe hated it! If West Brom were beaten then
Willie would invariably be blamed by the manager in the dressing room
after the match. In fact, Willie got so used to being blamed that he would
spread his arms out wide, displaying his palms, before Don Howe had even
started and would say: "Go on, Boss. Put the nails in."

One such occasion when Willie slipped the cuffs was in a game against
York. West Brom ran out comfortable 2-0 winners and the next day one
newspaper ran with the headline: WILLIE THE WIZARD. York manager
Tom Johnston became another member of Willie's growing fan club. "I

thought his close control was brilliant and he gave us a lot of trouble down both flanks" Tom told the newspaper. York captain Barry Swallow added: "Willie was skinning us. We thought we had found the answer in the second-half, but then he popped up in the middle to flick home a killer goal." The Scot, not for the first or last time, was voted Man of the Match.

One thing that had become evident about Willie since his arrival from Rangers was that he had never been sent off during a match. The media were also aware of that fact and it wasn't long before they asked the player to explain the change in his behaviour. Willie was never shy in talking to the press and grabbed the opportunity with both hands. "What you must remember is the fact that I've never been sent off for anything other than retaliation. I've always borne the brunt of horrendous tackles when doing what I do best – skinning defenders. I'm older now, though, and I've learned to control myself by counting up to ten following a bad challenge."

Impressive words – but the real reason he hadn't taken the long walk down the tunnel was quite different. Opposition defenders hadn't worked him out yet. He had played in Scotland since he was a boy and Scottish defenders knew there was only one way to deal with his style of play, and that was to chop him down! Would they work that out down south? Of course they would, and it wouldn't be long before Willie lost the mathematical ability to count past two. The day came in September 1973 in a game against Swindon – he was sent off for retaliation and suspended for three games.

Readers who know little of Willie Johnston should be enlightened at this stage regarding his bad-boy image. The image was something that was purely confined to the football park and didn't surface outside of the game. Willie wasn't like other players who were forever in the news for behaviour unrelated to football. Willie was a quiet man, and at times shy (and is still the same today – unless the subject is football), but on the pitch he became a different person. When he pulled a football jersey over his head he could be compared to Clark Kent stripping down to his Superman outfit. On the pitch he was an entertainer, a showman, a natural clown and a flying machine Oh yes, and he was volatile. Willie was also a dedicated professional. Nobody trained harder. He absolutely believes that the harder you work the better you become. Willie Johnston was an absolute athlete. He would step on to the scales every day and if he was as little as one pound overweight he would panic, get a hold of black bin liner, wrap it around his body under his training kit and sweat off the extra weight. This was Willie Johnston. He didn't need to kick players, he didn't need to cheat but, in the day when the tackle from behind was not only acceptable but expected, his mind would not allow him not to react towards assassins – and the reaction would often lead to an early bath.

In the 1973/74 FA Cup West Brom started on the road to Wembley by defeating Notts County in an emphatic 4-0 victory. In the fourth round they were drawn against Everton at Goodison. That was a hard-fought game which saw some of West Brom's youngsters grow in stature as they held Everton to a 0-0 draw. The Hawthorns was jam-packed for the replay and the players wanted to give the fans something to feel good about – and they did. Everton were sent home with their tails between their legs as the Baggies ran out 1-0 winners. Willie had performed well during the game, but (there's always a but) following a ridiculous tackle he saw red and once more the referee's finger pointed to the tunnel. Their fifth-round opponents were Newcastle and the Wembley dream was to come to an end when they were beaten 3-0.

As the League progressed, West Brom were finding that the campaign was not going as they had anticipated. Some thought the key factor was that Jeff Astle was often missing through injury and that this was hindering the team's progress. Others, including the majority of players, were of the opinion that because of his tactics Don Howe was the main culprit. Willie believed that if football was played on a blackboard Don Howe would win the World Cup. But football isn't played on a blackboard. Whatever the reason for the often indifferent performances, the club was languishing in mid-table and would finish the campaign in eighth place.

Willie: I found Don Howe to be a very nice man, but I never liked playing under him. Tactically he was probably the best in the country, but his playing systems curtailed players like myself and I was always frustrated during his time as manager. As a coach he would rank alongside the best in the country, but he lacked man-management skills and for this reason alone a number of West Brom players were happy when his services were dispensed with.

With the remaining League fixtures now becoming meaningless it was a difficult time for the supporters, as they prepared to face another season in the Second Division. In one of their remaining home games Willie thought he would try and put a smile back on the faces of the fans. In the dressing room he hid a clown's mask up his jersey and as the players came up the tunnel he put it on. As he ran on to the park the fans roared with laughter and Willie continued to wear the mask during the whole of the warm-up. The fans may have been amused but manager Don Howe certainly was not. At half-time he lambasted Willie and accused him of being unprofessional. Once again Willie shrugged his shoulders, spread his arms and said: "Put the nails in." There was another occasion when Willie fell foul of Howe, but this time it was for being all too professional.

> Willie: We were staying in a hotel the night prior to playing Ipswich. Don Howe was a strict disciplinarian and laid down certain rules – one of which was that all players had to be in bed by 10pm the night prior to a match. That night Asa Hartford and I were in the bar drinking half pints of lager shandy and discussing the tactics we would use on the left side of the pitch to make life difficult for the Ipswich defence. Don Howe entered and went ballistic. It was ten minutes past ten and he screamed: "I might have know it would be you two! I've got Englishmen, Welshmen, Irishmen … I don't know what it is about you Scots, but I just can't trust you!" This angered me and I replied without thinking: "Then why do you f***in' keep signing us then?" Don went red-faced, stammered for a split second and then replied: "You're uncoachable!" Then he stormed off.

If season 1973/74 had been difficult, there were few who thought 1974/75 would be any easier. Manchester United had been relegated and would be battling to go straight back up. Aston Villa would be no mugs, nor would Norwich or Sunderland. In the cups, West Brom would go out early doors – losing in the League Cup at the hands of Norwich, and faltering in the fourth round of the FA Cup, losing 3-2 to Carlisle.

Don Howe's robot-like tactics would not help matters as the League campaign got underway. Yet Willie had proved he could slip the bonds placed on him by the manager and that term he would be compared to Houdini as in game after game he broke free to turn in some great performances. Willie recalls, after one match at the Hawthorns, the players were in the bath and the talk was all about the tactics used that day. The subject changed when a hit song of the time was aired over the radio. Singer Ray Stevens blasted out the words from his hit The Streak. Len Cantello and a few others egged on Willie to do a streak around the stadium. Willie agreed, providing they would all pay him a fiver for doing it. Willie, as always, was quite happy to earn an easy coin. The players all agreed. Willie stepped out of the bath, left by the main door, and ran around the Hawthorns in full view of the passing public. When he returned to the main door it was locked. The players had locked it. Willie battered on the door, but to no avail. Eventually a police car drew up and two burly coppers approached Willie. Thankfully, they took the prank in good spirits and helped the streaker get back in the ground. It was a very embarrassed Willie who dressed quickly and joined his team-mates in the bar. Despite his demands for payment for his daring deed (according to Willie) no player paid him a penny!

Good performances would continue throughout the season, though they rarely produced the desired results and the club would yet again fail to win promotion, finishing in sixth place. Promotion would go to Manchester United, Aston Villa and Norwich. A club of West Brom's magnitude should not have been languishing in the Second Division. Something would have to change, and change it did. Don Howe was sacked.

Willie: It would be fair to say that when Don Howe was sacked from his managerial position at the Hawthorns not everybody was sorry to see him go. Striker Tony Brown was driving home when he heard the news announced over the radio and he immediately hit the brakes and the car screeched to a halt. Tony got out of the car jumped on the bonnet and started dancing. Passing motorists must have thought he had lost the plot. It would be fair to assume that he was no big Don Howe fan.

12

HERE'S JOHNNY

Willie knew that West Brom had to get out of the Second Division, not just for the club and the fans, but for his own personal reasons. He was happy at the club and had no desire to move on, but he so desperately wanted back into the Scottish international set-up. He was approaching 30; time was running out. Having great write-ups week after week would not bring the Scotland manager knocking on his door. Scotland had an abundance of good players at that time and many of them were playing in the English First Division. Willie would have to get there, too, in order put his hat in the ring. When it was announced that the new player-manager would be Johnny Giles, Willie saw a light at the end of the tunnel. Johnny was a creative midfielder possessing immense talent and of the same stature as Willie. Giles did not take punishment from defenders lacking in talent. He would often give them a taste of their own medicine (sound familiar?) and to hell with the consequences. Willie was certain that Johnny Giles would remove his handcuffs forever and let him express himself on the field of play.

Johnny was a Republic of Ireland international who had begun his English career with Manchester United, playing alongside Bobby Charlton and Denis Law. He had made the defence-splitting pass that had found David Herd and helped United to win the FA Cup in 1963. He had then been transferred for £33,000 to Leeds United where he formed a remarkable partnership with Billy Bremner. Leeds had gone on a 29-match unbeaten run in the First Division in 1974, but then Don Revie had resigned to take over the England job. Revie recommended that Giles (now 34 years old) should take over the managerial position but the board elected to ignore him and appointed Brian Clough as boss. The Leeds players had wanted Giles and the relationship between Clough and his squad was strained, to say the least. Finally the Leeds board realised their error and fired Clough, but Giles was overlooked again and the position went to Jimmy Armfield. Giles concentrated on playing for Leeds under Armfield while also managing the Republic of Ireland team. He had been at Leeds for 12 years, had made 521 appearances and had scored 114 goals when West Brom came along and offered the player-manager's job . He accepted immediately and Willie was looking forward to his arrival.

The presence of Giles was felt instantly. Don Howe's blackboard disappeared out of the window. Training became enjoyable, everything was about five-a-side football and ball skill techniques. Willie's enthusiasm for the game returned with a vengeance and attitudes within the squad were more positive than they had been since relegation. Willie was given the freedom he had longed for. Johnny Giles was a breath of fresh air.

Under Johnny, Willie repeatedly put in breathtaking displays. The media were writing good things about him almost every week. One newspaper ran with the headline: WILLIE JOHNSTON IS THE BEST WINGER IN THE SECOND DIVISION. Very nice – but Willie wanted to be the best winger in the First Division! Playing alongside and under the leadership of Johnny Giles, Willie knew this was possible. Giles had the knack of knowing exactly how opponents would play a game. He knew exactly where the dangers lay and how to snuff them out. Willie recalls a match against Bolton. For most of the season their winger, the ex-England and Liverpool star Peter Thompson, had been creating havoc with defences as he tore them apart. Giles had the solution, and the solution was simple – and, as far as Willie was concerned, suicidal. Giles wanted Willie to follow Thompson everywhere and snuff out his threat. How ridiculous could this be? Willie had enough trouble with players giving him a hard time. How could anyone expect him to become the aggressor? But this was Giles. Thompson was a flying machine, but Willie was faster. Willie did the job that day and the threat of Thompson was removed from the game. West Brom won 2-1, in a display that included a superb goal from the rookie Bryan Robson. (Incidentally, the teenager not only showed the West Brom fans they were looking at something special, but proved to Giles and the senior players in the team that they were looking at a future English international of outstanding quality.) Although Willie enjoyed the challenge of the role that Giles had set him that day he had no desire to make it a consistent part of his repertoire. However, he could not deny that the boss had got his tactics absolutely spot on.

In the 1975/76 season, one thing that caused West Brom concern was the lack of adequate cover up front in the striker department. Jeff Astle had repeatedly struggled with injury and had now left the club. Giles knew he had to do something and did so by bringing in a striker who was already an England legend – Geoff Hurst. Hurst's career at this point was winding down. He was 34 and the question was whether he could still do the business. Was his style of play (he no longer had the burst of speed which had been a feature of his game years earlier) suited to the rigours of the Second Division? Only time would tell. No one could deny his pedigree – he had made 411 appearances for West Ham, scoring 180 goals, before spending three season at First Division Stoke City. At the Hammers he had won a European Cup Winners' Cup medal and, of course, had scored a hat-trick in the World Cup final against Germany.

Hurst was introduced to the players in the dressing room following a home League match. Willie had just stepped out of the bath and was towelling himself down when he spotted Geoff. Willie couldn't resist the opportunity to have a dig. He pointed at Hurst and shouted: "The ball never crossed the line!" Willie was, of course, referring to the disputed goal that struck the bar and may or may not (depending on your view and, in Willie's case, your nationality) have crossed the line.

Geoff smiled and replied: "Yes it did, Willie."

Willie's reply was short and sweet: "Crap!"

Willie is first to acknowledge that Geoff was a total gentleman and that they got on well together during their time together at West Brom – but Willie would remind Geoff at every possible opportunity that he had won his European medal in Barcelona while Geoff had won his at Wembley.

Unfortunately, Hurst's time at the Hawthorns was not a happy one. Giles had paid £20,000 for Geoff thinking that his experience would guide his relatively young side towards promotion. In his autobiography *1966 And All That* Geoff admitted that playing in the First Division suited his game better. He recognised that he was nearly 34, his running power was beginning to fade and that the physical demands of the Second Division meant that he couldn't get by on skill alone. After only ten games and two goals his time at West Brom was over.

Willie continued to blossom under the tactics of Johnny Giles, whom he rated as an intelligent manager and a majestic and graceful player, as well as being a very nice man. Giles had the club on the fringes of promotion and Willie found himself getting back amongst the goals. In a League match against Blackpool at Bloomfield Road Willie struck a rocket shot from all of 25 yards and earned himself the goal of the season award from ATV.

By contrast, West Brom's League Cup exploits that season were far from impressive. They drew 1-1 with Fulham at the Hawthorns – the

Fulham team included two master defenders in Bobby Moore and Alan Mullery – but lost the replay 1-0. In the FA Cup they fared a little better, beating Carlisle 3-1, then Lincoln 3-2 in the fourth round. In the fifth round their opponents were Southampton, who held them to 1-1 draw. In the replay Southampton gave them a 4-0 drubbing and it was little compensation that the Saints went on to win the FA Cup.

Back in the League, things were coming along nicely. Johnny Giles had the dressing room buzzing; promotion was now becoming more than a dream and West Brom were very much in the frame despite Sunderland being almost certain to go up as champions.

Johnny Giles continued to get his tactics right against almost every opponent; the operative word being almost. Willie recalls a game against Luton. In the dressing room before the kick-off Johnny revealed his game plan, at the end of which he turned to Willie and said: "Bud, one of their defenders, Paul Futcher, is a bit of a hard nut. Avoid him. Keep out of his way."

Of course, what Giles was trying to prevent was Willie reacting badly to any tackles that were, shall we say, over the top. Willie nodded in agreement, and player-boss Giles led his team on to the park. The game was only a few minutes old when Futcher put in one of those kind of tackles that tells an opponent hospital treatment may be required before the afternoon is out. Inevitably, the West Brom player reacted badly and was duly sent for an early bath. No it wasn't Willie – it was Johnny Giles! At half-time Giles went into his team talk as if nothing had happened and told Willie to deal with the Luton defender. Willie smiled and gave a simple two-word reply, the second of which was "off!"

As the season drew to a close, the Baggies were still in the hunt. Sunderland had already secured promotion and Bolton, Bristol City and West Brom would fight it out to secure the other two spots. On 24 April 1976 West Brom travelled to Oldham, where a victory would snatch third place in the League from Bolton. Nearly 15,000 supporters travelled that day to encourage and cheer on West Brom. Their journey was rewarded and it was fitting that Tony Brown scored the winning goal to take the club back into the First Division. Tony was the longest serving player and had scored more goals for the club than any other man. Willie doubted that it would upset him to score another against Oldham despite being born there.

Willie: For that promotion season a great deal of praise has to be directed towards Johnny Giles. He had us believing in ourselves and we were playing open attractive football. As the season progressed it was obvious that a number of teams were battling to go up and for us it almost went to the wire. During the run-in I scored a goal against Blackpool from 25 yards (I really thought that it was 45 yards but I won't grumble) which would win me the award. But it was big Tony Brown who must take the real accolade; he kept hitting the back of the net almost at every opportunity. It was only fitting that he should score the goal against Oldham that would take us back to the big time.

The fans, the players and everyone linked with the club celebrated in big style – none more so that Willie. However, he had an extra incentive. Playing in the First Division would give him the opportunity to catch the eye of Scotland manager Willie Ormond. Willie Johnston wanted his international jersey back.

13

RETURN TO THE BIG TIME

West Brom's return to the top flight meant many things to the club, not least the financial advantage of playing in what was, and still is, considered the best league in the world. The division was overflowing with excellent teams, and for many players, experiencing life at that level for the first time could be frightening. Some players would be unable to make the transition.

They would either be not good enough or were simply past their sell-by date when it came to pace and talent. Willie had no fears in that department. He knew he was fast enough and talented enough for top-flight football. The big stage would hardly send shivers down his spine – remember the man who had the audacity to sit on the ball in front of over 100,000 fans during a final at Hampden Park simply to entice the opposition to attempt to take it from him? Fear just wasn't in his vocabulary – it was up to the opposition to second-guess what he would do next on the park, and Willie knew it!

In Willie's day the English First Division was overflowing with Scottish players who had a wealth of talent and many of them were internationals: Billy Bremner, Eddie Gray, Gordon McQueen, Joe Jordan , Kenny Dalglish, Archie Gemmill, Asa Hartford … the list just goes on and on. In each game Willie would hear enough Scottish accents to make him feel at home.

Willie: Billy Bremner and I started our international careers together when we were capped against Poland at Hampden in October 1965. We would play another four or five times together for our country and against each other on several occasions for our clubs. He was a class act, I've never known a player with such stamina – I did all my running in short, sharp bursts. Billy could run all day. He was the heart of that famous Leeds team of the late 1960s and 1970s, and a magnificent captain. How I would have loved to play alongside him week in and week out at club level.

Most teams that find themselves promoted from the Second Division have only one objective in mind: avoiding relegation in that first season with the big boys. West Brom may have had that very thought, but Willie didn't share it. He had been voted the best winger in the second tier, an accolade that meant little to him. He wanted to show everyone in football he was the best in the UK. Oh, to hell with it, one of the best in the world! Bring it on.

Good performances were instrumental in assisting West Brom to come through a difficult opening period in the League and saw them hitting mid-table. The League Cup threw up a money-spinning tie for the club when they were drawn against the mighty Liverpool in the second round. The tie was played at Anfield, and West Brom played much better than the odds offered on them by the bookmakers. In fact, the performance was outstanding and Willie and the lads came away with a 1-1 draw, ensuring they would live again at the Hawthorns. At home the bookmakers cut the Baggies' odds but still left Liverpool clear favourites – and they got it wrong again. Willie and his team-mates were in inspirational form and continually pinned Liverpool back in their 18-yard box. Their endeavours brought them the result they deserved, a 1-0 victory which took West Brom into the next round.

The opponents in the next round were less than glamorous: Third Division Brighton at the Hawthorns. West Brom had started the 1976/77 season well and could perhaps be forgiven for thinking that their League Cup opposition could be brushed aside with ease. How wrong they would be. Brighton put in a strong, solid performance that caught West Brom off guard. They turned out to be a physical side and most of that physical aggression was aimed at Willie. Brighton won the game 2-0 and the League Cup was over for the Baggies. The referee that day was Derek Lloyd who, Willie feels, did little to protect the ball players and simply let the assassins take whatever measures they desired to cancel out West Brom; to cancel out Willie Johnston. During the match, Willie lost the plot and was sent for an early bath, and some treatment to his battered legs. But this was a sending-off with a difference. Willie's retaliation wasn't directed at the player who had continually chopped him down – it was directed at the referee, as Willie attempted to boot him up the backside.

The FA took action, fining Willie £100 and banning him for five games. Thankfully, Willie didn't actually connect with the ref's rear end or our story may well have ended at this point.

West Brom also took action against Willie for the incident, and the Scot knew he needed to start practising counting to ten again. Yet despite the sending-off Willie had been performing well and, on numerous occasions, had been outstanding. So much so that the West Brom fans and large factions of the media were calling for him to be included in one of Willie Ormond's Scotland squads. The good performances continued following his suspension and Willie felt that a Scottish call-up was getting ever closer. In the League West Brom were in the top eight (although holding up that pile) and their next venture was the FA Cup. When the third-round draw was made, West Brom discovered they would be travelling to Maine Road to meet high-flyers Manchester City. City were challenging for the League title and contained several English internationals, including Dennis Tueart and Peter Barnes.

Naturally their squad also included Scottish internationals, namely Willie Donachie and Asa Hartford. Asa had, of course, been at West Brom with Willie and was a player he greatly admired. Willie knew that, despite being diagnosed with a hole in the heart, the talented youngster would go on to earn many caps for Scotland. He applauded his immense strength of character when the youngster took the news in his stride and continued to battle to prove he was a player of immense quality, worthy of playing for a top side and for his country. Willie looked forward to meeting him again.

Despite Man City's high League position, Johnny Giles took his team to Maine Road looking for a victory. It nearly came off. The Baggies played well. Willie was outstanding and rounded off the day by scoring a goal in what turned out to be a 1-1 draw, but there was a downside to the game. Willie was booked again. This really annoyed him, and he was convinced (and still is) that it only came about because his name was Willie Johnston. Trouble had broken out during the game following some bruising tackling and a heated skirmish erupted. Willie (for once) was not involved, but he did put himself in the picture when he went to pull one of his team-mates away from the situation. He caught the referee's eye and that was enough.

The ref ignored all the aggressors and took Willie's name, and the fiery Fifer had to restrain himself from kicking the man in black in the but. The following day the referee's action was condemned by the press, but that did little to quell Willie's anger.

The replay at the Hawthorns did not go West Brom's way. Despite hitting Manchester City with everything they had, they could not break down an outstanding defence. City scored against the run of play and Albion's hopes of a long run in the FA Cup were dashed.

In the League the good performances continued. In a match against Spurs at the Hawthorns, Spurs' new signing winger Peter Taylor, who would later go on to manage Crystal Palace, Hull, Brighton, Leicester and England's under-21 team among others, was having a sparkling debut and threatened to destroy the Baggies before the half-time whistle. He had made one goal and scored another himself, after an inspired run from Willie's former Rangers team-mate, Alfie Conn. However, Spurs didn't anticipate what the second half would bring. Willie put in an amazing, magical performance that saw him become the provider of four goals, steering West Brom to finish 4-2 winners.

Following the match Spurs captain, Steve Perryman, told the press: "That was the best first half performance we have played for a long time, but I just don't know what went wrong later on." Well the answer to that was simple; Willie Johnston single-handedly destroyed their rearguard.

Willie remembers that during the next home match (he can't recall the opposition) he went to take a corner kick. There was a fan who always sat in the same seat, and always spoke to Willie when the opportunity existed.

"How are you doing today, Willie?" he asked.

"Fine," Willie replied, "I've been busy in my garden all week."

"I've been the same," replied the fan.

Willie took the kick, then turned back to talk to the fan. "You don't know anybody who's selling a greenhouse?" he asked. The opposition's defence cleared Willie's corner and were now heading into the West Brom half.

"I've got one for sale," replied the fan.

"How much?" asked Willie.

They negotiated a price.

"You'd better get back on the pitch, Willie. They're attacking our goal!" advised the fan. Willie ran back up the park.

"What the f*** are you up to?" screamed Johnny Giles.

"I was buying a greenhouse," Willie informed his confused player-manager.

The 1976/77 season drew to a close and West Brom narrowly missed out on a European spot by finishing in seventh place. The team had grown in stature and had undoubtedly established themselves in the top division – but what of Willie and that international jersey?

14

SCOTLAND CALLS

Willie Ormond had been appointed Scottish manager in 1973 following the departure of Tommy Docherty. As a player Ormond had signed for Hiberian from Stenhousemuir in 1946 and became one of the Hibs' 'Famous Five' forward line. That quintet of Ormond, Bobby Johnstone, Lawrie Reilly, Gordon Smith and Eddie Turnbull made up perhaps the strongest forward line of its day, with all five scoring more than 100 goals for the club (Ormond scored 147). He also won six Scotland caps and three League championship medals. When he retired Ormond coached at Falkirk before taking the manager's job at St Johnstone in 1967. In 1969 he led the club to the League Cup final and third place in the League, guiding the provincial club into Europe for the first time. As manager of Scotland he took a talented Scottish squad to the World Cup finals in Germany. Scotland failed to qualify for the knockout stages and yet, amazingly, returned home as the only undefeated team tournament.

As a man and a manager Ormond was well respected by the players as he began preparing them for an assault on the World Cup qualifiers for 1978. He had been experimenting with various players to find the right combination that would take the country to the World Cup finals. Willie's form at West Brom brought him the call to join the squad that would take on Sweden in a friendly at Hampden. An excited Johnston joined his fellow players at Largs several days before the match. Willie's first impression was of how much things had changed since his last time in a Scottish squad (seven years had elapsed in what seemed like a blink of an eye). The whole set-up had become more organised and more professional, and only one player, Sandy Jardine, was still part of the squad from when Willie had last served his country.

Willie: It was my wife, Margaret, who took the phone call from Willie Ormond asking for me. Margaret had no idea who he was and shouted to me in the living room: "Billy, there's a Mr Ormond on the phone – will I tell him you're out?" I nearly broke my neck rushing to the phone. This was the call I had awaited for seven years and it would be impossible to put into words just how I felt when he told me that I was in his next squad. It wasn't till later that he told me I was part of his plans despite the SFA requesting my exclusion. They felt that my disciplinary record wasn't one they wanted associated with a Scottish international. But Willie Ormond was his own man and would select the squad he felt could do Scotland proud – and for that I've always been in his debt.

Willie Ormond had been a great player and on our first meeting I was left with the impression that he could be a great manager. Yet, like all people who are on the verge of greatness, he had a flaw. He liked a drink or two or three. The first sign I saw of this was when he gathered the squad together to name his team that would face Sweden at Hampden. The announcement went like this: "Alan Rough, Danny McGrain, Tom Forsyth, John Blackley, Don Anochie … all the players looked at each other with confusion, all were thinking the same thing. Who the hell was Don Anochie? Of course, Willie Ormond meant to say Willie Donachie. We all had a good laugh about it afterwards – especially Willie Donachie, who initially thought he had been dropped. Willie Ormond, first and foremost, was a magnificent person and a gentleman. he also had a great football brain, and I was gutted when he decided that the Sweden match would be his last as manager of Scotland.

Willie could not fault the manager's professionalism in preparation. The day before the game Ormond sought out Willie in the Largs hotel and asked him to join him in a walk. They strolled down to the shore sharing general chit-chat. Willie felt convinced that Ormond was about to announce that he would be in the team – which he did, but it was what followed the announcement that shook Willie.

"Bud, you're the best winger in England at this present time and that's why I want you in the team. It won't be my strongest team, I'm still experimenting and you'll have a couple of youngsters playing alongside you on the left side, but (another but) I need you to play well, and not to get yourself involved in any disciplinary action. I want you in my team but the SFA doesn't want you in the squad. Prove them wrong."

Willie was gobsmacked. He hadn't upset the SFA for a number of years and, oh, how he hated them now. He admired Willie Ormond's bravery to defy the governing body by including him in the squad. The day before the match Ormond announced his team: Rough, McGrain, Forsyth, Blackley, Donachie, Glavin, Dalglish, Hartford, Burns, Pettigrew, Johnston.

Willie was thankful that his former team-mate at West Brom, Asa Hartford, was playing alongside him. Asa was determined to battle his way into the team and become established prior to the World Cup qualifiers and Willie was equally determined to join him. He thought the fact that they had been team-mates together should assist them in achieving their goals. Everyone knew that the Swedes would be formidable opponents and could not be treated lightly. As it turned out Scotland dominated the match and ran out comfortable 3-1 winners. Asa strengthened his case by scoring one of the goals (Kenny Dalglish and substitute Joe Craig added the others), as did Willie advance his own cause by putting in an excellent display.

On the downside, rumours were rife that Ormond was about to resign and return to club management. Which is exactly what he did. Willie was all too aware that the next manager may not be strong enough to defy the SFA and keep him in the squad for the Home International championships.

The SFA didn't wait to long to appoint the new manager and that man was Ally MacLeod. He would have been the choice of the majority of Scottish football supporters and Willie felt (for once) that the SFA had got it right.

Willie: Ally MacLeod was one of the nicest people you could ever wish to meet. He was brilliant at man-management and a good motivator. Where he fell down was when it came to his tactical knowledge, which he lacked in a big way. Ally was old-school and simply believed that the team should go out, play well and win the game no matter who the opposition were. When it came to Argentina '78 it was the lack of opposition knowledge that would be the main reason for Scotland's failure in the opening two matches. Yet Ally should be applauded. Any man who could whip up such hype and get a whole nation behind him deserves that applause.

MacLeod, like Willie, had been a left-winger during his playing career. Amongst his clubs had been St Mirren, Blackburn Rovers and Hibernian. In the 1960 FA Cup final he had been voted Man of the Match despite Blackburn losing 3-0 to Wolves. On his retirement from playing he became manager of Ayr United. He took Ayr back to Scotland's First Division and maintained their status. He also steered the provincial club to a League Cup semi-final and also set a home attendance record of more than 25,000 as fans watched the club beat Rangers 2-1. Following this result Ally was named as Ayr's citizen of the year. In 1975 he took over the reins at Aberdeen, whom he guided to League Cup final success and second place in the League. He would now be faced with steering Scotland through the Home International championships, but more importantly, through to the finals of the World Cup. MacLeod was an extrovert bursting with ambition for the national team – but would he be brave enough to include Willie in his plans? The answer would not be long in coming.

MacLeod's first match in charge would be in the Home Internationals against Wales. The game would have a great deal more significance than normal. Wales were also in Scotland's World Cup qualifying group. A win would give Scotland a psychological advantage prior to the World Cup game. When Ally named his squad for the match Willie was more than relieved to find his name among the others. The game would be played at Wrexham on the 28 May 1977. When Willie and the rest of the squad met with Ally for the first time he introduced himself by saying: "My name is Ally MacLeod and I am a winner!" When the team was named Willie was disappointed to find himself on the bench as MacLeod went for a more defensive set-up. The team was: Rough, McGrain, Donachie, Rioch, McQueen, Forsyth, Masson, Gemmill, Parlane, Dalglish, Hartford.

The match was far from memorable and finished in a 0-0 draw. The Welsh snuffed out the two-pronged Scottish attack of Parlane and Dalglish by sheer weight of numbers. Willie came on as sub late in the game for Bruce Rioch but made little impact. MacLeod would have to put his thinking cap on for the game against Northern Ireland in four days time. At Hampden MacLeod made two changes to the team that had drawn with the Welsh; Joe Jordan took over in attack from Derek Parlane and Willie replaced Archie Gemmill, giving the team more power (Jordan) and pace (Willie). Willie would renew his left-sided partnership with Asa Hartford and Willie Donachie. A good performance was required and was duly delivered, with goals from Dalglish (two) and McQueen brushing Northern Ireland aside.

Willie: Joe Jordan was not only big in stature; he had an enormous heart. He would battle away all day, and no matter how good the opposition's defence, he would cause them mighty problems. There isn't a club in the world that wouldn't like to have a Joe Jordan in their team.

The player who impressed Willie most that day was Don Masson. Willie had not played with him before, but liked his style. Masson conducted affairs in the midfield, he was a ball-winner and play-maker of the highest order, Willie was beginning to sense that there could be something special about this team. The game against the 'Auld Enemy' (England) was looming and everybody wanted to be part of that. A few days later the players were on their way to Wembley and, like all Scottish squads, they so much wanted to do the business.

Three days before the clash with England, hordes of Scottish fans poured into London and took over the city. Two years earlier in 1975 they had witnessed the massacre of their team when they were beaten 5-1. Yet, there was a belief about this squad and the new manager. The Tartan Army knew this squad could play football and that, with Ally MacLeod as the new maestro, they could make things happen. They longed for a repeat of the performance from a decade before, the day the Scots became 'world champions' when they destroyed England 3-2 at Wembley. On that unforgettable day, Jim Baxter had played keepie-uppie with the ball and humiliated the English players. The Tartan Army invaded the pitch, the whole of Scotland went wild and Bobby Moore and company disappeared into the night. Now once again there was a feeling of expectancy – something was in the air.

This was the way of the Scots, fans and players alike. Nothing mattered more than stuffing England, and that included the World Cup, at least for this week. The clash would decide the Home International championship. If England beat Scotland they would win it. A Scotland victory would see them crowned champions. If it was a draw then Wales would take the title. To the Scots the championship meant very little if the 'Auld Enemy' couldn't be humbled. All this may sound as if the Scottish nation has an overwhelming hatred for the English. This is simply not the case and couldn't be further from the truth. It's the English sporting media who get right up the nostrils of Scottish fans and players. Their arrogance is second to none. They have their nation (no matter what the tournament) reaching the final stages before they've even qualified; they have them in the final before they've reached the semi, and so on. In other words they continually put their size-ten boots in their even bigger mouths, and their approach was no different in the run-up to this match. But Willie Johnston, Kenny Dalglish and company had other ideas.

The day prior to the match the manager privately announced the team to the squad before releasing it to the press. Willie listened with more than a hint of trepidation; he was carrying an injury from the match against

Ireland and had desperately tried, during training that morning, to prove to Ally MacLeod that he was fit. Before the left-wing position was named Willie knew he was in. The boss had selected Donachie and Hartford for the left side of defence and midfield and Willie felt certain the boss would keep the left-sided triangle that had proved so effective in the last game. He was not to be disappointed. The team: Rough, McGrain, Donachie, Forsyth, McQueen, Rioch, Masson, Dalglish, Jordan, Hartford, Johnston.

This would be Willie's third time playing against England and this was the one that would mean the most. He so much wanted to shine on the Wembley stage.

Willie recalls the evening prior to the match as being a relaxing affair in the confines of their hotel, with everyone retiring early in the hope of a good night's sleep. Willie, like a number of other players, placed his football boots outside his room before settling down for the night. During the night one of the backroom staff would come along and paint an extra two white stripes on each boot. This wasn't some strange voodoo ritual that would help bring about the defeat of the English; it was a money-earner for all the players concerned. *Adidas* had offered the Scotland players £300 each if they wore their brand of boots at Wembley. Willie, like most of the players in the team, wore *Puma* boots and no player was going to change his boots for such an important match. But neither were they willing to turn down the chance of earning 300 quid each! The problem was *Puma* boots have one white stripe on the side and *Adidas* have three. Solution: paint two extra stripes on each boot and take the money – job done! Earlier in the evening the team had decided that the money from *Adidas* would be clubbed together and invested sensibly. Lou Macari would act as the investor by placing all the money with a major bookmaker at odds of 9/4 (Scotland to beat England) and 9/2 Dunfermline (to win the Oaks), a return of over £5,000 per player if both bets came off.

In the dressing room prior to the match Ally relayed his thoughts to the players. He was confident that the team could be the first to win at Wembley in a decade. He emphasised his feelings on the comparison of the two teams. Scotland had more skill, more class and more heart. His only fear was the young English high-flying right winger, Trevor Francis. He felt he could cause the team problems. In the silence following, Willie piped up: "Don't worry about him, Boss … he'll be too busy chasing me."

It was 2.56pm on 4 June 1977, and Wembley was bursting at the seams with a sea of tartan as Ally MacLeod and his players walked down the tunnel on to the pitch to a rapturous reception. The famous Wembley roar, as per normal when Scotland were the visitors, had been transformed into one with a distinctly Scottish accent. At 3pm the match got under way and from the start Scotland set their stall out. Hartford collected the ball in midfield and sent it to Donachie, who played it along the byline to Willie. Already the left-sided triangle was in operation. The English full-back came towards him and Willie jinked one way and then the other four or five times before sending a perfect ball to the feet of the advancing Hartford, who hit a cracking shot from 20 yards which narrowly flew wide of the English right-hand post. The game continued in this vein with every Scot on the park playing superbly; but it wasn't until the 43rd minute that the deadlock was broken. Scotland were awarded a free-kick, just on the left side of the 18-yard line, and the English defence were at sixes and sevens trying to work out how to deal with the aerial threat of Jordan and McQueen as Asa Hartford took it. McQueen rose above the whole defence and headed the ball towards goal. Keeper Ray Clemence was beaten and Scotland were in front. An injury to Joe Jordan saw Lou Macari introduced to the match but the rhythm of play continued in Scotland's favour.

Willie: Gordon's huge frame was often enough to frighten off most forwards, but he could play a bit as well. He was a great header of a ball and not just to clear his lines. He could be found producing great headers in the opponents' 18-yard box and scored many a spectacular goal for both club and country.

At half-time in the dressing room Ally MacLeod was ecstatic and encouraged the players to give more of the same. Substitute Lou Macari added, to the bewilderment of MacLeod: "It's more important than you think, boys – Dunfermline's just won the Oaks!"

In the second half Scotland continued to pressurise the bedraggled English defence at every opportunity. In the 61st minute they were further rewarded for their efforts. Asa Hartford sent a defence-splitting pass down the left wing, Willie took off like a deer and ran the ball to the byline, sending over an inch-perfect cross before clattering into a photographer, who was sitting on the grass close to the corner flag.

Willie was furious with the photographer for being so near the field of play and questioned his parentage, as he watched Bruce Rioch head the ball back towards goal where it was met by Kenny Dalglish. Kenny's first shot was blocked but as the English defence gathered around him he managed to scramble the ball over the line and Scotland were 2-0 ahead. Victory was in their grasp. England could not get back in the game despite being awarded a penalty in the 88th minute – it gave them nothing more than a consolation goal, in what would go down as a richly deserved victory for the Scots. At the final whistle the Wembley crowd (that is the 90 per cent that were Scots) went ballistic and as the players gathered to salute them the fans duly invaded the pitch. Willie, with thoughts of Barcelona, bolted for the tunnel.

In the dressing room the celebrations between the players continued, unaware of what was happening outside. Ally MacLeod was delighted, the squad were delighted and Lou Macari was calculating the winnings! When things had settled down in the dressing room Ally took Willie outside and from a high vantage point they looked down at what was happening on the pitch. The playing surface was hardly visible for a sea of tartan, as the fans celebrated another memorable victory. They dug up the pitch and broke up the goalposts as souvenirs (the playing surface was due to be replaced anyway).

Ally turned to Willie and said: "It's like Culloden out there."

"Bannockburn," replied Willie.

"What?" asked Ally.

"Bannockburn, Boss. We got beaten at Culloden."

Back at the hotel the squad met for a celebratory drink and most would be going home for a well-earned break before their next venture. Willie, on the other hand, would be staying at the hotel for another day. His wife had travelled down and had been at the match and it was their 12th wedding anniversary, so the day represented a double celebration. Not only was Willie's wife in town, he had bought a number of tickets for friends from Cardenden, his home village in Fife, and they had witnessed the victory. Willie met up with Margaret in the hotel and romantically presented her with 12 red roses, then duly announced that he was going out for a drink with the Fifers – hell, they hadn't paid for the tickets yet!

It was still the close season and Ally MacLeod would soon be naming his squad, to embark in eight days time for a tournament in preparation for the World Cup qualifiers and the finals themselves. The tournament would be played in South America.

15

TELL THEM WILLIE BOY IS HERE

Scotland's South American tour would begin in Chile. Chile was a country of unrest and all the Scottish Players and the SFA would receive letters from footballing unions urging them not to visit the country and to pull out of the visit to South America. The SFA and Ally MacLeod thought that the tour would be essential for the build-up to next year's World Cup finals – providing Scotland qualified – which would be held in Argentina.

Every player in the Scottish squad elected to make the trip. No player would have been willing to put his World Cup squad place in jeopardy, no matter the political climate.

In September 1973, General Augustin Pinochet began a military takeover of President Salvador Allende's legal government. Backed by the CIA, as in the case of many Latin American coups, tanks crashed through the capital city of Santiago ready to install a new and brutal puppet dictator.

By 1977 the political situation had eased, but the country was far from the safest place in the world for Scotland to visit. The SFA responded to the Scottish squad who made the trip in their usual fashion; there would be no bonuses paid for the matches played on the South American continent. The SFA's Ernie Walker made the following announcement to the press before Scotland's first game in Santiago: "The players who are stripped for each match will be paid £100 and the rest £50. These are friendly matches and we do not pay bonuses for games in this category."

Does the category not change, slightly, when you're in a country where thousands of people have disappeared, many of whom were believed to have been executed?

Obviously not! Financially, it would mean that during the 16 days with the SFA party, each player was guaranteed £230 and the most any player could earn was £300. In addition to this, each player would receive a miserly £5 per day spending allowance. On reflection, those who played against England earned twice as much as those who were putting their lives at risk in South America. Certainly some lives would be at risk, especially Willie's, when Scotland played Argentina in their second match. Other European countries who also hoped to qualify for the World Cup finals made the South American trip. Among them were England, West Germany, France and Poland, and it is to be hoped they were better treated financially than the Scots.

The squad arrived in Santiago six days before their first game, which would be played in the Estadio Nacional. After they had settled into their hotel, the players were given a degree of freedom to explore the safer parts of the city, with a reminder from Ally MacLeod that a curfew existed and they all must be back in the hotel by 9.30pm. Willie left the hotel for a wander and met up with a couple of Scottish journalists, who he agreed to accompany to a local bar for a couple of beers. Naturally, conversation turned to football, a subject that serves to bring Willie out of his self-contained state and turns him into an extrovert. The journalists were keen to know how

Willie would perform on the tour and Willie was far from shy in providing them with his thoughts. "The South Americans will soon know that Willie Boy is here," he exclaimed.

Unfortunately they would know (or at least two of them would) much sooner than he intended. Beer followed beer before Dougie Baillie, a reporter with the *Scottish Sunday Post*, suggested that Willie should try one of the local drinks, known as planters' punch. Willie was game and a large bowl of the concoction arrived at the table. The bowl was decorated with a mountain of various fruits that would have delighted Del-Boy Trotter. In due course, a rather inebriated Willie headed out of the bar in the hope of getting a taxi back to the hotel. However, the streets of Santiago were deserted; the curfew was in force. Eventually two armed policemen spotted Willie weaving his way through the narrow streets. They duly apprehended him and Willie feared he might soon become one of country's missing thousands. Luckily, one of the officers was a football fan and recognised Willie from a newspaper photograph. The policemen escorted him back to his hotel, with a stern warning not to break the curfew for the rest of his stay. A relieved Willie picked up the phone in the foyer and dialled what he thought was his room number to inform his roommate, Don Masson, of his close shave. As he began to speak he recognised the voice who interrupted. It was that of Ally MacLeod. Willie had dialled the wrong number and he quickly banged the phone down and made for the lifts. As he approached the nearest lift, the door opened automatically and out stepped Ally MacLeod.

Willie attempted (and failed) to look sober and was subjected to a tongue-lashing from his boss before being ushered into the lift by a far-from-happy MacLeod. Ally pushed the button for Willie's floor and the lift gave a little jolt. The jolt was enough to activate the planters' punch into producing its final telling blow and Willie was violently sick all over the lift.

The following day Ally MacLeod gathered the squad together for a meeting where he announced that it had been his intention to play the team that had comfortably beaten England several weeks before. Then headded: "But that will not happen now. One of those players broke the curfew and will now be dropped." All eyes turned to Willie, who cringed and hung his head until the meeting was over.

For the remaining days prior to the match, Willie trained harder than anybody and kept a low profile when back at the hotel. On the morning of the match Ally MacLeod announced the following team: Rough, McGrain, Donachie, Buchan, Forsyth, Rioch, Masson, Dalglish, Macari, Hartford, Johnston.

MacLeod never revealed why he had a change of heart and elected to play Willie – and Willie was never brave enough to ask. When the squad arrived at Chile's national stadium they found it an eerie place. The stadium had been used for holding political prisoners during the coup and Scotland's dressing-room walls were riddled with bullet holes where many people's lives had come to an abrupt end.

The game itself was a spectacle. Chile were a typical South American team who played with flair and skill but, surprisingly, without the over-the-top physical contact so often expected from teams on that continent. However, if the Chileans had skill, on that day Scotland had more. The team, to a man, played with rhythm and style. Don Masson was an inspiration in midfield, but it was Willie Johnston who had all the Chilean fans talking as they left the ground at full-time. His explosive bursts down the wing, his tantalising runs with the ball and his cheeky dummies as he bewildered the Chilean defence served the fans with a brand of entertainment they undoubtedly enjoyed. On top of all this, Willie was the provider of three of Scotland's four goals as the boys in dark blue ran out 4-2 victors. He had run riot that day, being so much on song that the Chilean defence could not cope with him. His team-mates became aware of this and simply kept providing him with more of the ball. Willie responded and was the provider of three of Scotland's four goals, Dalglish, Macari and Hartford taking advantage of his fantastic play. Thus it was a happy Scottish squad that headed back to their hotel to prepare for their journey to Buenos Aires, where they would face Argentina.

Willie: The South American tour was a great experience for the squad a year prior to returning for the World Cup in Argentina. On a personal level I had a great tour. I went to South America totally believing in my ability and in the opening game against Chile I proved it to myself and, hopefully, to some of my critics. The tour was great preparation for the World Cup Little did we know it would be the only real preparation we would have.

16

ARGENTINA'S MAFIA HIT MEN

Scotland arrived in Buenos Aires on a high following their excellent performance against Chile. The squad was carrying a few injuries with Joe Jordan, who had missed the match against Chile, still struggling and captain Bruce Rioch doubtful for the clash with Argentina. Nevertheless, the atmosphere in the camp was good and everybody was eager to play against Argentina who, one year on, would host the World Cup finals.

Finally, When Ally MacLeod named his team, Rioch was missing, but Martin Buchan would deputise as skipper. Jordan was again absent. The team: Rough, McGrain, Donachie, Buchan, Forsyth, Gemmill, Masson, Dalglish, Macari, Hartford, Johnston.

The game would be played in extreme heat in the massive Boca Stadium and the Scots had no idea that they were about to be subjected to a 90-minute reign of terror. The Argentinians used every dirty trick in the book to stop the visitors playing attractive football. Willie Johnston would receive more than his fair share of abuse from his marker, Vicente Pernia. This was a man who could only be described as a thug masquerading as a footballer.

Scotland started the game well, and they played entertaining football throughout the confrontation. This must have been difficult as player after player was hacked to the ground by the Argentinian hit men. Eventually they singled out Willie, who was destroying Pernia, to be taken out of the game. In the first half Willie had been kicked, mauled, bruised and spat at, but in the second half Pernia decided to up the abuse. Minutes after the interval the defender sent Willie sprawling again. The Scot struggled to his feet and approached the hatchet man, saying something to him. Pernia responded by spitting into Willie's face in full view of the referee. Willie walked away cleaning his face with his jersey. Amazingly, the ref booked Willie, apparently for placing his face in the way of Pernia's spittle.

Only a few seconds later, with the ball at the other side of the park, Pernia ran past Willie and punched him in the kidneys. The incident went unseen by the referee, but was witnessed by the linesman. Willie climbed painfully to his feet and turned away from Pernia in disgust. He had not raised so much as a finger in the defender's direction. The referee stopped the game, spoke with his linesman and sent Pernia off. He then turned to Willie and sent him off as well! Willie was in tears and had to be assisted from the pitch by Asa Hartford and trainer Donnie McKinnon.

Willie: The Argentinians were no doubt aware of my performance against Chile and wanted me stopped. Pernia was the man delegated for the task. I just wanted to continue in the same manner as the Chilean game. I did, and Pernia came after me. Bad tackle followed bad tackle and eventually I snapped and retaliated. The ref immediately sent Pernia off and it was evident that I would escape with a warning. But the Argentina players were having none of it. They hounded the referee and demanded that I should go and he eventually gave in and issued me with my marching orders. The realisation of the sending-off struck me immediately. My disciplinary record was bad – this dismissal could end my World Cup dreams. I broke down and had to be helped from the pitch. Thankfully I was later cleared and received no punishment

Everyone in the stadium knew what had taken place, but only one thing was going through Willie's mind: was his disciplinary record about to end his international career? The game continued with the remaining Scots still taking more than their fair share of abuse. It finished 1-1, with each team scoring from the penalty spot. After the match, captain Martin Buchan revealed that, when Argentina were awarded a penalty for no reason whatsoever, the whole team was close to walking off. They didn't, and at the final whistle they were the only team that could leave the pitch with their heads held high, although their bodies were battered and bruised. The partisan Argentinian crowd certainly found out about Scotland the brave that day.

Back in the dressing room everyone tried to console Willie and assure him that all would be well. But he didn't believe it. He knew the SFA had not wanted him as part of the set-up and that this dismissal would serve as an ideal opportunity to dispense with his services. Even when Ally MacLeod assured him that he would be fine, Willie would have none of it. In his mind, Ally MacLeod may have been the manager – but he wasn't the SFA.

Amazingly, the Argentinian striker, Leopoldo Luque, appeared in the dressing room to seek Willie out. Not to give his apologies for the way he had been treated by the thug Pernia, but to ask Willie for his Scotland shirt, as Pernia wanted it as a souvenir. Willie's reply comprised two emphatic words.

Back at the hotel, as the team nursed their injuries with a few bottles of beer, Luque appeared again. He joined Willie at the bar and was more than friendly towards him. Before he left he whispered a few words to the Scot out of earshot of the other players. "John ... ston," he said in broken English. "You are very good player ... but be warned ... do not return to Argentina for the World Cup ... things will not be nice for you." And then he left. Willie would reflect on Luque's words, not that day – but in the not-too-distant future.

He felt slightly better about things the following day when Ally MacLeod assured him that the SFA would take no action against him, and that he would play in the next (and last) game of the tour against Brazil. Actually, the whole team would feel better when they discovered that the Argentinians had been slated by their own press in a number of national newspapers that morning. *La Nacion* reported that Scotland was able to expose the ineffectiveness of the Argentinian squad with little effort. It praised the performance of "that remarkable player, forward Willie Johnston." The paper also accused the Brazilian referee of giving Argentina "a non-existent penalty kick." The *Cronica* newspaper noted that the match was "full of fouls performed for the most part by Argentina," and claimed that the equalising penalty-kick was a "gift" from the referee. Another newspaper said: "Our world has fallen down. It is no use having the great stadia and everything in readiness for the World Cup if our players are going to play as they did against Scotland."

The president of the Argentinian FA, Dr Alfredo Cantilo, personally sought an interview with SFA vice-president Tom Lauchlan to express his regret for the way in which too many of his country's players had acted. Nevertheless, the history books will simply show the result as a 1-1 draw, but the Scottish players who took the park that day can claim that the moral victory was theirs. On their last evening in their plush hotel in Buenos Aires, the squad discovered that Joe Jordan and Gordon McQueen were due to get married – not to each other – on their return to the UK. To a man, they felt a celebration was in order and it was duly arranged in the hotel bar. Drink flowed all evening and by the end of the night the bar looked as if it had been hit by a bomb. The inebriated, comprising most of the squad, slipped off to bed.

The players met in the morning at breakfast, most of them still nursing sore heads. The meal was a quiet affair. Quiet, at least until an angry Ally MacLeod entered the dining area. He was waving a piece of paper about and screaming. The piece of paper, still flapping in the air, was the bill for the previous night's party. The squad had charged it to the SFA. I asked Willie, during our recent interview sessions, who had instigated charging the party to the SFA. He wouldn't say. He simply smiled at me in that rascally manner of his, and the smile alone told me he had played his part in putting one over on the squad's footballing bosses.

The next day, the team packed their bags and prepared for the journey that would take them to Rio de Janeiro, where they would face the mighty Brazil.

17

THE BOYS IN BRAZIL

Scotland arrived in Rio de Janeiro, the former capital of Brazil, and were met by blistering heat. Sweat streamed from their brows as they stepped from the plane. Still, it would take more than the tropical climate to prevent them from taking in the spectacular views and sights of that marvellous city. It is home to the famous statue of Christ the Redeemer, one of the seven modern wonders of the world; then there is Copacabana beach, Sugarloaf Mountain and, of course, the Maracana, where Scotland would soon face Brazil. Unfortunately the city also has a dark side. The crime rate in Rio is one of the highest in the world. Homicide is common with as many as 80 victims a week. Rio's lowly paid and ill-equipped police are known for their violence, killing as many as 1,000 people a year. One thing was for sure – Willie Boy had better not go walkabout here.

On the football front, the media were talking highly of the Scottish team. Ally MacLeod, forever the extrovert, soaked up all the praise, lavished it on his squad and added some more. Scotland were now joint first in the European rankings along with West Germany, a statistic Ally continually quoted when talking to the press. In an interview he gave prior to the Brazil game, he said: "Brazil are the number-one team in the world, but we know we're pretty good, too. We are looking forward to playing them on their own ground and beating them. I've told all the lads that this game is a rehearsal for next year's World Cup final." This was typical MacLeod, continually beating Scotland's drum and, on most occasions, it served to inspire and motivate the players.

The Brazilians, too, were giving Scotland a good press. Even the Brazilian manager, Claudio Coutinho, was getting in on the act and told the media: "Scotland will not be easy to beat. We have seen them here on

TV in their matches against England, Chile and Argentina. I rate them as one of the best sides in Europe, certainly better than England." Most people would have agreed with the Brazilian manager's words. Scotland did have an accomplished squad of players and they were getting better with each game that passed. The team, however, were still smarting from the physical abuse they had suffered during the game with Argentina. In reality, had the encounter with Brazil been the first game of the tour, Scotland would have been very much up for the challenge, but they were tired and weary, and some were bruised and battered. They had hardly seen anything of their families since the start of the Home Internationals over a month ago, and a number of them wished they could have gone home immediately following the game in Buenos Aires. Yet I've no doubt that when the players saw the magnificence of the Maracana, they would all have wanted to be selected to play against the greatest team in the world. The stadium holds more than 200,000 supporters and is one of the largest in the world. Pope John Paul II has visited the stadium; Frank Sinatra has entertained a huge crowd there. The question was: would Willie and company put on a show for the football-crazy Brazilians?

Several days before the game, the players were given a break from training and were given the opportunity to take in some of the splendour of Rio. Willie had arranged with one of the hotel staff for transportation to be laid on to give a day's tour. Willie would be joined by Don Masson, Tom Forsyth and Asa Hartford. Well, he couldn't be allowed out by himself. Outside the hotel, as arranged, the hotel porter's brother pulled up in his car – the word "car" is rather a loose term, as the Trotters Independent Traders' three-wheeled van was in better nick – to begin the tour. With all four squashed up inside the sagging vehicle they headed for the famous statue of Christ, then on to Sugarloaf Mountain. This monolithic peak of granite and quartz rises straight out of the water at the mouth of Guanabara Bay and stands 1,299ft above sea-level. Visitors can reach the peak by way of a glass-panelled cable car, which is capable of holding 75 passengers. Four of these passengers were Willie, Tom, Don and Asa, happy to escape the confines of their not-so-luxurious limousine for a short period. Willie was to learn one thing that day – he's scared of heights. Halfway up, passengers change cars and Willie would go no further. He travelled back down while the others continued to the top. Willie, naturally, waited in a bar until their safe return. Then it was on to Copacabana beach. Life is vibrant there. Like ants, thousands of people make their way to and from the beach. Either just strolling or exercising along the wavy Avenida Atlantica on roller-skates, jogging or on bicycles. You will hear many different languages, meet people with different social backgrounds. Then there are the sellers, entertainers, businessmen and beggars. Oh, and a few more bars. The sun was setting as the four adventurers returned to their hotel. They paid their guide and settled down for a few drinks in the bar before dinner. Next day it would be back to hard graft as they prepared for the forthcoming encounter.

On match day Scotland were still carrying injured players. Rough had a recurrence of an old shoulder injury, while Kenny Dalglish and Willie still bore the scars of the match in Argentina. Rough and Dalglish elected to play, as did Willie, but he needed the aid of a cortisone injection to achieve it. The drug was a type of steroid which was administered intravenously to relieve the pains and aches footballers regularly felt. What no one was aware of then was the long-term effect it would have on the thousands of players who received regular jabs to numb the pain and play on regardless of their own health.

Willie: Let's make it quite clear that players were never forced to take cortisone injections to help them play through injury. Most would take the injections to allow them to play in big important matches. It was vital for each player to retain his place in the team. Being out through injury could mean being out for a long time if your replacement happened to be playing well. Then there was the financial side of things, big bonuses for big matches. There were no bonuses if you didn't play. I personally believe that taking cortisone has had an effect on me in later life. I have days when walking is very painful because of all the injuries I received to my ankles.

Cortisone is no longer used in professional sport as the debilitating problems it caused in a generation of footballers have led to major knee, ankle and hip problems. That is due to players going out onto the pitch when, without the painkilling injections, they would have been sitting in the stand recuperating naturally. Ally named the following team: Rough, McGrain, Donachie, Rioch, Forsyth, Buchan, Masson, Gemmill, Dalglish, Hartford, Johnston.

The game itself was far from a classic. Scotland struggled in the heat and looked jaded. Willie didn't last the whole match. His injuries finally beat him and he was substituted. Scotland eventually went down 2-0. It wasn't a massacre, but it was not the fanfare finish with which they had hoped to end the South American tour. In terms of preparation for the World Cup finals in Argentina the following year the expedition had been a success. They had faced and learned from different levels of South

American play. They had acclimatised to the weather and had got used to the food. All they had to do now was to go home, win their two remaining World Cup qualifiers and then come back next summer and win the World Cup.

The South American matches had caught the imagination of the continent's people and media, mainly due to the amount of European countries that had been involved that summer. When the tour came to a close a panel from the South American press selected the 11 best European players they felt had been on show. Their selection read: Clemence (England), Battison (France), Russman (West Germany), Kaltz (West Germany), Vogts (West Germany), Platini (France), Bonhof (West Germany), Holzenbein (West Germany), Lato (Poland), Fischer (West Germany), Johnston (Scotland).

Willie Boy had, indeed, told them he was there!

The journey home was a relaxing one. The players had served their country well and were now looking forward to a short break with their families before the pre-season began with their individual clubs. Spirits were high, and some were also being swallowed in abundance. Willie was having a good time. Just how good no one was sure, at least until the plane landed, when he attempted (several times before succeeding) to get to his feet and pull down his overhead bags. Someone shouted: "Willie, what the hell are you doing?"

Willie was struggling with his bags and his speech, but eventually replied: "I'm getting off, we're in London."

"Sit on yer arse, ya idiot," said the same voice. "We're in Lisbon. We've only landed to take on fuel!"

The plane may have been low on fuel, but Willie'd had too much!

18

BACK AT THE ALBION

Back at West Brom things were not quite what Willie had expected. Johnny Giles had gone. Johnny, who had brought the Albion back to top-flight football, had seemingly got into a contractual dispute with the club. He had asked for a long-term deal, a request which the club had found unacceptable and he'd resigned.

The new manager was former a West Brom player, Ronnie Allen. Ronnie had joined the Baggies from Port Vale in 1950 for £20,000, a club record fee at the time. Initially he been a right-winger and although he stood only 5ft 8in, he'd developed into a talented striker. He played 405 games for the club and scored 208 goals before being transferred in 1961 to Crystal Palace. Between 1953 and 1955 he won five caps for England and scored twice for his country. His management career started at Wolverhampton Wanderers in 1965, and he guided them to promotion to the old First Division in 1967. This achievement attracted attention from abroad, which was unusual at the time for English managers, and he was appointed manager of Atletico Bilbao in 1968. He took Bilbao on to win the *Copa del Rey* in 1969, before leaving them in 1972 to take over at Sporting Lisbon. His time in Lisbon was not a happy one, and in 1973 he returned home to England to take the hot seat at Walsall. He remained at Walsall until 1977 when West Brom made their approach, and the opportunity to manage a club he had formally played for proved to be irresistible. Yet his stay at the Hawthorns would be both short and sweet.

Willie returned to training, sadly missing the presence of Johnny Giles being in command, but he was heartened by the news of Albion's pre-season matches. These would see Willie return to Scotland to play in a tournament that would involve his former club, Rangers. He trained like a demon, not only because he wanted to impress on his return to Scotland, but because he knew how important the next few months would be. Now, West Brom had a different look to their side. Several of the youngsters had staked their claim for inclusion in the first team, notably, Bryan Robson and Derek Statham. Also there was an exciting new addition signed from Leyton Orient – Laurie Cunningham. Albion had high aspirations and wanted to be up there in the League fighting for a European spot. Willie also aspired toward this goal, but he had an added incentive, that of being picked for Scotland's two World Cup qualifiers.

Willie: The difference between Ronnie Allen and Johnny Giles was like that between chalk and cheese. Ronnie was a laid-back character who'd rather be on the golf course than running a football team. Johnny, on the other hand, was totally dedicated to the task of taking the Albion forward. The players loved him, he was a good manager, a great player and a gentleman.

West Brom took a strong squad north of the border to participate in the Tennent's Caledonian Trophy, which would have Willie visiting his old stomping ground, Ibrox Park. The Albion's first match saw them pitted against St Mirren, and on the same day Rangers would take on Southampton. West Brom won their encounter 3-4, while Rangers brushed aside Southampton 3-1, leaving the two victors to meet the next day at Ibrox. Either side would win the trophy outright if they claimed a win.

Willie would have the honour of captaining West Brom that day, and he does admit to having some butterflies in his stomach, the first since he was a 17-year-old, as he led the team out on to Ibrox Park. He had some reservations about how the crowd would react to his appearance; at best, he expected a mixed reception of applauding and jeering. What he got was not expected – Ibrox erupted as he was greeted with a standing ovation. The experience was highly emotional for Willie and he had to draw in deep breaths to hold back the tears.

The match itself was entertaining but not a spectacle. Willie did, at one point, get on the wrong side of the crowd – some things never change – during a tussle with the opposing captain and former team-mate, John Greig. The issue was quickly rectified when Willie and John entertained the crowd with some friendly banter, then West Brom ran out 2-0 winners. It was very much Willie's day as he collected the trophy, eventually. Initially, and much to the delight of the crowd, he was jokingly presented with a trophy the size of an eggcup. It may have been Willie's day but it was young

Laurie Cunningham who'd stolen the show. The youngster scored both the Baggies' goals, and was presented with a cheque for £150, as his reward for being the best player in the two-day tournament.

Now it was back to the serious stuff, the English First Division. Although Johnny Giles had departed, Ronnie Allen took a firm hold of the reins and the Albion continued 1977/78 season just as they had finished the previous one – playing well. Allen had introduced Cyrille Regis to the team, and he joined Laurie Cunningham as one of the few black players in the First Division at the time. Bryan Robson was developing fast. Willie was continually entertaining, and putting on magical shows. West Brom had no need to fear anyone, and their results reflected just that attitude. The Baggies would lose only two of their first 12 matches.

19

THE WORLD CUP QUALIFIERS

International duty came calling for Willie again. It had been over two months since the squad had been together and now they would face East Germany in a friendly. Despite the friendly status of the match, it would serve as an important warm-up for the fast approaching World Cup qualifiers. The squad – and those who had been on the South American tour were very much in evidence – travelled to East Berlin. Willie recalls that the stadium was like a nightmare, with facilities that would have shamed many a non-League club in Britain. Alan Rough was missing in goal through injury and Dave Stewart (Leeds United) came in to deputise.

> *Willie: Alan Rough liked a good time and was always game for a laugh. On the park he was a top-notch goalkeeper who had only one flaw; occasionally he would have a lapse of concentration which at times would lead to the opposition taking advantage of the situation. This apart, he still ranks as one of Scotland's finest goalkeepers.*

The team: Stewart, McGrain, Donachie, Rioch, Forsyth, Buchan, Masson, Gemmill, Dalglish, Hartford, Johnston. Scotland lost the match 1-0, on a dismal night, in a dismal place. The result in itself was meaningless, but it was important in terms of the players being reacquainted for the first time in two months. The World Cup qualifying match against Czechoslovakia was only 14 days away and that would be a must-win encounter.

As the World Cup game drew nigh, Ally MacLeod worked closely with the players to ensure that they were prepared both mentally and physically. With the match almost upon them, Willie Donachie withdrew through injury. The two Willies had linked well together in the past, along with Asa

Hartford, on the left side and Donachie would be sadly missed in such an important match. Ally MacLeod elected to make a tactical change, bringing Sandy Jardine in at right-back and switching Danny McGrain to the left.

The team: Rough, Jardine, McGrain, Forsyth, McQueen, Rioch, Dalglish, Masson, Jordan, Hartford, Johnston.

It was 21 September 1977, and Hampden Park contained more than 85,000 fans singing their heads off. This would be a big night, and everybody knew it. The Czechs were a good side, with big aspirations. They were the current European champions and had the World Cup in their sights. As the players sat in the dressing room, confidence was high and the adrenaline was flowing. Just prior to walking up the tunnel Ally made one final announcement. He wanted to hit the Czechs hard and fast.

At the kick-off he wanted Willie, Gordon McQueen and Joe Jordan to line up on the left wing. He instructed the captain, Bruce Rioch, that no matter what, he was to choose the kick-off as opposed to the direction of play. At the kick-off the ball was to be passed to Don Masson, as Willie, Gordon and Joe sprinted up the left side of the park. Don was instructed to send a long ball up to the 18-yard box. Either Joe or Gordon would head the ball down to Willie, who would strike it home. Was he having a laugh?

Did he really think that the Czechs would be that gullible, or foolish, to fall for something so obvious? The Scottish players didn't, and glanced at each other in disbelief. The team took to the park to be met with the famous Hampden roar. Bruce Rioch won the toss of the coin and elected to take the kick-off. Willie, Gordon and Joe lined up on the left side as instructed. Everyone and their auntie could see the Czech defence glance at each other, and probably only the Hampden roar masked their laughter. The kick-off was taken, the three left wingers took off at speed, the ball was passed to Don Masson and he sent a long ball to the opposition's 18-yard box. The Czech centre-half beat McQueen and Jordan to the high ball and headed it back to his midfield. The Czechs immediately counter-attacked and only narrowly missed out on scoring before 30 seconds had elapsed.

Thankfully, the stupidity of the opening move would not be repeated by the Scots, as they settled into one of the most polished performances ever witnessed by the Hampden faithful. The Czechs were left in limbo as the firepower of the Scots struck them three times, with Joe Jordan, Asa Hartford and Kenny Dalglish, who had a masterful game, supplying the goals. The reigning European champions could only make one reply to go down 3-1. The Scots were another step closer to the World Cup finals.

Willie: Kenny Dalglish was the ultimate professional, a manager's dream. Next to Denis Law and Jim Baxter he is probably one of Scotland's greatest players of all time. I can give him no higher accolade than that.

The game against Wales was almost upon Scotland and it was considered foolish and downright dangerous to discount them. The Welsh were strong and resilient. They, like the Scots, had beaten Czechoslovakia in their qualifier at home. The 3-0 scoreline was nothing less than impressive. The winners of this clash would qualify for the World Cup finals in Argentina. In a nutshell, this was the game that meant life or death to both sets of players and fans.

Amazingly, the Welsh FA decided to switch the match to Liverpool's Anfield and there seemed no logic in the move. To Willie and the rest of the squad the switch was of no significance. They would have played in Timbuktu to gain the opportunity to reach the World Cup finals. The Welsh squad included some high-quality players such as Liverpool's defender Joey Jones, big striker John Toshack, tough midfielder Terry Yorath of Leeds, the more creative Brian Flynn from Burnley and Wrexham's flying winger Mickey Thomas.

Unsurprisingly, when the big day came the streets of Liverpool contained a throng of Tartan 'bunnets' and Scottish accents. The atmosphere inside the ground on the night was electric. The Scots had taken over and everybody knew it, but he team itself had been hit by injury again. Bruce Rioch was sidelined and Danny McGrain was out following an horrific injury.

Lou Macari would deputise for Rioch, while Willie Donachie would return in place of McGrain. Ally MacLeod named the following team: Rough, Jardine, Donachie, Masson, McQueen, Forsyth, Dalglish, Hartford, Jordan, Macari, Johnston.

Anybody who had thought Scotland would stroll through the match to an easy victory was soon given a sharp reminder that this would not be the case. The Welsh started the game confidently, while Scotland were exceedingly cautious and nervous in the opening quarter. The cots eventually settled and had begun to take control of the game when along came one of the most controversial moments British football has known. Scotland were hot on the attack when they were awarded a throw-in on the left side of the Welsh 18-yard box. Willie, a more than competent long-throw expert, took it and two Welsh defenders rose for the ball along with Joe Jordan. Several arms were raised in the air as the players leapt, and the

(Right) Marking the start of his incredible career, Willie won the League Cup with Rangers in 1964, just two months after his debut. Here Rangers' Jim Baxter 'crowns' Willie with the League Cup after the side's 2-1 win over Celtic.

(Below The team celebrate on the Hampden pitch with the trophy.

(Above) When Willie won his first Scotland cap in 1965 against Poland he was delighted to fulfil a boyhood dream of playing alongside his hero Denis Law.

(Left) Goalscoring Willie. Here he smashes home one of Rangers' five goals against Falkirk in the 5-0 victory in October 1966…

(Top) …while here he drives the ball past Celtic's John Clark to score Rangers' first goal in a 2-2 draw on 2 January 1968.

(Middle) Stylish on or off the pitch, Willie poses for the cameras after his first disciplinary hearing at the SFA.

(Bottom) Willie gets to grips with Celtic's Jim Brogan in typically aggressive fashion.

(Left) Willie scores the winning goal in his team's 4-3 win in the semi-final of the Glasgow Cup in April 1969. Celtic's David Hay and goalkeeper John Fallon can do nothing.

(Above) Left, posing with the first silverware Rangers had won in five years. Right, the two Willies, Johnston and Henderson, enjoy the moment.

(Right) One of Willie's favourite tricks was played on him by his great friend Colin Stein who had this photo taken in Italy and then superimposed Willie's head on the small man's shoulders!

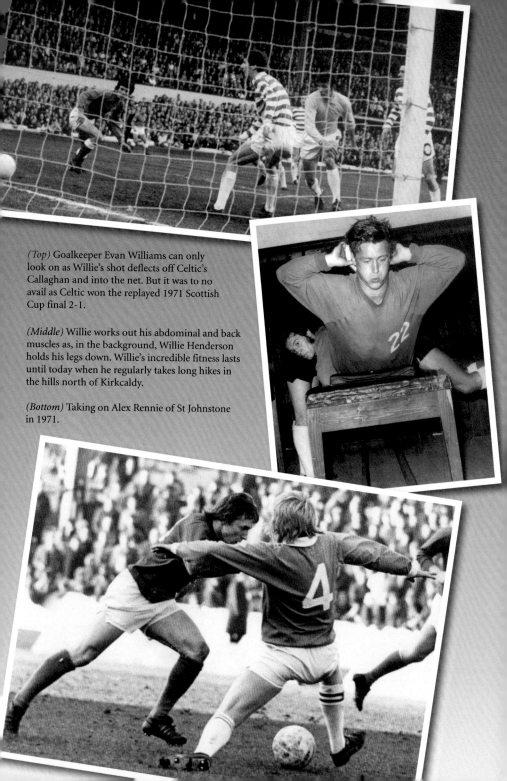

(Top) Goalkeeper Evan Williams can only look on as Willie's shot deflects off Celtic's Callaghan and into the net. But it was to no avail as Celtic won the replayed 1971 Scottish Cup final 2-1.

(Middle) Willie works out his abdominal and back muscles as, in the background, Willie Henderson holds his legs down. Willie's incredible fitness lasts until today when he regularly takes long hikes in the hills north of Kirkcaldy.

(Bottom) Taking on Alex Rennie of St Johnstone in 1971.

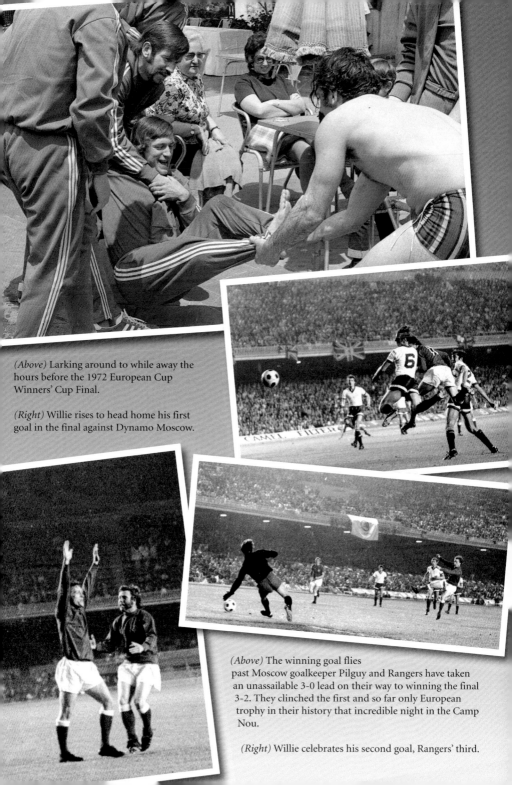

(Above) Larking around to while away the hours before the 1972 European Cup Winners' Cup Final.

(Right) Willie rises to head home his first goal in the final against Dynamo Moscow.

(Above) The winning goal flies past Moscow goalkeeper Pilguy and Rangers have taken an unassailable 3-0 lead on their way to winning the final 3-2. They clinched the first and so far only European trophy in their history that incredible night in the Camp Nou.

(Right) Willie celebrates his second goal, Rangers' third.

(Left) Willie shows off the European Cup Winners' Cup in the Nou Camp dressing room.

(Right) From left, Willie, captain John Greig and Colin Stein pose with the Cup Winners' Cup.

(Top) Thousands of fans gathered at Ibrox to welcome home the team.

(Middle) The last straw. Willie pleads with the referee not to send him off against Falkirk in September 1972. His protests were to no avail and he was dismissed, leading to a record 63 day ban. He would shortly be sold to West Bromwich Albion.

(Bottom) Looking slightly taken aback at the fever with which he is greeted by a host of young Albion supporters, Willie arrives in the West Midlands with a record £138,000 price tag.

(Top) Willie arrived at the Hawthorns amidst a welter of publicity…

…not least surrounding the size of his transfer fee

(Middle) but there were problems in the team as exemplified by the 1-3 defeat to Exeter in the third round of the League Cup at the Hawthorns in 1973, despite Willie scoring this goal.

WILLIE JOHNSTON … West Brom's big-money signing from Rangers

(Bottom) Willie entertained the Baggies fans with plenty of tricks on the pitch…

(Top) …and even more banter with the crowd, although he would receive plenty of abuse from opposing fans too.

(Middle and bottom) Willie in action for the Albion. Right, winning a trademark far post header against Leeds; bottom right, taking on a Carlisle United defender; and bottom left, firing in a shot.

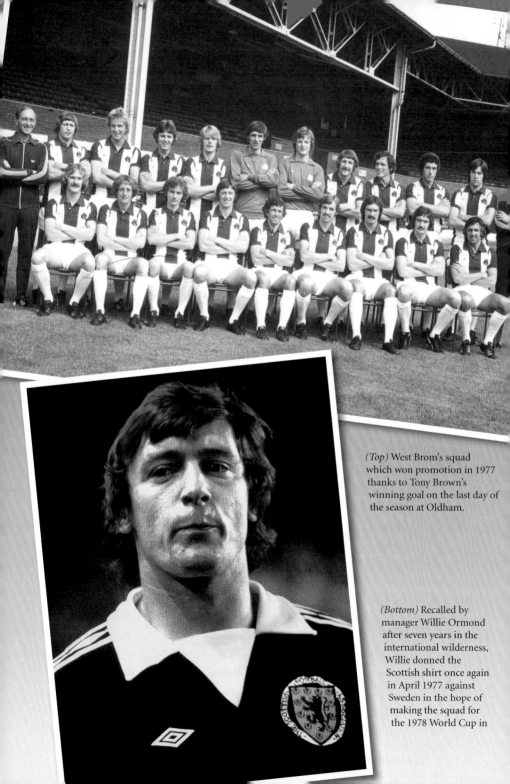

(*Top*) West Brom's squad which won promotion in 1977 thanks to Tony Brown's winning goal on the last day of the season at Oldham.

(*Bottom*) Recalled by manager Willie Ormond after seven years in the international wilderness, Willie donned the Scottish shirt once again in April 1977 against Sweden in the hope of making the squad for the 1978 World Cup in

(Top and middle) Scotland's 2-1 victory at Wembley in June 1977, in which Willie starred, brought about a wave of euphoria amongst the fans who broke the crossbar of a goal (left) and carried the Scottish players, including Bruce Rioch (right) shoulder high from the Wembley pitch.

(Bottom) During Scotland's tour of South America in the summer of 1977, Willie was targeted by some shameful tactics. Here Argentina's Vicente Pernia (left), who kicked and spat at Willie in an attempt to intimidate him, squares up to the wee winger yet again. Both players were sent off, although Willie's red card was later rescinded.

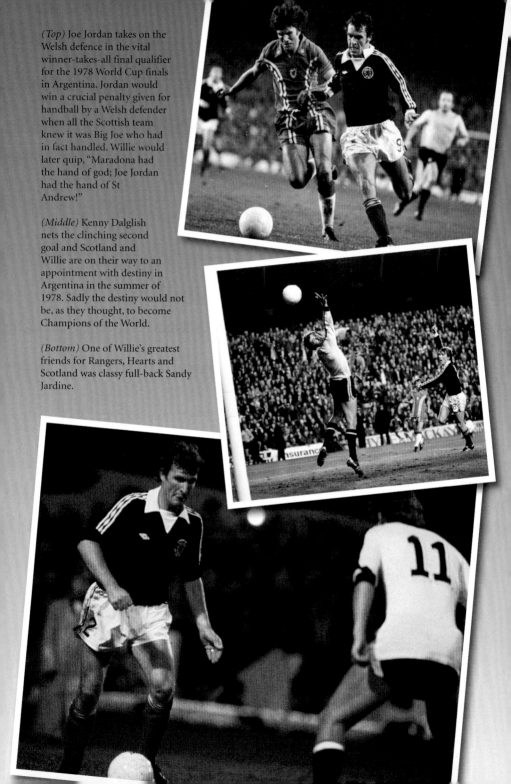

(Top) Joe Jordan takes on the Welsh defence in the vital winner-takes-all final qualifier for the 1978 World Cup finals in Argentina. Jordan would win a crucial penalty given for handball by a Welsh defender when all the Scottish team knew it was Big Joe who had in fact handled. Willie would later quip, "Maradona had the hand of god; Joe Jordan had the hand of St Andrew!"

(Middle) Kenny Dalglish nets the clinching second goal and Scotland and Willie are on their way to an appointment with destiny in Argentina in the summer of 1978. Sadly the destiny would not be, as they thought, to become Champions of the World.

(Bottom) One of Willie's greatest friends for Rangers, Hearts and Scotland was classy full-back Sandy Jardine.

(Top) Scotland manager Ally MacLeod (left) whipped Scottish fans into a frenzy with his rhetoric and had a nation believing his side would win the World Cup in 1978. This was never better exemplified than when 30,000 fervent supporters turned up to bid the team farewell at Hampden Park (right).

(Middle) Lou Macari would cause Willie plenty of headaches over his selling of stories from within the Scotland camp in Argentina to the press. Here Macari takes a shot against Wales.

(Bottom) Archie Gemmill was the man who refused to take a drug test after the Peru game, claiming dehydration despite having played only 20 minutes of the match, which meant Willie was called upon to give his fateful sample.

(Top, left) A lost soul. Willie trudges back to his hotel room after learning the devastating news that he had tested positive because of the Fencamfamin content of his Reactivan cold remedy tablet.

(Top, right) 7 June 1978 and a bemused Willie is accompanied by police on his return to the UK from Argentina. He was met by his West Brom manager Ron Atkinson, who looked after his star player and guided him through the dark days which followed.

(Middle) Willie escaped from the spotlight by joining Vancouver Whitecaps in 1979 and immediately struck up a great friendship with England World Cup winner Alan Ball, with whom he is seen here training.

(Bottom) Vancouver, with Willie starring, lifted the 1979 Soccer Bowl, beating the Tampa Bay Rowdies 2-1.

(Top) Back at Ibrox, the Rangers faithful heap praise on Willie after he re-signed for the club.

(Bottom) Willie weaves his magic to leave Dundee United's John Holt on the deck as he skips past him once again.

(Top) The aftermath of the shameful incident in the Old Firm derby in which Davie Provan fell to the floor claiming Willie had headbutted him. Nothing could have been further from the truth, but Willie still saw red and another ban anyway.

(Middle) Willie reacquaints himself with both the Scottish Cup and the Scottish League Cup at a Rangers Supporters convention in 2002.

(Bottom, left) The winning 1972 team reconvene at the Camp Nou, the venue of their triumph 25 years earlier, before Rangers take on Barcelona in the Champions League in 2007.

(Bottom, right) Willie with his five grandchildren; Christopher, Alix, Matt, Ellie and Jay.

ball struck an arm. The referee decided that the offender had been Welsh and awarded a penalty to Scotland.

The Welsh team protested en-masse, but to no avail – a penalty it was. Don Masson walked up to the spot and calmly struck the ball home. Scotland were 1-0 ahead in extremely controversial circumstances.

Willie: Handball incident ... what handball incident? Maradona had the hand of god; Joe Jordan had the hand of St Andrew!

A short time later Martin Buchan, who had come on as a substitute for Sandy Jardine, went on a devastating run down the right flank and sent over a superb ball. Kenny Dalglish was there to meet it, and with an equally brilliant header he sent the ball crashing into the net. Scotland had beaten Wales. The players went wild, the fans went wild, and the whole of Scotland would have a wild night. Scotland were on their way to Argentina.

In the dressing room after the game it would have been an understatement to say that the players were in high spirits. Willie was seated alongside Asa Hartford and Joe Jordan and in a rare moment of quiet and calm he turned to Joe and asked: "Did you handle that ball?"

Joe turned to Willie and smiled his toothless smile: "What do you think, Bud?" Willie didn't answer – Joe's smile had said it all.

The squad had a few drinks together that evening before the Anglos went their separate ways back to their own clubs. Well, most of them. Willie elected to travel to Manchester along with Asa Hartford and Willie Donachie (both City players) for a night out on the town. In Manchester they were joined by three of Willie's West Brom colleagues, Len Cantello and Scotsmen Ally Brown and Alistair Robertson. The drink flowed and in the morning the hangovers were severe. Willie had to check the morning papers to make sure qualification had not been just a dream.

20

WEST BROM MARCH ON

Willie returned to Albion, unaware that once again he had set a new record. He would now be West Brom's most capped Scottish international of all time, having played 19 times for his country. West Brom continued to be a presence near the top of the League table, and he continued to shine. Albion fans were now seeing him at his flamboyant best as he continued to entertain with dazzling runs, amazing trickery and inch-perfect passes. He was beginning to terrorise some of the best defenders in the country. Willie had never lacked belief in himself, but that belief had been bolstered by the desire to be named in Ally MacLeod's initial 40-player selection, eventually cut to 22, for the World Cup finals in Argentina.

Although the League campaign was progessing nicely, the same could not be said for the League Cup. West Brom had demolished Rotherham, before knocking out Watford – but then along came Bury. The Shakers were a Third Division side who should have been grateful to have a First Division team of West Brom's calibre visit their ground. After all, the game would generate good gate receipts, and then the minnows could subside quietly, accepting their inevitable demise. The problem was that nobody had told Bury this, and they went on to win the tie 1-0.

Despite that League Cup setback, the League form continued. Then an amazing thing happened. Manager Ronnie Allen announced that following their next League game the team would travel to one of the Arab Emirates to take part in an exhibition match.

The players could not believe it. There they were, battling it out at the top of the table, and the manager had announced that they would be travelling thousands of miles to participate in a contest that was no more than a mere bagatelle. Yet Ronnie Allen had arranged it, and the board had agreed. To the players this could mean only one thing – West Brom would be financially rewarded for making the trip. The players were unhappy with the situation, yet knew they could do little about it. The team – Willie was one of the instigators – asked for a meeting with Ronnie Allen. During the meeting they made it clear to the manager that they wanted to share in the financial rewards for making the trip. Amazingly, Ronnie agreed, and told them they would receive £250 a man for the Arabian adventure. This settled, the team would play their League game on Saturday, fly to Abu Dhabi that evening, play in excruciating heat on Monday, and fly home on Tuesday.

The Albion squad stepped from the plane in Abu Dhabi and were met by clear blue skies and a hot and humid climate of around 100 degrees Fahrenheit. As they were transported to their hotel the players became aware that Abu Dhabi was an affluent place.

Each car was bigger than the last and Willie sensed that if the car owner ran out of petrol, he would simply abandon the vehicle and buy another one. The hotel itself was located in the heart of Abu Dhabi overlooking the Arabian Gulf. It was the most luxurious, refined hotel Willie had ever set eyes on – hardly a place for Willie, Len Cantello, Ally Brown and company. They really would have to be on their best behaviour.

Willie remembers nothing of the game nor the scoreline. His recollections centre on the £250 each player received for being there. Ronnie Allen advised all the players to invest the money in gold, and had arranged how this investment would transpire. He told the players that on the following day the Royal Prince – Willie is uncertain if it was a prince, a sheikh or simply someone off the street – would meet the players and take them to the establishment where 22ct soft gold could be purchased. When the prince/sheikh arrived the players were whisked off to a nondescript building. They entered and Willie recalls: "The place was awash with money. People were shovelling it over the counter in exchange for gold." Willie had never seen so much money in his life; it was a weird, yet exhilarating experience. Eventually the players did their little bit of business and returned to the hotel. Later that day Ronnie Allen sat down with Willie for a private word. Willie always sensed that there was something about this trip that didn't ring true, and he was about to have his suspicions confirmed. Ronnie, after some pleasantries about the accommodation and how relaxing the trip had been, announced that his days as manager of West Brom were over. He had been offered the job of Saudi Arabia's national coach, on a salary of £150,000 a year. Willie nearly choked on his orange juice. In the 1970s £150,000 a year was an astronomical amount of money.

Was this contrived before the trip? Was Ronnie already in talks with the Saudis, and did he dent his club's championship chances by simply taking them abroad on a fools' errand to finalise the deal? Willie certainly thought so.

It was a confused and disheartened squad that made the journey back home. They had made the trip as title contenders and now returned managerless. The questions were: could they maintain their assault on the League title, or more realistically a European spot, and who would the new manager be? The answer to the latter wasn't long in coming.

21

WELCOME RON

Willie may have been selfish regarding who was to be the new manager at Albion. For him it was simple. If things started to go wrong at the club his World Cup place would be in jeopardy. He need not have worried.

The new manager would be 'Big Ron' Atkinson, a man with great presence, charisma and exceptional motivational skills. Ron's playing career had not taken him to any great heights. At the age of 17 he signed for Aston Villa, but never made the first team and was transferred to Oxford United in 1959 on a free.

He stayed at Oxford for the remainder of his playing career, making more than 500 appearances as a wing-half, and earning the nickname 'The Tank'. When he retired from playing in 1971, he was appointed manager of non-league Kettering Town. At Kettering he revealed signs that he possessed good managerial qualities, and Cambridge Town came in for his services in 1974. In 1977 he led the club out of the Fourth Division, and took them to the verge of promotion into the Second Division before West Brom stepped in and brought him to the Hawthorns.

Willie: Big Ron was a very charismatic character and an excellent manager. He wanted to play attractive, flowing football. His aim was to please the paying fans and he certainly achieved that. His style of play suited my game and I was playing some of my best football under his leadership. If the Albion won 5-4 Ron would be delighted – the four against were of no concern to him. Yes, Ron and I had the occasional run-in, but it was normally dealt with fairly and squarely and we'd both get on with our jobs.

In his opening games in charge Atkinson demonstrated he was capable of keeping the club on an even keel, and maintaining their challenge for the First Division title. His first signing was Brendon Batson from his former club, Cambridge. Batson would play alongside Albion's other two black players, Laurie Cunningham and Cyrille Regis, who were already in the first-team squad.

The three of them would be nicknamed 'The Three Degrees' after the famous black singing trio formed in the 1960s, and they would become the first three black players to be fielded together in an English League team.

The real plus for Willie was that Atkinson wouldn't attempt to shackle him and make him play to some prearranged system. Ron encouraged him to be flamboyant, take players on and entertain. So that's exactly what Willie did. He had two players breathing down his neck for Scotland's number-11 jersey, Leeds United's Arthur Graham and Nottingham Forest's John Robertson. At best only two of them would get the nod from Scotland manager Ally MacLeod. Graham had come on as sub against East Germany and had impressed. On the domestic front he was also putting in some fine performances; he had fired a hat-trick in five minutes against Birmingham and a brace when Leeds had destroyed Middlesborough 5-0. Also in his favour was the fact that he was more of a two-footed player than John Robertson. However, Willie was equally two-footed, and certainly more skilful. Ally MacLeod had already acknowledged that Graham was two players in one, equally comfortable on the right or the left. John Robertson, on the other hand, was a more direct type of player, and was turning on the style as Nottingham Forest challenged for the League title. His manager at Forest, Brian Clough, rated him highly and once stated: "John is an artist, the Picasso of our game."

Picasso or not, Willie had no intention of relinquishing his Scottish shirt to either of the two players.

In the FA Cup Blackpool were the third-round visitors to the Hawthorns and they were duly dispatched 4-1. The fourth-round draw wasn't so kind to the Baggies – Manchester United at Old Trafford. The match may not have been a classic, but the result suited Willie and his teammates. It finished 1-1, with Willie scoring the Albion goal, then it was back to the Hawthorns for the replay. This match had everything; it was a rip-roaring cup-tie between, two clubs who have a great history in that prestigious competition. Eventually the game went to extra-time, with Albion taking the honours as they ran out 3-2 winners. The only downside to the match came when John Wile was stretchered off with a broken jaw; this can happen when your jaw clashes with the elbow of Joe Jordan.

The fine League form continued, and the fifth round of the FA Cup saw the Albion drawn away to Derby. The Rams had done well to get so far as they were struggling in the League but, as expected, they found the Baggies too much for them and were brushed aside 0-2.

In the quarter-finals Willie got the draw he'd been praying for. West Brom would meet Nottingham Forest for a place in the last four. Forest were the current League title holders and were on course to repeat that achievement. So why would he want to meet them in the quarter-final? Simple: their left-winger, John Robertson, was in the Scottish World Cup 40. Willie wanted to put on a performance that would make Ally MacLeod, who was going to be at the match, well aware of who his number-one left-winger was. Confidence or what?

The match was more than a clash between two teams fighting to make it in the FA Cup semi-finals; it was more than a contest between two clubs of the most attractive teams in the First Division. It was a face-off between two high-profile managers. Ron Atkinson was already using his charisma to win over the media – Ron had never been shy – and to prove that he was a worthy acquisition capable of taking West Brom to dizzy heights. Clough, on the other hand, did not suffer fools gladly; he would make controversial statements to the press, and for that the press loved him. When Clough spoke everybody listened, and Big Ron would be a worthy adversary.

As the teams ran on to the pitch Willie immediately made the crowd aware of his presence. The West Brom fans cheered him, the Forest fans booed him, and Brian Clough went ballistic. Willie was wearing a tartan 'bunnet'. With normality restored, the match got under way and Willie didn't disappoint the Baggies' fans as he turned on the style. He then quickly tarnished his display by having an altercation with Forest's Scottish international, Archie Gemmill, which led to a booking from the referee and a blast of verbal abuse from Brian Clough. A few minutes later Willie attempted to trap the ball with his backside (his party piece) and failed. Clough had another go at Willie, who responded by going over to the Forest dugout and giving Cloughie a taste of his own medicine. For Willie it had been a good day, capped by a victory as West Brom ran out 2-0 winners. The result took the club into the FA Cup semi-finals for a record 18th time.

Willie: From what I can recall of the skirmish with Archie Gemmill it was nothing more than handbags at five paces. Unfortunately Brian Clough didn't see it that way and gave me a mouthful of abuse – and let's face it, it was some mouth. Clough had never liked me, for whatever reason; and I would have to say that I was no fan of his. I think part of the reason for his dislike was the fact that I was keeping his superb winger John Robertson out of the Scotland team. Cloughie didn't like that, he didn't like it at all.

On the day following the match, Ron Atkinson defended the arrogance of Willie's antics to the press: "When he attempted to trap the ball with his backside I nearly said to him, if you do that again Cloughie will fine you!" he continued, "You accept him for what he is – the best left-winger in Britain. There are managers around who wouldn't want to handle him. One thing I won't have with the football from my team is boredom. There's no chance of that with Willie around. Not only does he entertain, he produces and that's what counts. We beat Manchester United, the holders, in the fourth round and Jimmy Nicholl has still got a hangover from trying to catch Willie Johnston." Big Ron was obviously a Willie Johnston fan, and Willie was developing the same feeling for his new manager. In fact, Atkinson's Albion were becoming a feared force in football, featuring a number of household names.

Willie: During my time at Glasgow Rangers I played alongside many good players and a number of great players. Many of them would be heavy drinkers and smokers. My days at West Brom were no different and I was surrounded by players of immense talent and a delight to play with.

Tony Brown, beyond a shadow of doubt, was the best professional I ever had the pleasure to play with and it is unbelievable that he only ever received one full cap for England. He was nicknamed Bomber and went on to score more than 200 goals for the club. Unlike myself he was a non-smoker, but he did like the occasional drink and a game of darts. It would have to be said he was a better striker than he was a darts player.

Len Cantello was the first player I met when I arrived at the Hawthorns and we had a few beers together. During my time at the Albion Len and I would enjoy many a laugh and many a beer together. As a player he was a clever midfielder who, perhaps, never fulfilled his true potential in the game. Len and I remain friends to this day.

The Three Degrees, comprising Cyrille Regis, Laurie Cunningham and Brendon Batson, were a sensation at the Hawthorns. Unfortunately they received some harsh treatment from rival fans because of the colour of their skin. Black players were starting to break into top-level football during their time and racism within the game was at its peak.

Cyrille was another great striker and a true gentleman. I think he was only 18 years old when he joined the club and I recall him scoring on his debut. When I made my return to Glasgow Rangers I tried to get the club to sign him to play alongside me up front but, for whatever reason, they wouldn't. He would have been a sensation in Scotland.

Laurie was the quietest of the three, but what a player. He became the first black man to be capped by England at any level when he turned out for the England under-21 team in 1977 in a match against Scotland. Later, of course, he would be transferred to Real Madrid and would win six international caps. Sadly he died in a car crash in 1989 at the age of 33. Such a loss.

Brendon was a clever full-back who was equally happy when attacking or defending. I always thought that he would win England caps but sadly he never did, his career being cut short by injury in 1982. All three were very much part of the Albion spirit that existed among the players at the time; and all liked to indulge in a few after-match beers.

You can't mention the Three Degrees without saying a few words about the Irish quartet made up of Mick Martin, Paddy Mulligan, Ray Treacy and Johnny Giles. These four liked to party, although Paddy never had a drink in his life, and were great company to be around. Whenever an opportunity existed Ray would start playing his banjo and the whole team would join in the sing-song. I have great memories of those days.

Mick was an excellent player and despite winning a huge number of caps for the Republic of Ireland, he was very much underrated. Both Paddy and Ray were very good players, too. Johnny came to the Albion as player-manager and was the man who turned things around. You didn't mess with him either on or off the park. Johnny also liked a small libation now and then and I remember his arrival at the Hawthorns as if it was yesterday. That first evening he booked a hotel, hired a comedian and invited all the players and their wives to a party. The comedian was only a 17-year-old and a West Brom supporter. He was unknown to all of us – I think it was his first time in front of a large audience – but he was sensational. His name was Lenny Henry. Johnny Giles called the night out a bonding session. The players called it a great night on the bevvy!

Asa Hartford was another player who liked the occasional beer or three, but what a player. Asa had joined the club as a boy and was a *regular first-team player when I arrived. Asa, like me, was a left-sided player and was a delight to play alongside. He was strong, clever and talented, and it didn't surprise me that he went on to win 50 Scottish caps. By my reckoning he was one of the best midfielders ever to pull on a Scottish jersey.*

John Wile was another great professional, a great captain, a gentleman and a scholar. He was a hard defender who didn't take prisoners. I remember him playing with blood pouring from a head wound during the 1978 FA Cup semi-final against Ipswich at Highbury. He would never give in. I'm glad I never had to play against him; it might have led to another few red cards being added to my record.

Ally Robertson was another tough defender and a fellow Scot. It always surprised me that he never won a cap for Scotland. Ally and I would often have a little drink together and enjoy ourselves ... when I think about it, West Brom had the best drinking team in England at the time. Derek Statham was also a left-sided player. A defender with real class who could pass a ball and land it on a sixpence – a left winger's dream.

Bryan Robson, 'Captain Marvel', now what a player he was. When I arrived at the Hawthorns he was still a boy playing in the youth team, but as soon as I saw him in action I knew the club had something special on their hands. It was no surprise to me that he would go on to captain England and win 90 caps. He was everything a midfielder should be – he could tackle, he was a great passer, he was good with his head and he could score goals. Bryan and I became good friends and would often have a beer together ... well, he was good at socialising!

Scotland had a friendly match against Bulgaria and Willie had to withdraw through injury. He had played ten consecutive games for his country and having to pull-out of the squad gutted him. He feared the withdrawal would damage his World Cup chances. As fate would have it Nottingham Forest's John Robertson also withdrew and Ally elected to field a side with no wingers. Scotland won the game 2-1. The scoreline was an indication to all the wide players that their inclusion in the final 22 making the trip to Argentina was not a foregone conclusion.

West Brom's form in the League remained buoyant. Willie constantly entertained and continually added to his disciplinary points – there's no show without Punch! – which had by then reached 16. One more booking and he would be out of FA Cup semi-final against Ipswich. In the next

League game big Ron elected to leave Willie out of the team because he wanted him fresh for Ipswich. The decision proved to be disastrous as West Brom crashed to a 4-0 defeat at the hands of Arsenal. In the next game, against Bristol City, Ron would gamble, play Willie and hope that he didn't fall foul of the referee. The gamble paid off. Willie returned in style and scored the first goal in a 2-1 victory.

Along came the FA Cup semi-final. Ron Atkinson was up for it; the players were up for it; and the Baggies' fans wanted it. Unfortunately for West Brom, Bobby Robson's young Ipswich team wanted it even more. Albion played perhaps their worst game of the season and a 3-1 defeat put paid to the Wembley dream.

Willie: When we knew we had drawn Ipswich in the semi our expectations were high. And why not? We had already taken the scalps of Manchester United, Derby and Brian Clough's Nottingham Forest. We had played the campaign exceptionally well and felt we could go all the way. The match was at Highbury and we took a big support with us. Life is not a box of chocolates; we played our poorest football of the season and I had the worst game ever for the Baggies. Bobby Robson's young Ipswich side took advantage of our bad play and deservedly beat us 3-1. I've always accepted my fair share of the blame for the way we played that day. This West Brom team could and should have won the FA Cup.

Nottingham Forest and their contingent of Scottish international players, on the other hand, had reached the League Cup final. Liverpool were their opponents. Prior to the game Clough was always reminding the press that his three Scottish internationals – Kenny Burns, Archie Gemmill and John Robertson – should all be included in Ally MacLeod's final 22. MacLeod attended the final which finished 0-0 (Forest won the replay 1-0) and witnessed good displays from all three. After the game he told the press: "I wanted to see him (John Robertson) in a big-match situation and as Forest weren't at full strength it was also interesting to see how he would respond to that. But contrary to what is being said, Willie Johnston is the man in possession and it's a case of comparing John Robertson and Arthur Graham to decide who will be second choice." MacLeod had made himself abundantly clear – Willie would be in that final 22.

A few weeks later Nottingham Forest secured the League title. Liverpool finished in second place and West Brom took the number-three spot. European football was back at the Hawthorns.

Willie, now named in Ally's final 22 along with John Robertson, now turned his thoughts to the Home International championship, in which Scotland would compete against Ireland, Wales and England prior to leaving for the World Cup finals. Then disaster struck. During a five-a-side game his team-mate, Cyrille Regis, tackled him, there was a crack and Willie went down. Willie thought his ankle was broken and he could feel the Argentina dream slipping away. He was rushed to hospital and, prior to an x-ray, the nurse who'd first looked at the ankle confirmed his worst fears – it was broken. The first x-ray seemed to emphasise that fact. Willie confided in the doctor that this was the same ankle that he had broken during his time with Rangers. The doctor elected to have the ankle x-rayed again. This time he was able to confirm that there was no break. What he had seen in the first x-ray was a scar from the first injury. Willie's ankle was strapped and he was sent home to rest. Three days later he resumed light training and all seemed to be going well. Prior to joining the Scottish squad in Dunblane, West Brom were to hold a testimonial match for Willie's Hawthorns team-mate John Osborne. Willie elected to play, but following the match his ankle had swelled and he was in pain. He then travelled to Scotland where he spent a great deal of time on the treatment table. Argentina wasn't a certainty just yet.

22

WORLD CUP FEVER

From the minute Scotland qualified for the 1978 World Cup, the country was gripped in anticipation as to how the boys in blue would perform. It was like a fever. Ally MacLeod had Scotland as world champions, the press acknowledged this possibility, and the players believed it. Fantasy land, or what? Were the Brothers Grimm in charge of Scotland's destiny? They might as well have been, but the nation didn't care. Make no bones about it, Scotland had a good squad, capable of doing great things ... but winning the World Cup was a dream. However, reaching the last eight or even the semi-finals was a distinct possibility. England had failed to qualify and that bolstered Scottish belief. Scotland had a chance to do what the 'Auld Enemy' could not.

Ally MacLeod named his final 22 players who would travel to South America:

> *Goalkeepers:* Alan Rough, Jim Blyth, Bobby Clark.
> *Defenders:* Sandy Jardine, Willie Donachie, Stewart Kennedy, Gordon McQueen, Tom Forsyth, Martin Buchan, Kenny Burns.
> *Midfielders:* Don Masson, Bruce Rioch, Archie Gemmill, Graeme Souness, Lou Macari.
> *Forwards:* Kenny Dalglish, Joe Jordan, Derek Johnstone, John Robertson, Joe Harper, Willie Johnston.

There was no doubt that it was a high-quality squad, but it would have been impossible for the whole of the nation, fans and media alike, to agree with the final 22. Some felt that Aston Villa's Andy Gray should have been preferred to Joe Harper. Andy had won England's golden boot in season

1976/77, scoring 25 goals. In season 1977/78 he added four more goals to that tally and was voted the PFA's Young Player of the Year and their Players' Player of the Year. Still, these accolades weren't enough to earn him the nod from Ally MacLeod. Harper on the other hand, hadn't been part of the international set-up since 1975, when during an off-the-field incident in a night club in Copenhagen, he and several team-mates were involved in a disturbance which led to the SFA issuing Joe with a life ban from the international scene. The ban was later lifted and Ally MacLeod, his former manager at Aberdeen, obviously felt he was the right man for back-up to his main strikers Joe Jordan and Kenny Dalglish. There were also questions asked, mainly by the media, about whether the two Derby players, Don Masson and Bruce Rioch, should have been included in the squad. They were both in dispute with their present manager, none other than former Scotland boss Tommy Docherty. Yet not to include them would have been suicidal. The two, along with Asa Hartford, had been almost ever-present over the previous few years and were undoubtedly the players who made Scotland's engine room tick over. Criticism aside, this squad would now participate in the Home International championship before embarking on the journey to Argentina.

The hype in Scotland, and among Scots everywhere, continued to rise. Comedian Andy Cameron brought out a song, the lyrics of which sum up the nation's fever. It reached as high as number six in the UK charts.

Ally's Tartan Army

We're on the march wi' Ally's Army,
We're going tae the Argentine,
And we'll really shake 'em up,
When we win the World Cup,
'Cos Scotland is the greatest football team.
We're representing Britain,
And we're gaunny do or die,
England cannae dae it,
'Cos they didnae qualify!
We're on the march wi' Ally's Army,
We're going tae the Argentine,
And we'll really shake 'em up,
When we win the World Cup,
'Cos Scotland is the greatest football team.

Andy Cameron's song wasn't Scotland's official one. That distinction fell on the shoulders of Rod Stewart, with the song *Ole Ola*. Rod reached number five in the UK charts. The first verse and the chorus went as follows:

Ole Ola

When the blue shirts run out in Argentina
Our hearts will be beating like a drum,
And your nerves are so shattered you can't take it
Automatically you reach out for the run.
But there really isn't any cause for panic,
Ally's army has it all under control.
It's not merely speculations,
It's not just imagination,
To bring the World Cup home is Scotland's goal.

Ole ola, Ole ola,
We're gonna bring that World Cup back from over there.
Ole ola, Ole ola,
We're gonna bring that World Cup back from over there.

Ask anyone today if they bought either of the songs and you'll be met with strong denials – there are a lot of liars out there!

The Home Internationals were now upon us and Willie was struggling to shake off his ankle injury, plus a recurring shoulder problem. In other words, he was a lame duck. Deep down Willie knew that he would not make the first match against Northern Ireland. John Robertson would deputise and win his first cap. Willie would wish him well, albeit with tongue in cheek. He had no thoughts of relinquishing the number-11 jersey for more than one game, and he made it his all-consuming goal to be fit for the match against the Welsh. The game against the Irish finished 1-1. Martin O'Neill had opened the scoring and the young Derek Johnstone equalised for the Scots with a terrific header.

Nine changes were made for the game against the Welsh as Ally attempted to give all his players a runout before heading for South America. Willie was back, and the team taking the park that night at Hampden, in front of a staggering 70,000 fans, was: Blyth, Kennedy, Donachie, Burns, McQueen, Gemmill, Souness, Hartford, Johnstone, Dalglish, Johnston.

The match could hardly be deemed a classic, but Willie was happy to be back playing. Derek Johnstone opened the scoring for Scotland with another fine header. Yet the Welsh were not disheartened by this setback as they continued to look for a wedge to prise open the Scottish defence. With only five minutes to go the Welsh won a penalty. They missed it! But the drama didn't end there. With only minutes to go, Jim Blyth rolled the ball out of the area to Willie Donachie. The full-back was under no pressure and, knowing the full-time whistle would go at any minute, he began time-wasting before turning and passing the ball back to Blyth. There was only one problem – Jim Blyth wasn't there and the ball rolled into the empty net. Thus Scotland had to settle for a 1-1 draw because of what can only be described as a bizarre incident.

An injury to Gordon McQueen was the latest problem to hit the camp, and it was doubtful if he would make the first game in the World Cup finals, never mind the clash with England. If Ally was going to make any changes to the squad he would have to do it now. He elected not to and the criticism started. Furthermore, when the manager gave the squad a break from rigorous training, allowing them a day out, the flak increased. Willie and some other players – including Tom Forsyth, Asa Hartford, Derek Johnstone and Alan Rough – spent the day at Perth races. They had a good day, which included a few beers, a few bets and some £1,800 winnings between the group. Derek Johnstone met the American actor James Garner (*The Great Escape, The Rockford Files*) and enjoyed his champagne company for the remainder of the day. All in all it was hardly criminal activity. At the end of the day's racing the group received a tip from a bookie at the meeting. He had a pony and trap running at Bannockburn that evening, as Willie recalls, and it was certainty to win. The boys couldn't resist the idea and headed for the meeting. They duly put their £1,800 on the tip, and it duly lost. The bookie was conspicuous by his absence which, for the bookie at least, was probably a good thing. The press took the story of the day's events and turned the whole thing into a drinking and gambling orgy. The rot was setting in.

As the squad prepared for the England clash the press started their normal speculation on the outcome of the game. One newspaper reporter claimed the following: "Victory is vital. Apart from the prestige angle, we can't afford to go to Argentina with any self-doubts created by an English win". What a load of codswallop! The result wasn't critical in the slightest. Surely the important aspect of the game was for the players to come through it unscathed, without adding to the growing injury list. Yet the press wanted blood, sweat and English tears. In their eyes beating Scotland's greatest rivals was more important than the World Cup final itself. In fact, it was nothing more than a Home International, part of a championship of little or no significance. Yet there is something about the Scottish mentality, especially if egged on by journalists, that makes the nation want to slaughter the English at all costs – whether it be at football or tiddlywinks! If that victory didn't materialise, it would be the same sports writers who would set about pulling Ally MacLeod and his squad to bits.

They had even latched on to the fact that Willie had played against England in 1966, while Rough, Dalglish, Macari and most of the rest of the squad were still at school. England had won 4-3 that day. They'd even claimed that Willie was out for revenge after that defeat and they interviewed him on the subject. Willie being Willie gave them exactly what they wanted – he opened his mouth and jumped in with both feet! If the fans weren't fired up enough, they would be when Willie started: "The English team (of 1966) was nowhere near the same class as the Scottish side of today," he said. "They may have gone on to glory (winning the World Cup) but there's no reason why we shouldn't do the same thing in '78."

And so an encounter of no significance became the most significant game on the planet. On the day of the match Ally MacLeod named the following team: Rough, Burns, Kennedy, Forsyth, Donachie, Rioch, Masson, Hartford, Dalglish, Jordan, Johnston. Gordon McQueen was still missing through injury, and Willie Johnston, although playing, was still carrying an injury to his ankle. England, on the other hand, had no injury worries and named a strong team, and why not? Let's face it, they weren't going anywhere important after the game. England lined up thus: Clemence, Neal, Mills, Currie, Watson, Hughes, Wilkins, Coppell, Mariner, Francis, Barnes.

On paper there was no doubting that Scotland were the favourites, but the game would not be played on paper. Hampden Park was jammed with over-enthusiastic Scots. The atmosphere was electric and expectations were high. Unfortunately, neither team really delivered. Ally MacLeod had perhaps made some poor decisions on the day. There was a strong contingent of supporters (and the press) who had felt that Derek Johnstone should have retained his place at centre-forward, but that was not to be. And when it became obvious that the English defence were not going to be broken easily, MacLeod made the strangest of substitutions. He elected to take off Rioch and Masson, replacing them with Gemmill and Souness. Minutes later England scored through Steve Coppell, and there was no way back. The midfield engine room had been disturbed, the organisation had disappeared and England ran out 1-0 winners.

Yet the fans didn't desert the Scottish team and remained in the ground to give them their support for the adventure that was still to come. Willie recalls going back out on to the park to acknowledge the fans along with his team-mates. It was an emotional experience, but one which was unbelievably surpassed a few days later.

On 25 May 1978 some 30,000 banner-waving fans congregated inside Hampden Park to give the Scottish squad an emotional send-off for South America. The squad arrived in an open-topped bus and did a lap honour in the stadium. Pipe bands skirled, and the fans chanted, cheered and sang as each player walked to the centre of the park to be individually introduced to the crowd.

Willie: With the World Cup only weeks away the hype regarding our chances in Argentina was growing day by day. Ally MacLeod was adding to it by making rash statements to the press and the nation was beginning to believe that we could possibly win the World Cup. Did the players believe it? Not a chance. Oh, we knew we had a good squad, we knew we could do well – well enough to get through the group stages at least. Yet the hype kept building and then came the icing on the cake – the Hampden parade. There wasn't a player in the squad who wanted to take part in this American-style send-off. More than 30,000 fans were in Hampden Park that day. Majorettes performed, pipe bands played. Then comedian Andy Cameron told a few jokes before introducing each member of the squad individually to the fans. It was an ordeal that would not have concerned us had we been dressed in football gear prior to a match. But wearing a suit, collar and tie, and flat shoes with no studs was uncomfortable and daunting. It was embarrassing having to walk to the middle of the park and wave to the screaming crowd. Then we were made to parade up and down the pitch carrying the largest Scottish Saltire I've ever seen in my life. At one stage I nearly fell flat on my face. Little did I know that Ally MacLeod and the squad were only two games away from falling on their faces. My face, of course, would have more mud on it than any of the others.

Before they left the ground to head for Prestwick airport, Ally MacLeod made his final prediction to the press: "We will hammer Peru – and Iran have no chance!"

The lyrics of an Elvis Presley song come to mind: "Wise men say, only fools rush in ... "

23

DON'T CRY FOR ME ARGENTINA

The flight from Prestwick to Argentina was both long and boring. Most players passed the time by playing cards, with many of them losing a few quid into the bargain. The plane flew to the city of Recife in the north-eastern region of Brazil, then refuelled and headed for the Argentinian capital, Buenos Aires. From there they flew to Cordoba before setting off on a coach trip – two vehicles were used because of the size of the party – to the small market town of Alta Garcia, which would be the headquarters of the Scottish squad during the opening stages of the World Cup. By the time the two buses arrived in the market town the journey had taken its toll on one of them. It coughed and spluttered its way up the tiny main street. The bus would go no further that day (and perhaps, never again). After such an arduous journey many of the players were feeling in the same condition as that clapped-out coach and simply wanted to sleep. However, sleep was something that they wouldn't experience for a few more hours, at least. The locals had turned out in force to welcome the Scottish party. The squad had to listen to various speeches by local dignitaries – they didn't understand a word – before signing autographs for all the local kids. It was obvious that Scotland wasn't the only country gripped by World Cup fever.

The World Cup had returned to South America for the first time in 16 years, but the political instability of Argentina (not unlike the situation when Scotland visited Chile the previous year) had almost derailed the tournament before it had got off the ground. FIFA had become concerned about threats of violence from within the country. Argentina was under the dictatorship of General Videla who, following a coup, had deposed Isabela Martinez de Peron from the presidency in 1976. The military junta had killed thousands of people and things were far from stable. A number of countries, led by the Netherlands, talked of boycotting the World Cup because of the political situation. In the end all nations agreed to go. Yet a number of players took it on themselves to boycott the tournament, the most notable being two masters of the game, Holland's Johan Cruyff and Germany's Paul Breitner. However, Argentina had put over a strong case to FIFA, including a guarantee that there would be no bloodshed. Duly that was accepted and the tournament went ahead.

The Scottish squad, following the festivities in the market square, were ferried to their hotel in relays by the bus that still had some life in it. Every member of the squad was glad the journey was over. SFA secretary Ernie Walker and team boss Ally MacLeod had visited the Hotel Sierras in January. Walker had been jubilant at securing its accommodation for the World Cup and had told the Scottish media: "It's the best hotel we saw at any of the centres. For me it's a kind of Argentinian Gleneagles." Then he added: "Everything is there to keep the players happy. There's a golf course attached, tennis courts and a swimming pool."

Willie's recollections are slightly different. "When I saw the outside it certainly looked the part, but inside was less impressive. The rooms were uncarpeted and almost devoid of furniture. The food was unimaginative and nothing to write home about. The swimming pool was large, but lacked something ... oh yes, it didn't have any water." Gleneagles this was not!

The players settled in the best they could. The press reported that the financial rewards for success in the tournament were settled within a few days of arriving in Argentina. If Scotland were to win the World Cup they would receive £20,000 to £25,000 per man. The sports goods firm *Umbro* had also promised the squad £120,000 if they were victorious. Different payments would be made when and if the team progressed throughout the stages. What the press didn't report was the split in the camp regarding these financial rewards. Several players were unhappy about the sums of money that were on offer and wanted more. A players' meeting was called to resolve the issues and at times the discussions became quite heated. Willie identifies the two main players who wanted more cash as Lou Macari and Archie Gemmill. Macari insisted that he could earn more at Manchester United for reaching a cup final and Gemmill had the same feelings. Willie, on the other hand, felt quite different, as did most of the remainder of the squad. As far as he was concerned he was here to represent his country in the biggest event in football – money was of no consequence.

Willie: The demand for more money sickened me. We were in South America to play for our nation, and playing for our country should have been reward enough! Macari and Gemmill were wrong to start this debate. It only served to take the players' thoughts away from the real task at hand; preparing for the biggest matches of our careers.

At times the air was blue, but despite the feelings of Macari and Gemmill, the players would not approach the SFA with demands for better financial rewards – and so the first crack appeared in the harmony of the squad. Willie admits that he admires both players for their footballing talent, but that admiration doesn't extend to them as men ... and never will.

The players would now attempt to get down to the business of preparing for their opening three games in the World Cup. Scotland were grouped with Peru, Iran and Holland. From the four teams, two would qualify for the latter stages. Holland looked like being Scotland's toughest opponents from the section. Their style of play and temperament was similar to those of the Scots. Football in Holland was flourishing and many young players had broken into the squad to add to the experienced pool which already existed. They had the fast and dangerous Johnny Rep, the consistent Rudi Krol and Barcelona's Johan Neeskens. They were the fourth seeds in the tournament and had high hopes of doing well. Yet they would they miss the presence of their most famous son, Johan Cruyff. He had elected not to participate in the tournament because of the political situation in Argentina. Whatever, they would be Scotland's last opponents in the group and the destiny of MacLeod's men was in their own hands, via the two games prior to meeting the Dutch. As for Iran, one of the richest oil nations of the world, their football team were amateurs. They were the back-markers in the tournament and considered as no threat to any of the three other teams in the section. Peru, however, were an unknown quantity. Willie was amazed that, as the squad prepared to take this nation on, Ally MacLeod could tell the players nothing of note about them. In fact, MacLeod had never seen them play. Meanwhile Peru, on the other hand, had watched Scotland on several occasions. The Scottish players had to settle for watching a couple of videos of the Peruvians in action. Was this a mistake? Of course it was. They were the South American champions, after all!

In the confines of the complex their preparations for the first match against Peru continued, despite the training ground being a total disgrace and unworthy of Brigadoon United. Soon rumours began to reach the players that sections of the media were running a hate campaign against them. Stories were rife that there was unrest in the camp. The press were loving it and the players couldn't understand where they were obtaining their information. Later in the World Cup campaign it would be revealed that Lou Macari had been slipping out of the camp and feeding a journalist (for financial rewards) with all the muck the journalist required. Eventually the SFA became aware of Macari's involvement and he was banned from playing for his country for life.

Willie: Lou Macari was one of the players who supported me during my crisis in Argentina and for that I thank him. Yet I have never understood why he did what he did during that World Cup campaign. He kept a diary on the day-to-day activities within our camp and sold the contents to the gutter press. Harmony within the camp was disrupted because of his actions. As far as I viewed it he had betrayed his fellow professionals simply for financial gain and you cannot stoop any lower than that.

By the time Macari's subterfuge was uncovered it was too late. The hate campaign was in full flow and derogatory stories abounded. One such had Alan Rough and Derek Johnstone staggering back to the hotel in the wee small hours after visiting a nightclub. They reached the entrance and found the gates locked, so the pair vaulted over the wall. Inside the grounds they were stopped by gun-toting guards and Alan Rough shouted the immortal words: "Don't shoot me, I'm the goalkeeper!"

Willie recalls a similar incident which included himself, Alan Rough (again) and Asa Hartford. They had been in the local casino for a few hours before heading back to the hotel. Instead of going all the way to the main gates, they vaulted the wall and were met by a group of security guards pointing machine guns at them. Willie pointed to the badge on his jersey and blurted out: "Escocia ... Escocia!" Eventually the situation was resolved – almost certainly not through Willie's command of the local language – and they were allowed back into the hotel. The press had the story a day later (a fair guess will tell you who supplied it to them) and added that they were drunk into the bargain. Willie declares the drunken accusation as utter nonsense – the casino didn't sell alcohol. Sadly the Scottish nation began to believe all they read, started to turn against what was arguably the best Scottish squad of all time and the players began to feel the heat. The stories continued. There were headlines like WHISKY FOR BREAKFAST and SOLICITING THE SENORITAS – all utter nonsense but totally soul-destroying for the squad. There was only one way to resolve the situation, and that would be on the football pitch.

The opening game against Peru arrived and despite Willie feeling far from well – he was suffering from a bout of hay fever – Ally MacLeod named the following team:

Rough, Burns, Kennedy, Forsyth, Buchan, Rioch, Masson, Hartford, Dalglish, Jordan, Johnston.

McQueen and Donachie were missing from the defence through injury. It baffled Willie why Sandy Jardine wasn't used as cover at full-back, releasing Buchan to play in central defence in place of the young Kenny Burns. It was a question others would ask following the game. Willie himself was told by MacLeod that his role would be vital. He was asked to take on the defence, get behind them and supply high balls for Joe Jordan. It was the manager's belief that Peru would be incapable of dealing with the power of Jordan in the air. Time would tell.

More than 37,000 fans filtered into the Cordoba Stadium as the kick-off approached. Scotland started the game well and hit Peru with everything they had. Quiroga, the Peruvian goalkeeper, was playing out of his skin and stopped everything that was thrown at him. Yet it was no surprise when, after 14 minutes, Joe Jordan slammed the ball into the net to give Scotland the lead. Ally MacLeod had repeatedly said that the Peruvians were a team of pensioners and that Scotland's power, fitness and class would be too much for them. Unfortunately, he forgot to convey this to the South Americans and their blistering counter-attacks saw them fight their way back into the game. In the 43rd minute Cesar Cueto scored to level the match. Willie is the first to admit that he was playing poorly and perhaps should have been substituted at half-time. MacLeod didn't see it that way and there was no change to his tactics as the second half got under way. On the hour mark Scotland had the ideal chance to regain the lead. Bruce Rioch, following a blistering run, was fouled inside the Peruvian 18-yard box and Scotland were awarded a penalty. Don Masson stepped up to take the spot-kick. Nobody in a Scottish jersey thought for a moment that Don would miss. He was a cool customer and had scored from the spot against Wales to take his country to the finals. Yet miss he did. His shot was tame and easily pushed away by the Peruvian keeper. Willie believes if Don had scored, Scotland would have taken control of the game and victory would have been theirs. The outcome was totally the reverse. The Peruvians took the bull by the horns and went for glory. In the 72nd minute the South Americans were rewarded when Cubillas struck a tremendous free-kick with the outside of his right foot past the fully stretched Alan Rough.

Willie: The game against Peru turned out to be my worst ever performance for my country – yet we still could have won the match. My room-mate, Don Masson, had the opportunity to slot a penalty home to put us 2-1 up. He missed and the Peruvians became rejuvenated and went on to destroy us. Cubillas was their play-maker and the mastermind behind our demise, but he didn't do it alone. As a team they played well and seemed to know our strengths and weaknesses. We, on the other hand, knew nothing about them and the blame for that must lie firmly at Ally MacLeod's door.

When it came to both Peru and Iran the players knew absolutely nothing about them and it appeared MacLeod was no better informed than we were. Preparation for these two games was non-existent. MacLeod made a big mistake classing Cubillas as no threat whatsoever – he was a class act. Although Peru hadn't qualified for the 1974 World Cup the 20-year-old Cubillas had shown the world what he was made of four years earlier in Mexico. He scored in all four of Peru's opening matches and again in the quarter-final against Brazil. He ended the tournament as the third highest scorer, behind Gerd Muller and Jairzinho.

In 1975 he helped Peru win the South American championship and in the semi-final he scored two goals in a 3-1 victory over the mighty Brazil. Does this sound like a player who is no threat whatsoever?

In the game against Scotland he ran the show from midfield with clever runs and precise passing. The Scots didn't know what to do with him. Every move the Peruvians made appeared to come through Cubillas. As if his midfield performance wasn't enough, he finished the Scots off with a superb free-kick. No doubt Iran also thought he was of no threat when they played Peru in the second match of the group – and Cubillas scored a hat-trick against them.

At 2-1 down, Ally MacLeod made his biggest blunder of the game. He took off the heart of Scotland's midfield, Rioch and Masson, and replaced them with Gemmill and Macari. He had done the same against England and it had cost Scotland that game. Asa Hartford tried to hold the midfield together but the engine room had been removed and Scotland collapsed. That man Cubillas struck again in the 77th minute and the game was over.

The Scottish dressing room was like a morgue. The players were devastated. To a man they were aware that they had let themselves and the nation down. Some had tears in their eyes and Ally MacLeod was as white as a ghost. Everyone knew that to survive into the next round they would have to beat both Iran and Holland or the World Cup dream would be over. Things were bad, and for Willie a nightmare was about to begin.

He was lounging in the bath, still feeling unwell and unaware that two of his team-mates had been selected to take the statutory drug test which had been the practice since being instituted in England in 1966.

Willie: I admire Archie Gemmill's football talent and nobody can deny that he scored one of the best goals of the 1978 World Cup. It was after the Peru match that Archie was selected, along with Kenny Dalglish, to supply a urine sample. He failed to do so, claiming he was dehydrated. It's such a pity that I wasn't as dehydrated as he was that day!

In his book *Both Sides Of The Border* (published in 2005), Gemmill reveals that his selection to take the drugs test was a case of mistaken identity and he was not the player originally picked. Gemmill explains why he was unable to provide a sample: "When you're dehydrated after expending a lot of physical energy on a hot day it takes a good while before you feel the urge." Sounds like nonsense. Gemmill had come on as a substitute for Don Masson with only 20 minutes to go – how could he be dehydrated? How could it be a case of mistaken identity? Who selected the two Scottish players to take the drugs test? Presumably, FIFA officials. Did they draw names out of a hat? And if they did then how could they confuse the name Willie Johnston with that of Archie Gemmill? Let's face it – they couldn't! Still, Gemmill failed to provide that sample, and somebody had to. That person would be Willie Johnston. Why was Willie selected? Was it an official who directed him? No, while still in the bath unaware of what had gone before, he received a tap on the shoulder from Archie Gemmill, who informed him that he had been selected to take the drug test. Willie climbed out of the bath and without question went to the room where the tests were being held. In the room were three players (Willie made it four) and an official. There were four unmarked bottles. The four players (Kenny Dalglish, Willie Johnston and the two Peruvians, Cubillas and Diaz) were instructed to provide urine samples. They duly did.

Willie recalls that no names were written on the bottles, neither prior to the samples being given nor before the players were asked to leave the room – and that begs the question: which sample belonged to which footballer? Make no mistake about it, Willie has always admitted to taking two *Reactivan* tablets prior to the game. They were taken to relieve his hay fever condition and for no other reason. Why would he take pills for any other reason? Wasn't he already the fastest player appearing at the World Cup? Of course he was. His admission to having taken *Reactivan* still doesn't resolve the dilemma posed by the unmarked bottles – whose urine was in which container? Nevertheless, events would move on with Willie unaware about what was to come at him.

The dejected Scotland squad returned to their headquarters in Alta Garcia. Willie was lounging in his room with Don Masson. They were discussing the forthcoming game against Iran when Ally MacLeod entered, his face still registering all the pressure and humiliation he had suffered from the game against Peru. Willie was unaware of anything else troubling his manager. MacLeod spoke softly and asked Willie to walk with him. The walk took them to the room of the team doctor. In Doctor Fitzsimmons' room attitudes changed and Willie realised that something major was wrong. Fitzsimmons spoke: "Did you take pills before the game?" he asked:

"Yes," Willie replied.

"*Reactivan?*" the doctor asked.

"Yes," Willie replied.

"Didn't you know that *Reactivan* contains a banned stimulant?"

Willie's mind collapsed. He knew that what he was hearing would mean huge consequences. Consequences he didn't want to contemplate, but they came at him nevertheless.

"Your drug test was found to be positive," said the doctor. "You're in big trouble, Willie," he added.

Willie: When I learned I had tested positive my legs immediately turned to jelly. I felt weak and sick. Various thoughts went through my head. How would my family react to the news? Was my playing career over? But one thought kept returning more than most – had I been set up?

I have been asked many times about those two pills. Did I take them to enhance my play? NEVER! I was playing the best football of my career and I needed no artificial stimulants. Had I known that they contained a banned substance they would have been binned immediately and that's a fact. Did others in the squad take the same pills? I've heard all the stories, all the rumours and all the innuendos. Let me put them all to rest; as far I was aware no other player took any tablet of any description.

In the next few minutes following the revelation, many things flowed through Willie's mind, none of them heartening. He knew his international career was in jeopardy. Hell, his playing career was in jeopardy!

"Everybody takes *Reactivan* when they're feeling low."

Not the words the doctor wanted to hear.

"Willie, the problem is the stimulant *Fencamfamin*," said Fitzsimmons. Willie had never heard of *Fencamfamin* and doubted that he could even pronounce it. What he didn't know was that it was a banned stimulant and *Reactivan* contained 10mg per tablet. *Reactivan* was available over the counter in any chemists shop in the UK and was used (according to Willie) as a pick-me-up by many players in the English First Division.

What Willie wanted to know at this point was what action would be taken against him. The answer was not forthcoming and he was sent back to his room. Understandably, he had a restless night. What he didn't know was that the press had got hold of the story and he was about to be crucified by the media throughout the footballing world. That evening he, and all the others from the Scottish squad, attended an official function which was being given for the British Minister of Sport, Denis Howell. Willie was reluctant to attend. Nobody had told him anything regarding his situation and he was agitated.

Neither the SFA nor FIFA had approached him – but, unknown to Willie, a press statement was due to be released. During the official function the media, in the form of Trevor McDonald (now Sir Trevor), approached Willie and put him under the cosh. All who watched the live broadcast witnessed a confused Willie attempting to make sense of the questions McDonald threw at him. It was a travesty (allegedly, McDonald later apologised for it) which led Ally MacLeod to eject the reporter from the building. It was a harrowing night for Willie and he left the function and went out for a drink with those who were closest to him – Asa Hartford, Don Masson and Tom Forsyth.

The next morning was no less harrowing. Willie was summoned to the room of SFA secretary Ernie Walker. The questions came thick and fast. Where did the drugs come from? Who else took the drug? The pill had suddenly become a drug and Willie wanted to defend himself. But he couldn't, and his world collapsed.

"You're being sent home. You'll never play for Scotland again," said Walker.

"I want to appeal," said the ashen Willie.

"The SFA will not appeal. We have made our decision, you will be sent home," replied Walker.

Willie was devastated and only one person came to his mind at this point – Margaret, his wife.

"I need to phone my wife," Willie said.

"There will be no phone calls. You will remain in your room till told otherwise," said Walker. God had spoken.

Willie was made a prisoner in his hotel room, nobody was allowed near him. Some of his colleagues tried to save his bacon, but it was too late. He would be the sacrificial lamb to the Scottish nation. Don Masson sat before MacLeod and Walker and admitted to taking the same pill. Walker would have none of it. He simply told Don that if he'd taken the pill then he was on his way home as well. Don retracted his statement but took no further part in the World Cup and would never win another Scottish cap.

Certain factions of the media had for some time been calling for the exclusion of both captain Bruce Rioch and Don Masson because they were not getting regular games for their club. The defeat against Peru would result in MacLeod listening to these so-called media experts and Rioch would take no further part in the tournament. Indeed, he would never play for Scotland again.

Archie Gemmill took over as captain (such acceleration within the squad) and scored the goal of the tournament in the 3-2 victory against Holland, slipping the ball between two players' legs before curling it home with his left foot. It made no difference, Scotland were still on their way home. However, prior to these events Willie would make the long, lonely journey back to the UK. The SFA had kept Willie in his room, with no phone calls, no communication with the outside world. He was a total prisoner. If he had committed murder he would have been treated better.

Willie sat in his room feeling cold, and was trembling all over. He played the whole scenario through his head several times and it didn't seem to get any better. He thought of his previous trip to Argentina the year before. On that occasion he had been the star of the mini-tournament – this time he was the felon. He recalled the words of Luque, the Argentinian player, after Willie had destroyed their defence throughout the game. "John … ston, you are a very good player, but be warned – do not return to Argentina for the World Cup … things will not be nice for you!" These words began to haunt him. Was there a conspiracy against him? Was he being set up to take a fall? If he was, he knew the SFA weren't going to help him. They had made their position very clear. They were sending him home in disgrace. This didn't surprise Willie and why should it? Hadn't the SFA made it perfectly clear to the Scottish managers, Ormond and MacLeod, that they didn't want him part of the set-up? Now they were in command

and they were calling the shots. All these thoughts made Willie feel exhausted, vulnerable and dejected.

The next day the SFA decided Willie should be removed from the country. They threw a blanket over his head, bundled him into a car and removed him from the complex. How was he feeling? Nobody asked him. Nobody seemed to care. In the car was a driver, an SFA official and Willie. They drove the 700 kilometres to Buenos Aires, with no food, no phone calls, no talking. The only stop was for Willie to get out of the car and have a cigarette, like a condemned man. Finally they arrived at the British Embassy. Now Willie was placed in a room, again denied food and all communication, to await the next stage of the move. How did he feel? The answer is simple. He was distraught, humiliated and anxious. The SFA had ostracised him from the squad and his family. How low could you get? He was left alone in the small room for what seemed an eternity. Eventually the door opened and a smiling fellow entered. "Are you Willie Johnston?" the friendly face asked in a Scottish accent.

"Yes," Willie replied.

"Do you fancy a beer?"

Willie: When I had been placed in the room at the Embassy, fear was running through me. I couldn't think straight and felt certain that something bad was about to happen. Instead a wee bloke from Edinburgh came into the room, smiled and asked me if I wanted a bottle of beer. A minute or two later we were having a beer together and having a rare old chat. He was a nice, friendly character and made me feel at ease. For the life of me I can't remember his name – but I'd love to have another beer with him!

The stranger made no mention of the drugs scandal – it was the first time in days he had spoken to someone without having to discuss it – and for this Willie will remain eternally grateful. When the beer was finished the little man from Edinburgh announced that he would have to get on with his duties. Willie never learned what his position within the Embassy was. All he knew was that he'd gained a friend in the middle of the nightmare. When he was alone once again, Willie's anxiety returned and his antipathy towards the SFA grew. Eventually officials arrived in the room and once more he was bundled into a car, transported to the airport and placed in a small lounge. Another long wait came to pass before two armed Argentinian guards entered. They were intimidating characters, and when they prodded Willie with the barrels of their machine guns he was overcome by fear.

Where were the men from the Embassy? Where were the men from the SFA? What was happening?

Eventually one of the guards spoke: "John ... ston ... you leave now."

Willie got to his feet and his legs turned to jelly as he was led from the building. They placed him in a deserted coach. One of the guards drove while the other kept his machine gun pointed at the distraught Scot. The journey seemed to take forever and Willie had visions that his life was in jeopardy. He sensed they were driving him to some secluded spot where they would pull the triggers and Willie Johnston would be no more.

Willie: Being bundled into a car like a criminal and thrown out of the country at gunpoint was more than terrifying. There were times I feared for my life and there was no one I could turn to. Reflecting back I now feel certain that the SFA had treated me as the sacrificial lamb. I would take all the heat, all the blame for the disappointing 1-1 draw against Iran and the disharmony in the Scottish camp. I'm certain the SFA felt that the media would have a field day destroying me over the two pills and would pay less attention to their huge mistakes in Argentina, such as the poor accommodation, the lack of preparation for the opening group matches and their total amateurism throughout such a big event as the World Cup finals.

Willie cannot describe the relief he felt when he saw the bus pull up alongside a large aircraft. Willie was ejected from the bus and roughly bundled aboard the plane. They placed him in a seat at the back of the plane before disappearing from his life. The plane was empty; he was the only passenger on board. Surely they weren't going to take him all the way back to the UK as the only passenger? What the hell – Willie certainly felt a modicum of relief that he was, at least, about to leave the country. Eventually the plane filled with other passengers and the plane prepared for take-off. As it rose to the heavens Willie let out a huge sigh of relief, but the nightmare was far from over.

The plane made the relatively short trip to Rio where the passengers disembarked and Willie joined the flight that would take him to Paris. There was no sign of the press and Willie began to feel more relaxed than he had over the past few days. The trip to Paris also passed without incident. As the plane taxied to a halt in the French capital, Willie only had one thought. He would disembark and make a phone call to his wife, Margaret.

If only things were that simple. As Willie emerged on to the steps to disembark, all he could see was a sea of cameramen and reporters. The media had caught up with him. Willie pushed his way back on to the plane – there was no way he was facing such a terrifying horde.

Passengers disembarked, the plane took on fuel and new passengers (destined for London) came aboard. Within minutes Willie sensed that something was wrong. A number of the new passengers were not what they first appeared to be. A large percentage of them were from the media. Cameras began to flash and notebooks and pens where pushed in front of Willie's face. Questions abounded. Willie said little, but the media persisted, and the short journey from Paris to London turned him into a nervous wreck. His arrival in London would bring all the severity of the situation fully home to Willie.

24

UNDER THE MICROSCOPE

If Willie thought Paris was packed with press and other media, London was worse. The airport was saturated with them and they all wanted a slice of his hide. Amongst the throng Willie saw a friendly face, that of his manager Ron Atkinson. Police officers escorted him through the hostile crowd as questions abounded, and cameras flashed. Willie tried to keep calm, but the experience was harrowing. He was pushed this way and that, like a ball in a pinball machine. Eventually Big Ron grabbed his arm and pulled him towards a waiting car.

As they walked Ron asked: "Have you got any of those pills left, Willie? I'm knackered!"

Willie tried to smile, but it was forced. Inside the car it was Willie's turn to fire a question at Ron: "Where are my wife and kids?"

"Don't worry, they're perfectly safe," Ron assured him. "The kids are with neighbours and Margaret is in a hotel in Cambridge."

"I need to be with Margaret," said Willie anxiously.

Ron put his arm reassuringly around Willie's shoulders. "Take it easy, son. I'll get you through this mess. I've already got a new contract for you."

"New contract? What new contract?" enquired Willie.

"With *Boots* the chemist," Ron quipped.

A genuine smile crossed Willie's face and he suddenly felt more relaxed than he had at any time during that past 48 hours. Ron then asked Willie to do him one favour before they made their way to the hotel in Cambridge. Allegedly, Ron's friend, Bob Wilson, was in danger of losing his job as a sports presenter at the BBC. If Willie would agree to do a TV interview on BBC's *Nationwide* programme, then Wilson's job would be safe. Willie was reluctant but eventually he agreed. They drove to the television studio, where Willie discovered that the plan was for him to be interviewed by a panel which would include Lawrie McMenemy and the legendary Jock Stein. Willie realised that facing a panel would be dangerous. He was jet-lagged and certainly not clear-headed. He wasn't about to allow a panel of football experts to rip him apart.

Finally a compromise was reached whereby Willie, with Big Ron alongside him, would be interviewed by the *Nationwide* presenter alone. Willie recalls little of the interview and was just glad to get it over and done with. Favour now complete, all he wanted to do was make the trip to Cambridge and be with Margaret. As he was about to leave the building Jock Stein approached him for a quiet word. Jock was sympathetic towards Willie's plight and offered his support. Jock had never hidden his admiration for Willie's talents, but his next sentence took the troubled footballer by total surprise. "When this settles what's in your plans, Willie? Because if you want to return to Scotland I'll make a bid to West Brom and bring you to Celtic Park."

> *Willie: When Big Jock approached me that day in the studio and told me he wanted to sign me for Celtic I was slightly taken aback. It was obvious that he didn't see my Argentina nightmare as a problem and insisted that I take his phone number and call him when I'd had time to think it through. I never did make that call.*

Willie thanked Jock and left the building. As he walked to the car he gave a little shake of the head. He knew that the drugs scandal would be with him for years and that would be hard enough to stomach. But pulling on the green-and-white hoops of Celtic – well, that would haunt him forever.

After Willie and Margaret were reunited, they they made a joint decision, with the blessing of Ron Atkinson, to get themselves and the family out of the country for a week or two. They headed to Majorca. While on the island Willie bumped into the Nottingham Forest assistant manager, Ronnie Fenton. Fenton felt empathy towards Willie, especially as the named pill was *Reactivan*. Fenton told him that the tablet was widely used throughout English footballing circles, and that many players were using it at that time as a pick-me-up. Willie thanked him for his understanding – but the information regarding the fact that other players were (or had been) taking the tablet offered him little solace. Everyday the newspapers carried some sort of report relating to Willie and his "drug abuse".

Not all reports were completely derogatory. Ron Atkinson publicly defended him on numerous occasions. The sportswriter Ian Wooldridge wrote an unusual article, part of which went as follows: "In pursuance of a small, new experience, not to mention the bleak hope of finding out why Scotland are playing like Basutoland Wednesday, this column comes to you in unusual circumstances. It is being written under the influence of Willie Johnston's funny pills. Three hours before typing the opening line I swallowed two *Fencamfamin*-based *Reactivan* tablets. This was the same dosage Willie admitted taking three hours before the start of his last game for Scotland. For all the good they have done it might have been *Rentokil*. I do not imply that other members of the Scotland team are on them. But if they were it could explain a great deal."

In 1979, August 20 to be precise, a headline in a Scottish national newspaper read: SFA BOSS SLAMS MacLEOD. The reason for the headline was simple. Ally MacLeod had alleged that more than one player possessed banned drugs in Argentina. In the article Willie Harkness, the SFA president, said bluntly: "That's not the facts he gave us during the World Cup finals."

MacLeod's disclosure of more than one player being involved had emerged in a book that the former Scottish manager had written in an attempt to defend his reputation, which had been torn apart following the team's collapse in South America. Were these allegations by MacLeod true? Maybe – but we will never known to what extent.

There was one story linked to the drugs scandal of 1978 which, if for nothing more than its humour, deserves to be told. Allegedly, the team had boarded the bus and were heading for the second game against Iran. During the journey MacLeod had gone to the back of the bus and placed his hat on the back seat. He turned to all the players and announced: "I'm going to the front of the bus to talk to the driver. I expect, when I return to fetch my hat, to find any illegal pills to be inside it. Then he walked to the front of the bus. The story goes that on his return, the hat was filled with various pills. Ally went to speak to the driver and ordered him to stop the bus. He then walked over to a field full of horses and threw the pills over the fence. After the miserable 1-1 draw with Iran the bus passed the same field. Apparently the horses were having a rare old time. They were doing cartwheels, somersaults and other strange things. If there was even a modicum of truth in the story, and I doubt that there was, it would certainly set the cat amongst the pigeons. Or more appropriately, the pills amongst the horses.

Were other Scottish players taking the same tablet? No matter how I pursued this with Willie he would not be drawn on the question. I named a few players and was met only by that rascal smile of his. What Willie didn't know, or had conveniently forgotten, was that at least one other player, years after the event, had admitted taking the same tablets. That player was Asa Hartford. His admission came in a newspaper article six years after the World Cup. The headline of the article was: DRUGS LIE THAT HAUNTS ME.

In the article Asa went on to admit: "I took the same kind of pill as Willie ... but I escaped because I wasn't one of the players tested for drugs after the game."

Asa also confessed that he lied to the team doctor and manager Ally MacLeod when the Scots launched an investigation at the training camp. He felt sure that Ally MacLeod suspected him of taking the tablet but no one could prove that was the case. Asa added: "It was the worst experience I've ever had and I think any of the players who were there would agree. The defeat against Peru was bad enough, the drugs storm was worse. Today (1984) it is hard to believe the fuss which was caused over a small tablet. People saw the 'drugs' headlines and seemed to think all the players were on heroin or cocaine or something.

As a stimulant it was not in the same league as those used by so many stars in athletics."

In his book *Hand of God – the Life of Diego Maradona* (1997), Jimmy Burns makes reference to the 1978 World Cup, and the Argentina team in particular. He states:

"Argentina had players who had been regularly provided with amphetamines while playing for their league teams, and who found in this World Cup a suitably lax regime when it came to urine samples." Relaxed regime when it comes to urine samples? That would imply to me that not all samples would belong to the players credited for them. Which, no matter how you view things, takes you back to Willie's claim that at no time during his drugs test were the samples of the four players marked to indicate just who had provided which sample.

Burns continues: "FIFA had yet to develop an efficient system for controlling the taking of drugs during the competition, while for political reasons Argentine officials appear to have ensured that none of their own players were shown positive in the periodical testing that did take place. According to other reports, Kempes and Tarantini were so 'high' after playing one particular World Cup match that they had to keep going for another hour before they came down again."

Burns then turns his attention to Scotland. "The sacrificial lamb of the competition was the Scottish player Willie Johnston, who was sent home in disgrace and banned from international football for one year after his dope test had proved positive."

Archie Gemmill, in his book *Both Sides Of The Border,* makes the claim: "Three other players were on the same pep pills that got Willie Johnston sent home from the World Cup in Argentina 1978. I know who they are and I know they brought the stuff with them from their clubs. It's not my job to expose the trio more than 25 years later and I have no inclination to cause them embarrassment, but I hope they have had time to consider the dreadful damage they might have caused Scottish football and learned the error of their ways."

He continues: "I'm glad it's not a guilty secret that has ever cost me any precious sleep. It's all water under the bridge, much like the evidence, which was flushed down the toilets when we returned to the team hotel in the wake of a dreadful 3-1 spanking by Peru. It was like Niagara Falls, there was so much rushing water that night. Any casual guest would have thought we were all suffering from Montezuma's Revenge after a spicy South American supper."

Interesting ... and confusing? If there were only three other players who took the tablets, then only three others would have to flush them away. It would hardly cause so much rushing water as to be compared to Niagara Falls – would it? No matter. These words would be nothing more than speculation in the distant future.

The Argentina episode has become a Scottish national obsession because the media kept bringing the subject up at every opportunity. Even 30 years later there is no hiding place for Willie. If a chemist took an overdose of *Nightnurse* and hit the headlines then Willie and his two pills would be guaranteed to feature somewhere in the story. It has been a noose around his neck which he has chosen until now to stay silent about. The story told here is the full truth of the matter. It is shocking and controversial and, for Willie, life-changing in so many ways.

Back in 1978 the immediate consequence was that Scotland banned him from playing for his country for life; while FIFA had deemed that a year's ban was sufficient. The SFA would not fall in line with football's governing body and Willie would never play for his country again.

25

BACK AT THE HAWTHORNS

Returning to Birmingham was far from easy for Willie and his family. Hardly a day would pass without small snippets appearing in the press regarding Argentina. Apart from training, Willie had become almost a recluse, choosing to hide himself away whenever the opportunity arose. All the garbage written about him had taken its toll. The press had been murdering him. He was slipping into depression, and his children were being hounded at school by the media. Willie even went so far as to consider leaving the game altogether and returning to Scotland – to do what? He had no idea. Without the support of Ron Atkinson and his fellow West Brom players, Willie believes his playing days would have been over.

Back in training he found it hard to concentrate, and having to meet the rigorous demands of playing in the First Division, that affected his game. Ron tried to motivate him and even offered an extension to his four-year contract, which he had signed just before heading for Argentina. The extension would undoubtedly have taken him to the end of his playing career, but he was reluctant to sign. He wanted first-team football and coming off the bench or playing for the reserves wasn't in his make-up. In addition, West Brom were in the UEFA Cup. Willie had played a big part in securing their place, yet it was a tournament he could not take part in. FIFA had banned him for a year, which included not only international but also European competition.

By the turn of the year he had played no more than a handful of first-team games and he asked for a transfer. Ron refused his request. But the barracking he was taking from opposition fans, even when he was on the bench, was hard to stomach. It became a morning ritual to knock on Big Ron's door and ask for a move. Every morning Ron refused and their relationship was becoming strained. As the season moved along Albion were playing well, both in the League and in Europe, and Willie was finding the frustration of rarely being involved soul-destroying. Eventually he was able to have a meeting with Ron away from the Hawthorns. Willie recalls that the meeting took place either in a café or a hotel lounge. Ron was seated when Willie entered. As he approached Ron smiled at the logo on Willie's T-shirt, which read "I love Big Ron". They discussed the situation, with Willie continually asking to be freed, Ron continually telling him he was very much part of his plans. It was a stalemate and the meeting came to an end.

Willie is uncertain why, shortly after the meeting, Ron agreed to listen to offers for his unhappy left-winger. Maybe it was what the manager read on the back of the T-shirt as Willie left the meeting: "Big Ron's a bastard!"

Willie knew it would be a big wrench to leave the Baggies. The club, the players and the fans had been his family for seven years – but he needed to get his career back on track. Queen's Park Rangers were first on the scene and Willie was aware that they were in negotiations with Atkinson. Ron had put a £120,000 price on Willie's head, which was a huge fee for a 32-year-old at that time. Perhaps it was Ron's way of showing that he was still in command.

Willie had no idea how the talks with QPR had been coming along, but was aware that the Canadian club Vancouver Whitecaps had also tabled a bid. During a break from training Willie and a number of his team-mates headed to Cheltenham for some horse racing. It was always a big day out for the lads and Willie was happy to have a break away from all his problems to enjoy the racing and have a few beers.

During the race meeting he felt a tap on the shoulder. He turned to see a well-dressed man who was unknown to him. "I'm from Queen's Park Rangers," the stranger announced. "Mr Gregory, the chairman, would like a word with you."

Willie felt sure that West Brom and QPR had agreed a fee and a smile crossed his face.

"Fine, where is he?"

"In London. We have a limousine outside waiting to take you there."

"London!" exclaimed Willie. "I'm not going to London today."

"But Mr Gregory wants you there today."

"I don't care, I'm having a day out with the lads. Tell him I'll phone him tomorrow."

The man scurried away and Willie rejoined his West Brom team-mates. He never made that call to London. The following morning he received a call from Tony Waiters, the head coach at Vancouver Whitecaps. After introductions, Tony's message was simple. "Don't sign anything until you've spoken to the Whitecaps, Willie. I'll arrive in England tomorrow along with the club president . We have a very good offer for you."

Willie was intrigued and agreed to do nothing until he met with them. The following day he received another call from Tony Waiters telling him that the Whitecaps had agreed a fee with West Brom for his services, following a meeting at the Hawthorns. They wanted to meet him in a hotel that evening to discuss the contract. Willie agreed to meet with them.

Willie took his friend and West Brom team-mate, Paddy Mulligan, with hi n. Paddy had had more clubs than Seve Ballesteros, and was an expert on cor tracts. The meeting went along well, and eventually they got down to the nitty gritty of the contract. Mr Best, the president, went through every cla .se and then passed the contract to Willie. Willie in turn passed it to Paddy. Paddy studied it in detail, before glancing up at the two men from Vancouver and asked, in his thick Irish accent: "This signing on fee … is it in Canadian dollars?"

"No," said Best. "British pounds."

Paddy turned to Willie, looked him in the eye and whispered two words: "F***in' sign!"

But Willie had never been one for signing things impulsively and asked for a copy of the contract to take home and discuss with his wife Margaret.

That evening Willie spoke with his former manager Johnny Giles, who arranged a meeting between his lawyer and Willie for the following day. The lawyer sat with the contract, and every so often he would put his pen through a particular clause, look up and announce: "That's out."

That evening Willie returned to the hotel and produced the revised contract for Mr Best to view. He accepted all the changes. Willie signed. He was on his way to Vancouver.

26

A WORD FROM BIG RON ATKINSON

When I first arrived at West Brom I was very aware of Willie's disciplinary record, but in fairness this didn't really cause me too much concern. I knew the ability he possessed and that was of more interest to me.

My real first impressions of him came in my second game in charge when we played Manchester United in an FA Cup tie at Old Trafford. The game finished 1-1, and it would have to be said that United were very fortunate to get a draw. Willie performed well that day and scored our goal. Yet it was his lightning bursts down the flank that were a joy to behold. In the replay at the Hawthorns Willie was outstanding and we ran out 3-2 winners. He had almost destroyed the United defence on his own. It was a tremendous performance by a very talented player. As I got to know the player better his personality became more and more evident. He was a likeable scallywag – I've always liked a few of them around my teams, they give the team character. He had an eye for the big occasion and when we met Nottingham Forest in the FA Cup he turned on the style. The game was played at Forest's ground and Willie, forever the showman, annoyed Brian Clough when he sat on the ball – right in front of the dugouts. I came out of the dugout to give him a rollicking only to find that Brian Clough had beaten me to it. Willie continued to put on a show and was instrumental in us being the first team to beat Forest that season.

Willie's performances for the rest of the season continued to impress me and to delight the fans. West Brom qualified for Europe for the first time in a number of years and the part Willie played in this achievement was significant.

Then came the ill-fated trip to Argentina, which was to change his life. I'd heard of the drugs claim on the radio and was gobsmacked. Willie was a flying machine and had no need to take any type of pill to enhance his performance. Nevertheless, he was on his way home. I was finally able to discover his arrival time at Heathrow airport and set off to meet the plane. Colin Addison was with me that day and he was shocked by the number of press that had gathered to meet Willie's flight. The media attendance was something that would have been worthy of the Beatles. This was Colin's first day as my assistant at the Hawthorns, having joined me from Newport County. "I'll tell you this, Ron. This never happened at Newport," he said to me, somewhat nervously.

I was allowed to go forward to meet Willie as he disembarked. I had only one objective and that was to protect him from the media. I took Willie's bags from him and led him through the throng of waiting pressmen; every so often I would use the bags to clear a path through the hordes. On one occasion I swung the bags and knocked over Ray Maloney from *News at Ten*. Finally we got to the car and headed out of the airport. I told Willie that the BBC's *Nationwide* wanted an exclusive interview. Willie agreed and we headed for the studios. On the journey I saw two motorcycles in my rear-view mirror and soon got the impression that they were following us. I tried to give them the slip, but they kept on our tail, and it turned into a chase that would have been worthy of an American movie. We never did manage to shake them off and it turned out they were two outriders from the BBC, hired to protect us as we made our journey to the studios. After the interview was over I took Willie to a reunion with his wife. Margaret had been "kidnapped" by the *Scottish Daily Record* newspaper and whisked off to a remote hotel.

By the start of the new season Willie was still struggling with all the adverse publicity, which appeared as if it would never go away. His form suffered, but a lesser man would have walked away from the game. His appearances were few and far between, but that was not all due to his form. West Brom were involved in Europe and Willie was banned. In the end it seemed logical that he should be given the chance to re-launch his career in pastures new. It was with some sadness that I agreed a fee with Vancouver Whitecaps and his West Brom days came to an end.

In my time, I have been manager over some excellent wingers and wide men, such as Laurie Cunningham and Gordon Strachan. Then, there is the Scot that I never had the privilege of managing, the world-class Jimmy Johnstone, but Willie is right up there alongside him.

INTRODUCTION TO VANCOUVER WHITECAPS
BY TONY WAITERS

(Tony was a former goalkeeper with Blackpool and Burnley. He was capped five times for England during the 1960s. When he retired from playing he was appointed as manager of Plymouth Argyle, where he stayed for five years. In 1977 he became manager of Vancouver Whitecaps. In 1981 he was appointed manager of the Canadian national side and guided them to the Olympic quarter-finals in 1984. In 1986 his management skills took the Canadians to the World Cup finals. Tony was inducted into the Canadian Soccer Hall of Fame in 2001).

I arrived in England to look for several players to add to the Whitecaps squad. I wanted two wingers and Willie Johnston was always going to be my first target. I was well aware of his talent and I knew the Canadian rules would suit his style of play. The offside rule in the North American Soccer League was different from the UK rule – a player could only be offside within 35 yards of the opposition's goal. I felt certain Willie would take full advantage of this newly introduced rule.

I signed Carl Valentine from Oldham, who would play wide right for the Whitecaps. Then I went into negotiations with West Brom to get the services of Willie. I was delighted to get my man. The Whitecaps would now be playing with two orthodox wingers, by then unheard of in the NASL.

Willie was a revelation and soon became a firm favourite with the fans. He became good friends with Alan Ball, and the two of them would play a huge part in getting us to the Soccer Bowl final.

Willie was quite a character both on and off the field. I recall the incident when he took a drink of beer from a fan's bottle during a match. The crowd loved it, but I wasn't amused – yet I couldn't resist smiling at his showmanship.

Ten years after the Soccer Bowl victory the Whitecaps brought all the players who'd taken part in the final back together for a reunion. During the evening Willie was presented with a silver salver with a bottle of *Bud* sitting proudly in the middle. Even ten years later the beer incident had not been forgotten.

It was a sad day for the club when both Willie and Alan Ball were released to return to the UK. Willie's skill, trickery and showmanship will never be forgotten in Vancouver.

27

TURNING OVER A NEW MAPLE LEAF

Archaeological records show the presence of Aboriginal peoples in the Vancouver district dating back some 9,000 years. The coastline of present-day Point Grey was first explored in 1791 by the Spanish explorer Jose Maria Narvaez. The British naval explorer George Vancouver, who explored the inner harbour of Burrard Inlet in 1792, followed him. Vancouver was responsible for giving various British place names in the district.

The Cariboo gold rush of 1861 brought over 25,000 men to the mouth of the Fraser River and by 1862 this location would become known as Vancouver. Lumber soon became the main trade and Vancouver would slowly grow into the beautiful city it is today. It has often been hailed as one of the most desirable cities in the world. Now it would soon be receiving a citizen who might slightly dent that image.

Vancouver Whitecaps played in the North American Soccer League, which was formed in 1968. It followed the success of a one-off tournament the previous summer which had featured British clubs such as Wolves, Stoke City and Aberdeen playing on behalf of cities across the continent. The Whitecaps joined the NASL in 1973, and home attendances at their Empire Stadium gradually began to grow as their performances improved. Yet, real success had eluded them, and by 1978 they had failed to progress beyond the first round of the Soccer Bowl. Reaching the final of the Soccer Bowl is the ultimate goal of every club in the league. It is America's equivalent of the European Cup final, and brings huge financial rewards to the winning club.

Willie had only one thing on his mind as he made the long flight to Vancouver. He could now put his career back on track. A different country, different mentality, surely Argentina would be behind him? What he didn't anticipate was that the media would be out in full force when the flight landed on Canadian soil. Thankfully, his new manager, Tony Waiters, would be waiting to greet him as he stepped from the plane. Tony ushered his new signing through the media masses.

"We have to attend a press conference, Willie. Just leave the talking to me."

Willie knew that the press would want one thing and one thing only – what did happen in Argentina? He was not looking forward to facing the media. Tony Waiters hushed the crowd of pressmen and made his opening statement: "You all know that Vancouver is the third largest drug capital in the world … Willie Johnston will feel at home here!" Job done. No embarrassing questions came his way and the remainder of the conference went smoothly.

Vancouver Whitecaps were minnows in the NASL. But Waiters was a shrewd manager and had quietly and quickly put together a good squad of players. Willie and Alan Ball would be the final cogs in the Vancouver Whitecaps machine. Yet Willie didn't settle quickly into the new set-up. He now found himself playing most games on *Astroturf* and likened it to playing on a snooker table. Once Willie mastered the playing surfaces, he soon became a regular feature in the Whitecaps team. He was enjoying himself and the crowds loved him. The fans were well aware of the nightmare of Argentina, but he was no longer receiving the verbal abuse that had become a feature back in England.

The game in the NASL was different. There were no draws and each game was played to a finish. After 90 minutes with the game still level, an extra 30 minutes would be played. If the game was still level then, a shoot-out would take place. The fans loved it and Willie revelled in it. The shoot-out players would be given the ball 35 yards from the opposing goalkeeper. They would have five seconds to beat the goalie. Willie could do it every time. His favourite trick was employed when the goalkeeper moved off his line, to close the attacker down. He would flick the ball in the air and lob him on every occasion. It was like taking candy from a baby.

Willie: Tony Waiters was right. Moving to Vancouver was the best thing I could have done following the events of Argentina. The Canadians made little of it and I was allowed to get on with my life. Vancouver is a lovely city, the standard of living was high and the people were tremendous. More importantly, my family loved it. I was able to dismiss the demons of Argentina and was soon back playing good football.

Vancouver were making every team sit up and take note. The squad had a good contingent of British players: Willie Johnston, Alan Ball, Trevor Whymark, Phil Parkes and John Craven to name but a few. With the manager, Tony Waiters, also being British, there was a strong English influence to their style of play. Willie had mastered the alien playing surfaces and was in his element, turning in entertaining performances game after game.

Willie: All the playing surfaces in the North American League were artificial and the ball reacted differently on them in comparison to grass. It took a number of games to master all the differences, but when I did I was soon back to my best. What was interesting was the different attitude to football as a sport in Vancouver. All the American clubs would have a mascot and cheerleaders in abundance prior to the kick-off. They treated it as showbiz. This wasn't the Vancouver way – we would do our entertaining on the park.

During one match, in extreme heat, he delighted the crowd as he walked towards the corner flag. He pretended to be struggling with the heat and gave the impression he was about to collapse. He placed the ball by the flag, walked to the crowd and took a drink of beer from a fan's bottle. Duly refreshed, he took the corner and the Whitecaps scored – the fans went wild. Willie was once again back in the limelight for the right reasons. Good results continued and home crowds were soon hitting the stadium's capacity of 32,000. Progress in the Soccer Bowl was also coming along nicely. So we were getting the "Good" – then along came the "Bad" and the "Ugly".

The match was in the League; the venue was New York; the opponents, the mighty New York Cosmos. Cosmos were a team who were heavily backed in finance by Warner Brothers. Their colours had originally been the green and yellow of Brazil – a ploy used to lure the great Pele to the club. Pele was by then retired, but the club was saturated with class players, amongst them were Franz Beckenbauer, Giorgio Chinaglia, Johan Neeskens and Carlos Alberto. The players took the pitch. During the warm-up Andranik Eskandarian approached Willie and gave him some serious verbal abuse. Eskandarian was one of the Cosmos defenders; he was also an Iranian and had played against Scotland in the World Cup 1-1 draw in

Argentina. The main point of this abuse was to inform Willie that he was a useless Scotsman of dubious parentage. Willie was quick to point out to Eskandarian that he hadn't played in the game in Argentina – he was on his way home as his countrymen had flopped – and also reminded the big defender that he had little to brag about for his part in the Iran versus Scotland game.

After all, Eskandarian had slotted the ball into his own net, giving Scotland the 1-1 draw.

Willie then added: "Playing against me today will be your worst nightmare, sunshine!"

Willie skinned the Iranian time and time again. Players began to lose the plot. The Brazilian, Carlos Alberto, started kicking every Whitecaps player he could find. Chinaglia scythed down Willie, who retaliated (*deja vu*). Chinaglia threw a punch – and all hell broke lose. A battle broke out in the middle of the park. Willie recalls that only two players didn't take part in the battle – Cosmos' Franz Beckenbauer and Whitecaps' Alan Ball. They both elected to sit down in the centre circle, smile at each other and let events take their course. Chinaglia was shown a red card and trotted off. Willie was shown a red card and refused to go (*deja vu*). Eventually Willie did leave the field in New York, and at least it was not at gunpoint this time. As he walked down the tunnel, he was surprised to see Chinaglia standing in his path. The former Italian striker was leaning against the wall, wearing a dressing gown and casually puffing on a cigarette.

"John ... ston ... you are dead," he said as Willie approached.

"Piss off!" replied Willie, who walked on and entered the dressing room.

Chinaglia followed and continued to rant. It was obvious to Willie that a punch-up was about to take place. Chinaglia would not let things go. Suddenly the door flew open and a Whitecaps player, big John Craven, burst into the room. Craven had been the next player to receive a red card and was far from amused. "Shit!" he shouted as he entered. He eventually noticed Chinaglia and turned to Willie: "What's going on here?" he asked.

Willie smiled: "Nothing, now that you're here, John."

Chinaglia glanced towards the raging Craven and made a wise decision, he pissed off. The media got hold of the story, and it even filtered back to Scotland. The headline being the typically understated: WILLIE JOHNSTON IN RIOT IN NEW YORK.

Willie's mother was watching the news and remembered his last confrontation in New York with Glasgow Rangers and Fiorentina, when he was sent off at gunpoint. This time she felt sure he'd been shot. He hadn't been, of course, but the necessary disciplinary action was taken against both the clubs and the players involved.

Vancouver's good League form continued and they won the Western Division by finishing ahead of Los Angeles Aztecs. They marched on to the quarter-finals of the Soccer Bowl, where they defeated Dallas Tornado over two games. In the semi-final they brushed aside Los Angeles to reach the Conference Championship where they would play New York Cosmos. The winners of this match would find themselves in the much-coveted Soccer Bowl final. The first game was played at Vancouver's Empire Stadium in front of a 32,000 capacity crowd, who witnessed a Vancouver victory. In New York the Whitecaps stunned the Cosmos by running out as the eventual winners, in what was described as one of the most exciting games in recent years. The icing on the cake for Willie was scoring a great goal against the much-fancied New Yorkers. Whitecaps would meet Tampa Bay Rowdies in the Soccer Bowl final.

Willie: My revenge against Chinaglia was simple. Throughout the match he had given me the evil eye following the incident the previous time we'd met – but he was never fast enough to get close to me to cause me any damage and I would just keep smiling at him. When I scored the goal, a header from 20 yards, I raised my arms in celebration and turned towards him. He was seething with anger and if looks could kill I would have dropped dead on the spot. This time as we ran down the tunnel at full time as winners, Chinaglia was not in sight – no doubt he was in the dressing room banging his thick skull against a wall and crying.

It would be the biggest day in the history of the Whitecaps. The date was 8 September 1979. The venue was New York City. Willie recalls that prior to the match some of the home-grown players were particularly nervous in the dressing room. Experienced players like Willie and Alan Ball did their best to settle them. Unlike in the UK on such a big occasion, where both teams take to the park together, in the States each player is introduced individually to the fans. When it was Willie's turn he strolled on to the pitch with a ball stuck up his jersey, giving everyone the impression that he was pregnant. The crowd loved it, and it served to ease the nerves of the Canadian players in the team. The match itself was a cracking one. Two goals from Trevor Whymark saw the Whitecaps run out 2-1 winners.

Alan Ball, who had a tremendous game, was voted player of the tournament and Willie would be voted their most popular player by the Vancouver fans.

The trophy was presented to the Whitecaps by Henry Kissinger, the former Secretary of State in the USA. He was a famous figure and had been responsible for breaking down the barriers between the USA and communist China. During the Whitecaps' celebrations Kissinger sat in Willie's company. He praised the Vancouver side on their great performance and asked Willie what the team's plans were for the evening.

"We're going to have a party," replied Willie.

"I would like to join you," said Henry.

"No chance," replied Willie, "it's only for the players."

"But I'd really like to be there," Kissinger asked again.

"I'm sorry, you can't come," said Willie.

Once again the press got a hold of the conversation, and the next day back in Vancouver the newspapers ran the story: "Henry Kissinger, the man who broke down barriers with the Chinese, gets a knock-back from Willie Johnston when he asks to join the Whitecaps' party."

Whitecaps' season was over and several British players had secretly booked flights back to the UK from New York. This angered the Whitecaps management who wanted all their players back in Vancouver for further celebrations. It also angered Willie, who wished he'd thought of booking himself on a flight instead of having to make the 3000-mile journey back to Vancouver. Margaret and the kids were already back in the UK and Willie wanted to join them.

Tony Waiters would have none of it, and Willie was on his way back to Vancouver.

The Whitecaps had become only the second Canadian team to win the Soccer Bowl in the history of the competition and more than 100,000 fans turned up to welcome them back to Vancouver. The players were given the freedom of the city and some thought that gesture was the green light to have a good drink, Willie being one of them. He put his return to the UK for the close season on hold. He moved in with fellow Whitecaps player, Roger Kenyon, formerly of Everton, and they went on a drinking spree. They had seen a sign somewhere that read "Drink Canada Dry" – and for a week they tried to do just that!

Willie recalls very little of the drinking spree. Quite simply, they had moved from bar to bar. They were treated like kings and got as drunk as lords. George Best would have been proud of them. Then the two of them turned up for a large presentation ceremony, which related to the Soccer Bowl win, and they were still absolutely inebriated. The management, wisely, refused to let them go in front of the TV cameras to receive their awards. The situation jolted Willie back to reality and he realised it was time to have some "Betty Ford" days, or weeks. He made the decision to return to the UK and join his family.

What he wasn't aware of at the time was that he would soon be making his debut for another club.

INTRODUCTION TO BIRMINGHAM CITY BY JIM SMITH

(Jim Smith, affectionately known as 'The Bald Eagle', started his playing career in 1959 when he joined Sheffield United as a trainee. His playing career saw him at a number of clubs including Aldershot, Halifax and Lincoln City before he moved into management in 1972. Outside Birmingham he has managed Blackburn Rovers, Queen's Park Rangers, Newcastle United, Portsmouth and Derby County, among others. Jim is currently a member of the board at Oxford United).

Willie had arrived with us at Birmingham on loan from Vancouver Whitecaps and his influence was felt immediately. He gave the whole team a big lift in the dressing room. Adding to his influence, of course, was the fact that he was a great player and a great character. On match days when all the team gathered for the pre-match meal I would ask Willie what he would like to eat. His answer was always the same: "Two wee lamb chops, Gaffer." He was very food-conscious in a time when diets and eating the right kind of food were unheard of in the game.

I think Willie was 32 or 33 when he came to Birmingham but his fitness rivalled that of a 22-year-old. He would train for fun. Willie could never see enough of the ball. I recall a game against Fulham where the full-back marking Willie was a big strong lad. Willie came to the touchline and said to me: "Tell the lads to give the ball to me, Gaffer. This guy's useless. I'll destroy him all day. He's useless!"

I passed the word for the players to supply Willie, and when they did our lively left-winger didn't disappoint. The full-back would come at Willie like a raging bull; Willie would jink one way, then the other, before leaving the player in his wake.

That particular season Birmingham were struggling in the League, lying second or third from bottom. For whatever reason, probably the weather, we found ourselves with a long break from competitive football. Big Ron Atkinson and I arranged a friendly between Birmingham and West Brom, to be played in Jersey. Both clubs flew out together and the plane went through a turbulent patch. Willie didn't like this at all and expressed a few superlatives on the matter. His old colleague from West Brom, Len Cantello, turned to Willie and said: "Don't worry, Willie. Birmingham can't go down twice in the same season." Willie smiled but he hated the whole flight. The match itself finished in a 2-2 draw and Willie had an outstanding game.

Sadly his loan period was soon over and he had to return to Vancouver. Even though his time at the club was short, the fans loved him. Players like him are few and far between in the modern game – and football is so much the sadder because of it.

28

BACK IN BRUM

Willie joined Birmingham City on loan during the NASL close season in the immediate aftermath of the biggest transfer in British football history. Trevor Francis had just been sold to Nottingham Forest for £1 million, the first transaction ever to reach that barrier. Birmingham were nothing more than an average team at the time, and Francis' performances caught the eye of everyone in football. The Birmingham supporters were far from happy with the sale, and Jim Smith tried to appease them by spending a portion of the £1 million. He bought Archie Gemmill from Nottingham Forest, Frank Worthington from Bolton and Colin Todd from Everton, for a club record fee of £300,000. As for Willie Johnston, he was brought in on loan – well, they couldn't afford to buy him, could they? Happily, Willie had retained his house in Sutton Coldfield from his time with West Brom and the whole family felt they were back home.

Willie's first game for Birmingham was against Sunderland and he was satisfied with his debut. Yet, he recalls, an angry Jim Smith bursting into the dressing room following the game.

"That was pure shit," screamed Smith. Archie Gemmill started to make a reply but Smith would have none of it. "You can shut up," interjected Smith. "I brought you here to do a particular job – and you didn't do that job today."

Willie then piped up: "Boss ... we did win 1-0."

Smith looked at Willie, and the dressing fell into silence as the manager contemplated his new signing's words. Eventually Smith replied: "You're right, Willie. Take the lads for a pint." Willie duly did as he'd been ordered.

Playing for the Blues was an enjoyable experience for Willie and he soon became good friends with Colin Todd and Frank Worthington. They would have many a drink together. Frank Worthington was a real character and a die-hard Elvis Presley fan. Around his neck was a necklace with the letters "TCB" inscribed. It was a replica of the one Elvis gave to all his entourage – TCB meaning Take Care of Business. Frank once said to Willie that he wanted to visit Gracelands, lie on Elvis' grave and never move again. Willie feels reasonably confident that when Frank made the statement a lot of alcohol had been consumed.

Another well-known name at the club was Alan Curbishley, who had been signed from West Ham for £225,000. Willie remembers Alan as being a quiet lad, who thought really deeply about the game. It came as no surprise to Willie that Alan went on to become a top-class manager when his playing career came to an end. Also at St Andrew's was fellow Scot, Jimmy Calderwood (the present manager of Aberdeen), another talented player. Willie could see that Jim Smith was trying to build a good team despite the loss of Trevor Francis.

But not all players at Birmingham took Willie's fancy. For instance, left-back Mark Dennis had been sent off almost as many times as Willie, but not for the same reasons. Willie didn't rate him in the least. Dennis was the type of player that often hurt wingers of Willie's calibre. During games Willie would never part with the ball in the direction of Dennis, and many a verbal confrontation would ensue between them.

> Willie: At Birmingham I played alongside a number of strong characters. Frank Worthington and Mark Dennis immediately spring to mind. Frank was such a talented and flamboyant player who could also score goals for fun. He was so fit it really didn't surprise me that he would play into his forties. He also liked to party … and boy could he party! He was a great guy to be around. Mark Dennis was a no-nonsense full-back who didn't take prisoners. You messed with Mark at your own peril. He earned the nickname 'Psycho' and it was well deserved – there were a number of psychopathic tendencies lurking within that mind of his. Off the park he was more mild-mannered and a very nice man, but I would rather play alongside him than play against him.

Willie's third appearance for the club saw Birmingham up against Swansea at home. He remembers the game well. He had constantly destroyed their defence throughout the encounter. At one point in the match Willie went to take a throw-in and stuck the ball up his jersey. The Swansea players were confused and were taken unawares when Willie produced the ball and took a long throw-in. The ball landed at the feet of Archie Gemmill, who slotted it into the net. The fans loved it and Willie was beginning to really enjoy being part of the Birmingham revival. As matches progressed Birmingham began to move steadily up the league.

Willie played a total of 15 times for the Blues before having to return to the Whitecaps. His last game was against Leyton Orient on 9 February 1980 at St Andrew's. Willie had a good game and the club ran out 3-1 winners. The fans gave him a thunderous farewell as he left the pitch after 90 minutes, and there was sadness in his heart that he would now need to return to Canada.

29

BACK AT THE WHITECAPS

Willie was joined on the flight back to Vancouver by the Whitecaps' new signing, goalkeeper Bruce Grobbelaar. Grobbelaar had formerly played for the South African team Jomo Cosmos. He'd eventually left the club after being dropped from the team. Bruce had claimed that he was being overlooked because of his colour – Jomo were predominantly a black team at the time. He had quit the game, though still only 20 years old, and signed up for National Service, serving two years in Rhodesian National Guard. He would go on to be something of a cult hero at the Whitecaps before he was eventually signed by Liverpool. And the rest, as they say, is history.

> *Willie: I had first met Bruce Grobbelaar at West Brom. Unfortunately West Brom couldn't get a work permit for him and he was released. We joined up again at Vancouver Whitecaps. He had by them matured a lot and was showing signs that he was something special. Playing football wasn't his only task in Canada. If Margaret and I wanted a night out then Bruce would get the job of looking after my children. Stephanie and Dean have fond memories of Bruce the babysitter. As a player he had class, style and a sense of fun. He was unquestionably the fittest goalkeeper I have ever come across.*

When the pair arrived in Vancouver Willie had a slight problem, and Bruce had to borrow a wheelchair to get Willie from the plane and through the airport. Willie wasn't ill as such – he was as drunk as a skunk! Bruce had to use all of his wits and guerilla guile to guide Willie away from the media, out of the airport and into the relative safety of a taxi.

Returning to the Whitecaps, Willie didn't quite feel the same excitement as he had at the end of the previous season. He was growing tired of all the travelling – which would often be a few thousand miles to away matches – and he was beginning to feel homesick. Yet he would still have moments of magic – and some that he wished he could make disappear! – during games.

Willie recalls a match against Seattle Sounders., which qualified as a local derby, the Whitecaps having only 500 miles to travel. In the Seattle team was his former Scotland colleague   ruce Rioch. They may have played together on numerous occasions for Scotland, but there was certainly no love lost between them. Following a Scotland game, Willie and Rioch were signing autographs for the fans. Willie noticed that Bruce was signing his name followed by the letters COS.

"What the hell is COS?" asked Willie.

"Captain of Scotland," replied Bruce with a smile.

Willie shook his head and thought: "You're an arse."

Willie: What can I say about Bruce Rioch COS (Captain Of Scotland)? Well, really I can't say a lot … in fact, I'm going to say nothing at all.

During the game in Seattle, Rioch had gone out of his way to deliberately foul and taunt Willie. Following one of these rash challenges, Whitecaps player Ray Hankin had stern words with Bruce. Rioch responded by spitting in Hankin's face. How Ray kept his cool Willie will never know.

The game finished 1-1 and would be decided by a shoot-out. The scores remained level with Willie still to take the last kick. He responded by doing what he did best – he bamboozled the keeper and slotted the ball into the net. Whitecaps were the victors. Willie rushed over to the sideline in celebration. Cavorting done, Willie spotted the Seattle manager Alan Hinton and asked him: "Where's that arse, Rioch?" Hinton replied that he was still on the field of play. Willie spotted him and caught his attention. Willie then turned, bent over and dropped his shorts. The cameras clicked and the newspapers ran the story the following day. One headline read: WILLIE MOONS IN THE AFTERNOON. Unfortunately, NASL officials were not impressed, and neither were the Whitecaps management. Willie was fined $2000 and dropped from the team for a while.

Following the mooning incident, an adult magazine approached Willie. They made him a proposition, wanting him to appear in their centre pages alongside a well-known model. She would bare her breasts and Willie was to bare his backside. Willie would be paid $100,000. It sounded good to him and he responded favourably. His wife Margaret's response was slightly different: "Over my dead body!" she informed him. The idea was shelved.

Soon Willie was back in favour and back in the team. Yet again he was performing brightly and entertaining the fans. They had played Los Angeles Aztecs away from home and although Willie played well they had been beaten. A certain Johan Cruyff had ripped them apart almost single-handedly. Cruyff was a truly world-class player with unbelievable pace. He had been voted European Player of the Year on three occasions, 1971, 1973 and 1974. Although he was 33 years of age, his skill and pace had not deserted him. It was then time for the return game in Vancouver. The talk in the home dressing room was very much Cruyff-orientated. Roger Kenyon had marked Cruyff on the previous occasion and it was felt that the role should be his again, although this time with some assistance from midfield before the Dutchman could get to Roger.

Alan Ball said: "I'll nail him."

Willie laughed: "You're too slow, Bally!"

"I can do it," exclaimed Alan. There was some debate, but Alan was the captain and eventually he was given the task of slowing down the mighty Cruyff. Early on in the game Cruyff had the ball at his feet and Alan Ball made a move toward him. Cruyff moved up a gear and was soon 20 yards past Ball, who was rooted to the spot. He turned to Willie and blurted out: "He is fast, isn't he?"

Willie took over the role of snuffing out Cruyff and matched him for pace. Several tackles later – some good and some touching on the illegal – Cruyff gave up and was substituted. Whitecaps then took the game by the scruff of the neck and went on to win. Job done.

That evening Willie went on a night out with a number of the lads and they ended up outside a nightclub. Willie was debating with the rest of the players about what he thought was an exorbitant entry fee of $25 – Willie is well known for being careful with money. The other players pointed out that there was no fee to gain entry. The $25 was to purchase a piece of cake once they were inside.

"$25 for a slice of cake," screamed Willie. "Is it filled with gold coins?"

"No," replied one of the players. "Marijuana."

"Count me out," said Willie. "I've had enough trouble with illegal substances!"

As the season was drawing to a close, it was evident that there would be no repeat of winning the Soccer Bowl. Willie was by then approaching

34 and no longer wanted to continue with all the travelling. He and Alan Ball asked to be released in order to find clubs back in the UK. Whitecaps agreed that they would consider any offer that came their way.

Several English clubs declared their interest. Heart of Midlothian did the same, and this approach was the one that attracted Willie the most. Scotland seemed the right place for him to end his playing career. Hearts play in Edinburgh, just across the Firth of Forth from his native Fife. It would be the right place to go. But unfortunately Hearts failed to agree terms with Vancouver and the deal fell through.

Back in the UK, another Scottish Club, Dundee, stated an interest. To Willie this was equally as attractive as joining Hearts. Dundee was also close to Fife, albeit in the opposite direction to Edinburgh and over the Firth of Tay. Dundee's offer was tempting, and warranted consideration. Before anything was finalised, Willie received a call from John Greig, his former playing colleague at Rangers. John had been appointed as the manager of Rangers. Initially the conversation was simply general chitchat, and then John said something that nearly blew Willie away. He had agreed a fee with Vancouver to secure the winger's services back at Ibrox. The conversation ended with Willie agreeing to travel up from Birmingham to talk things over.

The meeting at Ibrox went well and the financial package was a good one. John Greig had been honest, and had made the point that Willie would not feature in the first team on a regular basis. John wanted him as a good addition to the pool of players, and also to kick a certain gifted young left winger up the backside. The young winger was Davie Cooper. Greig felt that the lad had mountains of talent, but needed to be guided by someone who had done it all. Willie was definitely the man for the task.

Willie: When I returned to Rangers the media treated me reasonably well. They didn't make a big thing of Argentina, although in certain quarters they couldn't stop themselves from reminding the Scottish nation that I had been a bad boy in the past. It was when I started playing again for the club that the Argentina incident would find its way back into the press, especially if the sports writers were short on juicy stories at the time. Talk of Willie Johnston apparently sold papers!

Everything agreed, an emotional Willie became a Rangers player again.

30

BACK IN BLUE HEAVEN

The day after Willie signed for Rangers, the Ibrox club were playing in the Anglo-Scottish Cup against Partick Thistle. Rangers were beaten 3-2. Thankfully it was the second leg and Rangers held a 3-1 lead from the first encounter. If there was any team in Scotland that would send a shiver up Willie's spine it would be Partick. It was during a fixture against Thistle, eight years previously, that he was ordered off for the last time in Scotland. He had thrown a punch at Partick's Alex Forsyth and the dismissal led to a nine-week ban. That suspension led to his exit from the club. Ironically, Forsyth was one of his new team-mates at Ibrox. Willie did give a sigh of relief that he was not involved, as he had only signed the day before. He was quite happy to miss the Thistle game so soon after his return to his homeland.

Willie, as always, put his heart and soul into training. John Greig was impressed and expressed this to the media. The date was Friday 15 August 1980. John told the media that evening: "Willie Johnston will play tomorrow. He is in on merit. I have one or two fresh ideas I want to try and, given the way Willie has played in training, I couldn't leave him out." God works in mysterious ways; the opposition the following day would be none other than Partick Thistle.

Former Celtic star Bertie Auld was the manager of Thistle at the time. He told the press: "It's good news for us that Willie Johnston is playing, because it helps make this game even more attractive than we expected."

The game itself probably went exactly how manager John Greig wanted it to go. Rangers dominated and ran out 4-0 winners. How did Willie play? Well I think the headline in the Scottish Sunday Mail the following morning said it all: BRILLIANT BUD SPURS SUPER SHOW.

The article goes on to comment: "Willie was given a tremendous reception by the Ibrox support, and the cocky wee man from Cardenden reacted by being a very important player. His long-range passes and explosive running on the left flank gave the Ibrox men a whole new dimension. He had a superb game."

But the writer, Allan Herron, couldn't resist telling his readers that: "Willie Johnston was the winger who embarrassed all Scots in Argentina two years ago." Was this necessary? Hadn't Willie and his family been punished enough? It is of little surprise that Willie has a hatred for the press and other media, who seem to go about their job looking for sensationalism.

Media aside, Willie was happy to be back at Rangers, and delighted to be teaming up with a number of players who he'd played with back in 1972. Peter McCloy, Sandy Jardine, Colin Jackson, Derek Johnstone and Alex McDonald were all still at Ibrox.

Willie was well aware that he wouldn't feature in every game Rangers played. When not involved with the first team, he would find himself working with the youngsters and the reserves. Passing on his experience was an aspect of the game that he thoroughly enjoyed and found extremely satisfying.

Willie: I thought my Ibrox days were over and it was a great honour to make the return. But I was under no illusions, I knew I would never be a first-team regular and would make many of my appearances from the subs bench. My main task at Ibrox would to coach and bring out the best Davie Cooper. Cooper, of course, went on to be a fantastic player on the wing and I would like to think I played my part in getting him there.

That September John Greig informed Willie that he would be part of the squad in an important league match against Aberdeen at Ibrox. Willie was more than happy to oblige. His feelings would be rather different when the match was over.

Matches between Rangers and Aberdeen are always torrid affairs, with little quarter given. This game turned out to be no different. Willie started the match on the bench. Sitting alongside him was defender Gregor Stevens. As the match progressed it was evident that Aberdeen's Willie Miller was running the show. Miller was a strong central defender who took no prisoners and he certainly wasn't taking any that day. A number of Rangers players felt the brunt of his tackles. Willie turned to Gregor Stevens and said: "If you get called on, deal with that bastard."

Gregor looked at Willie and simply nodded. Willie continued: "Because if I get on, he won't know what hit him!"

Willie was eventually told to strip and was sent on to the field of play. His arrival would lead to a really nasty unsavoury incident. Sadly, the culprit was none other than Willie.

Willie: The John McMaster incident when playing for Rangers against Aberdeen is one that I would rather forget. Yet, like Argentina, it will never go away.

Willie Miller, Aberdeen's captain, put himself about a bit. He was a highly experienced defender who knew every trick in the book. He could be classy but he could be dirty when he wanted to be. He wanted to be that day. My anger grew as I looked on from the substitutes' bench and when I was called on I only had one thing in mind – to deal with Miller. I was only on a few minutes and was running with the ball when I saw, out of the corner of my eye, an Aberdeen player heading towards me at speed. I was convinced it was Miller and that he was coming in strongly to hurt me. When he arrived I shoulder charged him, knocking him to the ground. My next reaction was instant and unpremeditated – I stamped on his head. Of course, it wasn't Miller, it was McMaster, and I had hurt him badly. Never in my career, apart from that afternoon, have I set out to intentionally injure a player. I can make no excuses for my actions and have always deeply regretted the incident. It still sends a shiver through me when I think about it.

McMaster had to be given the kiss of life as he lay on the ground. Naturally, a lengthy ban followed. Willie was once more the bad boy of Scottish football, although this time it was at least deserved.

By October Rangers' League campaign was progressing nicely. They'd played every other team and hadn't lost a game. But by the turn of the year, all that had changed. Celtic were starting to open up a points gap, and Rangers were battling it out with Aberdeen for the second berth. They'd even suffered a degrading defeat in the insignificant Anglo-Scottish Cup at the hands of lowly Chesterfield.

Rangers focused their attention on the Scottish Cup as a means of bringing home silverware. Willie himself was still performing well when the opportunity of first-team football presented itself, and he wanted so much to add another Scottish Cup winner's medal to his list of achievements. Rangers came into the competition in the third round. Their opponents were Airdrie, away from home. Rangers thumped them 0-5 to march on. St Johnstone were the next opposition, again away from home. The game finished in a 3-3 draw, with Rangers winning the replay 3-1 at Ibrox.

In the quarter-final they met Hibs at Ibrox. Willie had been suffering from a niggling pelvic injury, yet manager John Greig wanted him to play in this one. Injury or no injury, Willie was more than happy to play.

Hibs had Bertie Auld as their new manager, and he would always prove a worthy adversary no matter which club he managed. Rangers started the game well and grew in stature from there. Jim McArthur, the Hibs keeper, was immense that day. But he could do nothing about Bobby Russell's first goal, and even less when Willie directed a free-kick straight to Colin McAdam to score the second. At half-time Willie was in some pain from his injury and was struggling. John Greig asked him to continue: "Go out and kill them off quickly and I'll replace you," he said. Willie agreed, and within minutes had set up young John McDonald to slot home the third. Greig, as promised, took Willie off the park. The decision was met by boos from the Rangers fans, who weren't aware that Willie was injured.

Rangers won the match 3-1.

Willie's injury would prevent him taking part in the semi-final clash at Celtic Park against Morton, which Rangers won 2-1. The final took place on Saturday 9 May 1981. Rangers' opponents were the current League Cup holders Dundee United. This was expected to be a difficult, close encounter. Dundee United had some classy players in their squad including David Narey, Paul Hegarty, Richard Gough (later Rangers' captain), Willie Pettigrew and Paul Sturrock. They would win the Scottish Premier League and reach European finals and semi-finals over the next few years.

Willie still had that pelvic injury when John Greig announced his team for the final. To Willie's delight he was named in the side, and he realised it might be his last chance to win a Scottish Cup medal. The game did not turn out to be the showpiece everyone had expected. It was a dour affair and finished in a 0-0 draw. The replay was scheduled for the following Tuesday. Rangers would win 4-2 in a classic game, but Willie was not part of the on-the-park celebrations. His injury had flared up following the first encounter and he had no chance of being fit for the replay.

The 1981/82 season would start with Rangers going on a Scandinavian tour. The tour would make it evident to the older players in the squad (and there were a few of them) that playing for a place in the first team was about to get harder. Younger players were knocking at the door; in fact, a few of them were battering it down.

It came as no surprise to Willie that he would find himself playing a lot of reserve football in the new season. It was a sad time for him, and he recalls sitting in the dressing room with several of the other older players. The others already knew they were being freed at the end of the season.

Alongside Willie were Alex Miller, Sandy Jardine and Peter McCloy, all of whom had played in that famous European victory in 1972.

Willie looked at each of them and then spoke: "Listen boys, I've got an idea. The Hearts are in big financial trouble, and their directors are looking for an injection of cash."

"So?" replied one of his colleagues.

"So," said Willie, and continued, "we chip in £50,000 each. We buy the club and continue playing. Hearts have a number of good young players, and our experience will turn them into even better players!"

His colleagues were stunned – but there were no takers for this proposal, and the idea drifted off into oblivion.

By December Willie had played only six games, which gave him the clear message that his Ibrox days were coming to an end. He would come on as substitute on 19 December 1981, his 35th birthday, against Dundee at Ibrox. He didn't know it at the time, but this would be his last game for Rangers. If he had known, he most certainly would have done something outrageous on the park to leave the Rangers fans with a final memory of him.

A few days after that match, he discussed his situation with the manager, and John Greig agreed that he would listen to any offers made for Willie's services.

Ironically, it was Hearts who showed the first interest in buying Willie. John Greig would have none of it, but agreed to free Willie, providing he left the country. Why wouldn't John Greig allow Willie to join Hearts? Did he think there was life in Willie's old legs and didn't want them in action against the Gers? Whatever his reasons, Willie agreed to his terms because he wanted first-team football. With great sadness, he packed his gear away and left Ibrox for the last time as a Rangers player.

Goodbye Blues – hello again Vancouver.

A WORD FROM ANDY CAMERON

(Andy is a well-known Scottish comedian, after-dinner speaker, and radio and TV presenter. He started working in clubs in 1972 as a stand-up comedian. However, his big break came in 1978, when he wrote the football anthem *Ally's Tartan Army*. Oh yes, I nearly forgot – Andy is a diehard Rangers fan).

Faster than a speeding bullet ... it's Superbud!

Bud was having a *Bud* as we waited for the call to board the Globespan Jet to Calgary for the North American Rangers Supporters Association convention on 4 June 2008. I was having a cup of tea. Around the table were Jim Hannah, the fans' liaison officer for Rangers; Ian Durrant, who is as quick with his quips as Bud was with his feet; Colin Stein, the first £100,000 player in Scotland, and me. I was the only one I'd never heard of! To say that the patter was flying wasn't quite accurate; it was in orbit.

Durrant was in his element and everybody was in his firing line. When 'Jasper' is in this kind of mood you just sit and listen and laugh. Meanwhile Bud and Colin Stein were reminiscing about playing for the Glasgow Rangers and others. By the time we touched down in Calgary ten hours later and made our way to our hotel we were all still flying. It was the start of a great few days which will have a special place in my memoirs forever.

To share the company of three of the greatest Rangers players I ever saw was magic. To hear their stories and laugh at their escapades was even better. Bud was 15 when he came to Rangers and he became a fans' favourite from his first outing until he moved on to West Bromwich Albion. It's a fact that in all his years in football he was always known as Willie Johnston of Rangers.

I was a bus driver in the 1960s and one night I took overtime on a football special rather than go to Hampden and see Scotland play Poland in a World Cup qualifier. Jock Stein had given Bud his international debut and was I sorry to have missed it. As I stood at the back of the bus waiting for it to fill up with punters, I was expecting them to be moaning about the fact that Poland had come back from a goal down and beaten Scotland 2-1. All they spoke about was the display of the "wee fella on the left wing who was magical."

Now I knew, as a Rangers fan, that he was magical but to do it in his first international was a bonus for all of the Bluenoses who were looking for a star to play on the left with Slim Jim Baxter. "Ya hooer sur! Thur twa Fife boays wis somthin' else oan that left wing. Ah'm telling ye!"

Bud was a player and a half. He could score goals, he could create goals, he was two-footed and his biggest asset in my opinion was that he could beat a greyhound over 100 yards wearing pit boots! He was faster than a Scouser wi' a handbag.

I was introduced to Bud by a mutual friend, Big George Mullholland from Toronto. We had some laughs together. Like the time we were down at Wembley for a game against the 'Auld Enemy' and Jocky, Bud's pal from the Ballingry Club, had everybody in stitches with his patter. As we got into a taxi to go for dinner, all of us covered in tartan, the London cabbie asked: "You all down for the game, lads?" Big Mullholland rasped back: "Naw, we're doon fur the Chelsea Flower Show!" Even Jocky was laughing at that one.

Bud has always liked a laugh and I've had a few with him, but it hasn't all been fun. The papers would tell you that Bud had a chequered career with Rangers, West Brom, Vancouver Whitecaps and Hearts. The Argentina affair, which got him a sponsorship with *Boots* the chemist, represented a bad patch and the fact is well documented that he has had more red cards than Joseph Stalin on his birthday! But Bud has come through it all intact. Okay, there are a few teeth missing and his hair is disappearing faster than the £1 litre of petrol, but look into his eyes, the sparkle is as bright as his play was all those years ago. He has lost none of his zest for life. He likes a drink, as we all do. He likes a cigarette or two and if you see him nipping out for a fag at a hotel you'll know that he has lost none of his pace. As always Bud is still smokin'.

31

HELLO AGAIN VANCOUVER

The day Willie left Ibrox for the last time as a player, he was uncertain where his future lay. He was aware that his old manager from West Brom, Johnny Giles, was manager of Vancouver. Willie took the bull by the horns and phoned Vancouver. Giles answered and was met by Willie's request: "Gizza job!"

Willie went on to explain his dilemma. John Greig would not allow him to join a Scottish club. He was honest in the sense that he had no desire to be in Vancouver for a long period of time. "I only want to be there till a Scottish club comes along," he said.

"No problem, Willie," said Johnny. "Get yourself over here and play on a monthly contract."

Willie was on the next available flight.

Things had changed somewhat since Willie's last spell with the Whitecaps. Apart from Johnny Giles being the new manager, Nobby Stiles and Peter Lorimer were on the coaching staff. There was also a new, young, exciting player in the squad, who went by the name of Peter Beardsley.

Willie not only found himself playing but coaching schoolkids in between matches. Coaching was a project he really liked and he put his heart and soul into the task.

Willie: There is no greater satisfaction than coaching kids in the art of football – I loved it and could have stayed at Vancouver for the rest of my career and beyond in a coaching capacity. But, just like when I was a boy at Manchester United, I was homesick and longed to return back home to Fife.

Once more the travelling was getting him down and he really wanted to return to Scotland. The Whitecaps were playing a match in Florida when Willie had a chance meeting with Mario Caira. Mario, who was on holiday from Scotland, was at that time the chairman of Raith Rovers. Raith were in the Scottish First Division and hailed from Kirkcaldy, Fife, Willie's home county. Willie had already bought a house in Kirkcaldy and wanted to buy a bar in the town when he finished his playing career. He indicated to Mario that the Rovers would be the ideal club to see out his playing days. Mario showed enthusiasm towards the idea, and said he would arrange things and be back in touch.

Mario didn't disappoint. He contacted Willie a few weeks later with the news that the Rovers would be delighted to have him at the club.

Willie arranged a meeting with the chairman of the Whitecaps to explain his situation, describing his desire to return to Scotland and buy a bar. The chairman's response was not what he'd expected: "Willie, we want you to stay here. Coach the kids and we'll buy you a bar in Vancouver as part of the signing-on deal."

Willie was astounded. It was an amazing offer. But it was one he wouldn't accept. Scotland was calling. Another episode in Willie's long career had come to an end. He had enjoyed Vancouver, apart from the travelling. The city had been good to him and he would always have great memories of his time there. Returning to Scotland would be his final move – or at least that's what he'd thought.

32

BACK HOME

When he arrived back in Kirkcaldy, Willie was convinced that this was the final leg of an incredible journey. Apart from a short time down a coal mine he had known nothing other than professional football. He'd played at the highest level since the age of 16 and considered himself both privileged and fortunate to have made his living from the love of his life – football. Kirkcaldy would be his final stop. Kirkcaldy would be his home, and he would finish his career playing for Kirkcaldy's Raith Rovers – or at least that's what he anticipated.

When Willie started training with the Rovers, he was friendly with the husband-and-wife team who ran the Port Brae bar, just off Kirkcaldy's High Street. Willie and Margaret were given part-time jobs behind the bar to learn the trade that would see them into their retirement. Several weeks passed and Willie had trained hard with the Rovers until he reached peak fitness. He still hadn't signed for the club, but the time was right and he asked for a meeting with the manager, Gordon Wallace.

Gordon was a young manager, just a couple of years older than Willie, and had an illustrious playing career despite never being capped for Scotland. He'd played for Raith Rovers, Dundee, Dundee United and Seattle Sounders. He scored 30 goals in 1967/68, and in that season became the first player outside the Old Firm to be awarded the Scottish Footballer of the Year accolade. He held the Scottish scoring record of 264 League goals, a mark that was surpassed by Ally McCoist many years later.

The meeting was tense. At first Willie couldn't understand why. He had trained hard, he was ready to play, but still Gordon showed reluctance to sign him. Suddenly Willie understood – Gordon feared that the man with 22 caps for Scotland might take his position as manager.

"I don't want a manager's job, if that's what's troubling you, Gordon!" exclaimed Willie.

"I'm not sure that we need your services," Gordon replied.

"Fine," replied Willie. Before adding: "Stick it up your arse!" and walking out. The club that had rejected him as boy had now rejected him as a veteran – and Willie was livid!

When Willie arrived home, and had calmed down slightly, he picked up the phone and made a call to his former Rangers colleague Alex McDonald. Willie explained his situation and rambled on that he still had another few seasons to offer in top-flight football.

"I'm sure you have, Bud," McDonald replied. "I'll sign you tomorrow." Alex was player-manager of Heart of Midlothian. It's never over till the fat lady sings …

INTRODUCTION TO
HEART OF MIDLOTHIAN
BY ALEX McDONALD
and SANDY JARDINE

ALEX McDONALD

(Alex McDonald joined Rangers from St Johnstone and was a member of the Cup Winners' Cup-winning team in 1972. During his time at Ibrox he played a total of 503 games and scored 94 goals for the club. He won three League Championships, four Scottish Cups and four League Cup medals. In 1980 he joined Hearts for £30,000, becoming their player-manager in 1981. He took them to within eight minutes of winning the Scottish Premiership title in 1985-86. McDonald was capped once by Scotland, against Switzerland in 1976).

When Tom asked me to write part of the introduction to Willie's career at the Hearts, I told him the opening line would have to be "Once upon a time." Well, isn't it true that all kids' stories start that way? Even today Willie still has that schoolboy scoundrel image about him. And a large part of his playing career had all the attributes of a fairy tale. Now, most fairy tales have a few nightmares scattered here and there, and Willie's story would be no different.

Hearts signed Willie in 1982 when he was 35 years old. But his age didn't disturb me; I knew the mettle of the man and had no doubts that he could do a job for us at Tynecastle. Willie didn't let me down. We had a young squad and my plan was to introduce several older players to guide the youngsters and teach them their trade. Willie was a master at this. He not only taught them about football, he taught them about life. He gave them guidance both on and off the park. He taught them how to handle pressure. I remember a cup-tie against Celtic; the match had been delayed for one reason or another. Back in the dressing room the youngsters were becoming nervous, agitated even. Willie recognised this and proceeded to change things around, he started to tell jokes and clown about. The young players had no idea what he was up to, but they all had a good laugh, and their nervousness disappeared without them being aware of it. There was no doubt about it – Willie was a real asset to the club.

But let's not forget his own ability on the park. He was a flying machine with two good feet and he was exceptional in the air. He also could play anywhere – up front, right, left, inside-forward or as a striker. But he was temperamental, and was perhaps better suited to playing on the wing. In that position he had only one defender to fall out with. Playing through the middle, he would be likely to fall out with every bugger in the opposition defence.

Because I played alongside Willie at Rangers I'm often asked how I rated him as a player. The answer is very, very highly. If Willie were in his prime in this day and age he would command a transfer fee in excess of 15 million – that's how good he was!

SANDY JARDINE

(Sandy Jardine was a truly world-class full-back who would go on to play 674 times for Rangers, win three League championship medals and four medals for each of the Scottish and League Cups. He was a member of the team that won the European Cup Winners' Cup in 1972. He also earned 38 caps for Scotland during his Ibrox career from 1964 to 1982. Jardine would then join Hearts as player-assistant manager).

Willie and I both joined Rangers as boys around the same time. He was a nice lad and throughout his long career his personality never changed. Everybody liked Bud. As a player he was typical of the old Scottish wingers that the country was so famous for producing. He was tricky, intelligent and was undoubtedly the fastest player I have ever played with, or played against. His explosive bursts over the first 20 yards were incredible. He was good with both feet and scored a phenomenal amount of goals for a winger. What an ability he possessed! He was a player of truly enormous talent.

What a lot of people didn't realise about Willie was his desire to train. He wanted to be the fittest player in the squad and he strived to be so. At Rangers, under the management of Jock Wallace, he would come to pre-season training with some strange ideas. He would wear pit boots during sessions in the belief that his legs would be stronger come the start of the season, and that he would be even faster than he was the season before. For Willie it worked, at least psychologically. And no more so, than during the season we won the Cup Winners' Cup.

He was such an important player for the club during that run. He terrified defences wherever we went.

When Alex and I brought him to Hearts, we both knew what we were getting, and we knew what we wanted from him. The Hearts squad was full of promising young players such as John

Robertson, Gary Mackay and Craig Levein. These players needed experience, and the best way for them to get it was for us to put experienced professionals on the park alongside them. Willie fulfilled that role perfectly.

Off the park we knew Willie as a "tea jenny" – he would do anything for a cup of tea. So we set up a tearoom. The young players would come in and sit with the older players like Jimmy Bone and Willie. The young guns didn't know it, but being in that tearoom was all part of their development – they would learn from the masters. And

Willie was a master.

If Willie had a flaw, and all great players do, then it was his temperament. He couldn't control it. When his mind told him he had taken enough punishment for one day the bubble would burst.

Temperament apart, there is no doubt in my eyes that Willie is one of the finest wingers Scotland has ever produced.

33

THE BOYS IN MAROON

When Willie joined Hearts in September 1982, he was 35 years old and fast approaching 36. Most players have thrown in the towel by that age, but Willie simply kept his close by in his kit bag. He was under no illusions, he knew the end was near – but hell, he was still fast and could still play a bit. A Zimmer frame was not yet needed.

Willie: I was absolutely delighted when the move to the Hearts came along. I've always had a soft spot for the Jambos, and helping them get back to top-flight football provided a great end to my career. There was also the added bonus of teaming up with my old playing buddies Sandy Jardine and Alex McDonald, and I was interested to see how they performed as a player-management team. I wasn't disappointed. They were as shrewd in management as they had been as players at Rangers.

Hearts are one of the biggest and proudest clubs in Scotland. They had been going through a rough patch, and were languishing in the First Division. Alex McDonald and Sandy Jardine had taken over as manager and assistant manager respectively. Both were still playing in order to give the young Hearts squad the benefit of their experience.

They brought Willie to the club for the same reason and added several more old heads in an attempt to win promotion to the Premier League. The veterans wouldn't play in every game, and when they did play it was not always for 90 minutes. However, their experience and encouragement would be vital if this team was to achieve success.

Willie: Alex and Sandy had put together a relatively young side and it was rare to see so many youngsters playing in the first team together. As with most youngsters they tended to lack self-confidence and belief in themselves. What they needed was some old heads to lift them both on and off the park. Part of my deal in coming to Hearts was to coach these youngsters; and it wasn't difficult – they were a talented bunch. The one thing I have never lacked is confidence in my ability and I spent so much time with these boys it wasn't long before they had become almost as cocky as myself.

When Willie arrived at Tynecastle the dressing room was like a morgue. The young players' heads were down and something had to be done to lift their spirits. Willie used to arrive a good half-hour before training began and used to sneak off for a cup of tea and a quick fag. Alex McDonald and Sandy Jardine came up with the idea of creating the tearoom just for Willie – but it was a decision made with ulterior motives. Willie was aware of these motives, and encouraged the young players to turn up early for training and have a cup of tea. The rookies slowly began to drift in, partake of a cup of tea, and listen to Willie's experiences. The other old heads, like Jimmy Bone and Willie Pettigrew, also came along and added their experiences to the conversation. Before long, harmony and belief returned to Tynecastle.

Hearts steadily moved up the table. Willie was playing from the start in most games. He entertained the fans while still being creative. A young John Robertson did the rest and rattled in the goals. In the centre of the park, the youngsters Gary Mackay and Davie Bowman were starting to shine, helped by their manager, the ageing Alex McDonald. In defence the callow but classy Craig Levein was making his mark under the guidance of veteran Sandy Jardine. All was going well.

Then along came the Scottish Cup. Hearts had been held to a 1-1 draw away from home in the third round against Queen of the South. Willie had come in for some heavy treatment from the opposition in the first match – but it could not compare to the GBH that would come his way during the replay at Tynecastle. The date was 2 February 1983. Hearts would eventually win the match 1-0, but Willie would see red before the final whistle. He had been on the receiving end of a number of harsh tackles – off the park many of them would have been classed as assault. Eventually he snapped and retaliated. The referee called Willie over, Willie pleaded his innocence. The ref shook his head. Willie knew that a sending-off could easily end his career.

"Name?" asked the referee, producing his little black book.

"You can't send me off," pleaded a distressed Willie.

"Name?" the ref repeated.

"It's not me that should be going in the book. What about those dirty bastards?"

"Name?"

"You know my name," replied Willie.

"Name!" screamed the ref.

"Roy Rogers!" Willie roared back.

"Well, you'd better whistle on Trigger – because you're off!" came the ref's reply. Another early walk down the tunnel came Willie's way and he would be out for the next round.

Willie: Time has eroded my memory of the sending-off I received at Queen of the South, but you could bet your boots it would be following a bad tackle on me and that I did my usual by retaliating. At this late stage in my career referees were well aware of Willie Johnston's disciplinary record and I'm almost certain some of them put my name in the book even before kick-off.

Hearts moved into the last eight with a 2-1 victory over East Fife without the presence of Willie. The quarter-final draw saw them paired with Celtic away from home. Celtic Park had always been a happy hunting ground for Willie and it was a match he didn't want to miss – and he didn't miss it. Well, at least not all of it. Playing against Celtic is always tough for any club and this was a big ask for Hearts. Celtic were in the hunt to win the Premier League, while Hearts were fighting for promotion from the First Division. The match was an intense affair and the tension grew when the Hearts full-back Peter Shields was carried off with a broken ankle following an horrendous tackle. The final result didn't fall in favour of Hearts, they were well beaten 4-1. However, there was an incident during the game that would cause a lot of controversy – and naturally Willie was right in the middle of it. The incident was to take place just prior to half-time. Willie set up to take a long throw-in, only to find a Celtic player, Davie Provan, blocking his path only a yard from the touchline. Willie hesitated with the throw and had a word with Provan.

"Get out of the way, you arse. Don't you remember what happened the last time you did this?" shouted Willie.

Willie was referring to a similar incident when he was playing for Rangers against Celtic. Provan had been standing in the same position as

Willie was about to take a long throw. On that occasion all eyes were on Willie and Provan, and no one saw Alex Miller move into an open position to receive the ball. Willie took a run and threw a long ball to the feet of Miller, who duly hammered it into the roof of the Celtic net. Yet despite the reminder of his previous failings Provan would not move. Willie shook his head, took the run up and sent a long ball up the park. His momentum carried him on to the park and his hand, following through the natural arc of taking a throw, struck Provan gently on the side of the head. Provan's reaction was unbelievable. He hit the deck like a ton of bricks, and rolled around the ground as if a bullet from a Kalashnikov assault rifle had hit him.

Willie: The Provan incident has always needled me. I was about to take a long throw and he stood so close to me I could almost feel his breath. I told him to back off, but he wouldn't listen. I took the throw and during the follow-through one of my hands gently brushed the side of his head – and I mean gently! He went down as if he had been hit by Rocky Marciano. I was sent off. Davie Provan should have been ashamed of himself that day. He intentionally set out to have a fellow professional dismissed from the game, and in my book that makes him a cheat.

The referee, Brian McGinlay, had clearly not seen the incident, although he was standing only yards away, for he elected to run 50 yards to the linesman. A conversation took place between the two officials before McGinlay trotted back to Willie. McGinlay produced a red card and informed Willie that he was being sent off for head-butting Provan and kneeing him in the groin. Willie went ballistic and had to be restrained by several of his team-mates, before leaving the action. The Celtic manager, Billy McNeill, followed Willie into the tunnel and shouted at him. What Willie describes as a confrontation took place between the two. The police were called, all was calmed and Willie continued on his way for an early bath.

As Willie lay in the bath his mind was in turmoil. He had now been sent off 20 times in his career, and he was certain of the consequences that would follow. Thirty years previously, Rangers and Scotland centre-half Willie Woodburn had been suspended *sine die* after being sent off four times. Willie had now surpassed that five-fold and knew that the end of his long career could come sooner rather than later. Willie left the ground and avoided all the press before travelling back to Fife. He and his wife Margaret were now doing an occasional stint behind the bar in the Port Brae in

Kirkcaldy. They had become friendly with Mr and Mrs Wood, who were running the establishment for the brewers, and serving behind the bar was an ideal way of learning the trade, one which Willie intended to move into when his football days were over. Perhaps he should start learning faster.

The sports columns that Sunday morning were full of the Provan incident. Some supported Willie, but the majority were calling for his head. Argentina was mentioned in virtually every article. Willie was distraught. On Monday morning there was no let-up from the press and Willie was at least thankful that Hearts had issued a statement in his support. The Hearts chairman, Wallace Mercer, had launched his own investigation into the incident. He had spoken to Willie and other Hearts players over the weekend which resulted in the following statement being released to the press:

> "There is no way one of my players is going to be pilloried on such flimsy evidence. Willie Johnston is a victim of his own reputation and we are not going to stand by and do nothing if his career in the game is put at risk over this incident. The player has assured me and the manager that he did not head-butt or knee the Celtic player in the groin. The referee did not see the incident and Johnston was given the ultimate penalty on the word of a linesman who was about 50 yards away. If Willie was to face further punishment we would have to look at taking this case through the law courts."

The incident was now the talk of bars and clubs up and down the country. Football fans were split on their views on the incident. Some wanted Willie banned from the game, others thought that Davie Provan should join the Royal Academy of Dramatic Art, while the majority sat on the fence.

Then came a little twist in the tale. Two policemen, who had been on duty at Celtic Park that day, came forward and made statements to the media. They claimed that they were both only a few feet from the incident and had witnessed the whole affair. Willie Johnston had neither butted nor put his knee into the groin of Davie Provan, and both were willing to make statements to that effect to the SFA.

As Willie travelled to Park Gardens to face the disciplinary committee he was well aware that the words of the two policemen would play no part in the proceedings. The only statements that would be considered were those of the two officials, the linesman and the referee. Willie was far from naïve; he knew the SFA had no love for him. When he was at West Brom they had tried their best to convince the Scotland manager not to include him in any international squad. They had treated him like a criminal following the affair in Argentina. Now they had the opportunity to finish him off – and he felt certain they would do so.

Sandy Jardine accompanied Willie to the hearing and had done his best to calm him down. As it turned out there was little need for concern, as Willie received a three-match ban and that was the end of the matter. Willie was relieved to say the least – but still, a three-match ban for something you didn't do was harsh. Willie could sleep at night over the incident, but he would often wonder if Davie Provan could do the same. Willie was convinced that if Provan had gone to acting school he could have become a huge Hollywood star. Perhaps even as big a star as Homer Simpson, but maybe not as smart. The sending-off had been his 20th in his career and it would be his last. Yet it would not be his last time in front of the disciplinary committee – he had one more visit to go.

Following his ban Willie returned to play against Clyde in March 1983. Hearts won the game comfortably 3-1, with Willie providing assists for two of the goals. The following week he scored twice against his home-town club Raith Rovers, but unfortunately Hearts lost the game 4-2. In the final League outing Willie scored the goal that ensured victory against Hamilton. That strike saw Hearts finish in second place and gave them promotion to the Premier League. There was life in the old dog yet.

For season 1983/84 the Hearts management team had only one objective in mind – to remain in the Premier League. Willie spent less time playing from the start during this campaign and found himself in the role of Hearts super-sub. And a truly super substitute he turned out be. In September he came on against Hearts' greatest rivals, Hibernian, when the Jambos were 1-2 down, and created the two goals which saw Hearts walk off the pitch at full-time as 3-2 victors. He then came on as sub against Rangers at Ibrox and played a crucial part in a 0-3 victory. In an important game against St Mirren, Willie came off the bench when the Hearts were 1-0 down and scored to secure a much-needed point. The "young guns" and the "old heads" were performing beyond their management's expectations. Not only were they going to retain their status in the Premier League, they were fighting for a European spot.

Wallace Mercer, the Hearts chairman, wanted that European place so much that he introduced a new bonus scheme to encourage the players. The scheme was simple – the bonus would be £200 per man following a win. If they won the next game the bonus would double to £400 for that game, then £800 for the next and so on until the end of each month, when the players would be paid and the scheme would start over again. One day as the players travelled to an away game against Dundee, the chairman asked Willie to join him at the front of the bus. Hearts had won their last three games and Mercer said: "Listen, Willie, about this game against Dundee ..."

"Don't worry about it, we'll win easy," Willie interrupted.

"That's the point. If you win I can't pay out the bonuses next week," admitted Mercer.

Hearts gave Dundee a lesson in football that day and ran out easy winners. The players had to wait two weeks for their bonus and Mercer scrapped the scheme.

The good form continued and that European spot was within their grasp. It was the 37-year-old Johnston who made certain of it. The match was against Celtic. Hearts needed a draw to claim the European slot. With Hearts 1-0 down Willie was brought into the fray and scored an excellent equaliser from all of 30 yards to give Hearts the result they so much craved. The Jambos were back in Europe for the first time in a number of years.

During the close season Willie found himself working more and more behind the bar of the Port Brae – and he turned up equally as often on the customers' side. He knew his playing career was all but over; the following season would be his swansong.

Hearts' season did not get off to a good start and they lost their first two League games. A combination of the management team and the old heads in the squad steadied the ship and they won the next four games on the trot, three in the League Cup and one in the League. Willie played in all four and added another goal to his tally, though Hearts suffered another League defeat the week prior to facing their European opponents Paris St Germain. The first leg of that tie was played in France. Willie recalls that prior to the game, Sandy Jardine gave the longest team talk he had ever heard in his career. In fact, it was so long that Willie fell asleep during it.

He was on the bench that night and could only watch as the game proved too much for the Hearts youngsters. Willie was brought on, but by then it was already too late. Hearts were 4-0 down and that was still the score at the final whistle. In the second leg at Tynecastle Willie played from the start as Hearts regained some of their pride with a respectable 2-2 draw. The European dream had been short and sweet.

On the home front Hearts had once more reached the semi-final of the League Cup only to falter at the hands of Dundee United. The League campaign was a case of swings and roundabouts – a victory here, a defeat there and an occasional draw. Only a month before his 38th birthday Willie scored his last goal for Hearts. It came against Celtic – which made it even better – although unfortunately Hearts lost the game 1-5, which took the edge off his achievement.

Back at the Port Brae, circumstances had changed. Unfortunately Mr Wood had died and Mrs Wood had no desire to continue running the bar. Willie discussed the situation with his wife, Margaret, and they both agreed that they should apply to the brewers for the tenancy. However, nothing was guaranteed. Another Kirkcaldy couple, George and Betty Pratt, also wanted the bar and they had years of experience in the trade. Willie had a word with Wallace Mercer regarding the situation. Wallace owned bars and nightclubs and was well known in the licensed trade. Mercer was very helpful and assured Willie that he had nothing to worry about. "I'll have a word in the right ear and the bar will be yours," he said.

It was around this time that Willie was pulled up in front of the SFA disciplinary committee for the last time. On this occasion it had nothing to do with his actions on the football park. Willie had released a book on his career to date. Part of the book referred to the Davie Provan incident, and that excerpt had appeared in a newspaper. The SFA were far from happy. Willie travelled through to Park Gardens and sat in front of the disciplinary committee, one of whom – Willie cannot remember his name – tore into the Hearts man as soon as he had sat down.

"You're an absolute disgrace to Scottish football!"

Willie was not slow in responding: "Who the hell are you – and what have you ever done for Scottish football?"

SFA chairman Ernie Walker intervened: "Calm down, Willie."

"Calm down? I'm here to talk about a book, not my career as a footballer, and certainly not to listen to some big shot from a two-bit club who has done nothing for the game!"

"Okay, Willie. Then let's talk about the newspaper article," said Walker. "Did you get paid for it?"

"Yes," replied Willie.

Walker looked from Willie towards his colleagues and then back to Willie. "Could you leave the room for a few minutes while we discuss the matter," he said.

Willie was more than happy to vacate.

Less than a minute later they called him back into the room. Willie was informed that he had been fined £200 for bringing the game into disrepute. He rose and leaned on Walker's desk. "I suppose you'll all be going to lunch now?" he asked.

"Yes," replied Walker.

"Well, obviously the wine's on me ... you arseholes,' said Willie before turning and leaving the room. As he walked down the steps at Park Gardens for the very last time he couldn't prevent a cheeky grin from crossing his face – and why not? He had received £1,000 for the article.

Willie: It would be fair to say that the SFA disciplinary committee were not my favourite group of men. At that time they were an amateurish bunch that were making big decisions in a professional sport. Most (if not all) never played the game at top level and to give them such responsibility was folly.

A few days later Margaret and Willie were asked to attend an interview at the brewery along with George and Betty Pratt. What George and Betty didn't know was that Wallace Mercer had indeed done as he'd promised. George and Betty were only there to make up the numbers. The decision had already been made and the pub would be Willie's.

Back at Tynecastle Hearts' season continued to stutter along. A European place was not be achieved that season, but they did enough to comfortably ensure their place in the Premier Division. In January 1985 they were invited to take part in a competition that was still in its infancy – the Tennent's Sixes. The competition was played indoors with a maximum of six players from either team on the park at the same time. Each team would register a maximum of 12 players to form their squad. Tennent Caledonian Brewers sponsored the competition, which was run by the SFA. Willie had been chosen as one of the Hearts squad. This was the second year of the competition, Rangers being the first club to win it. Hearts progressed through to the semi-finals and at this point Willie had only one thing on his mind. He wanted to finish his career on a high, he wanted to win one last trophy. In the final they met Greenock Morton and Willie scored a cracker of a goal in a 4-1 victory. It was time to celebrate.

The players went back to Tynecastle with the trophy, the boardroom was opened up, and the drink began to flow. Willie missed his last train back to Fife and went out on the town with the youngsters. They visited pubs and nightclubs before eventually agreeing to go back to John Robertson's flat. It was two o'clock in the morning and there were five of them left: Willie, John Robertson, Gary Mackay, George Cowie and Kenny Black. Willie made the taxi stop at an all-night bakery and he bought a dozen fresh rolls. John Robertson assured him that there was plenty of food in his fridge to fill the rolls. When they arrived at the flat the youthful quartet sat down in front of the television to watch a recording of the Tennent's Sixes, while

Willie was to be mum and make up the rolls. He opened the fridge to find it was almost bare except for the smallest tin of luncheon meat he had ever seen. As Willie struggled to open the midget tin, John Robertson's cat entered the kitchen, glanced at Willie and left. The boys were in their element, watching themselves on the TV, but eventually hunger got the better of Kenny Black.

"Bud, where's these f***in' rolls?" he shouted.

"They're coming," Willie shouted back. But Willie had a problem, the luncheon meat would barely cover two rolls. He tried to cut it thinner.

"F***'s sake hurry up, Bud!" screamed Kenny.

Willie's short fuse came into play. He bent down, picked up the cat's dish and spread cat food over four rolls and took them through to the living room. Willie returned to the kitchen and enjoyed his two rolls with luncheon meat.

"These rolls were great, Bud. Any chance of another?" called Black.

Willie duly obliged and spread another four rolls with *Whiskas*, which the youngsters swallowed with enthusiasm. A few days later at training Willie told them the story of the *Whiskas*. None of them ever believed him, but the cat knew the truth.

Several days on, Willie received the official news that the Port Brae Bar was now his and his decision was instant – he would play a few more games and then retire. His final appearance came on 20 February 1985, when he was 38 years old. The opposition were Brechin at Tynecastle in the Scottish Cup. It was a game of little note and hardly worthy of seeing a legend's career come to an end.

Now Willie would take up residence in the Port Brae bar. There would be no more football. The fat lady had sung.

34

THE LANG TOUN

K irkcaldy is the largest town in the Kingdom of Fife, with nearly 49,000
living within its boundaries. The town is known as the Lang Toun, the
name being derived from the original settlement, which was a thin strip
parallel to the sea-front. It lies on the north shore of the Firth of Forth
looking towards Edinburgh. In the 18th and 19th centuries its port
developed extensively and supported a large fishing fleet. Sadly, today the
harbour is all but derelict and the fishing fleet is no more. In the 19th and
20th centuries Kirkcaldy became famous for linoleum manufacturing. Both
Willie and I can remember the days when, if travelling to the town by train,
you could smell Kirkcaldy (the horrible odour of linoleum) well before you
reached the outskirts.

The sea-front is also home to Europe's longest street fair, known
locally as the Links Market. The fair celebrated its 700th anniversary in
2004 and the town boasts of having been home to famous people such
as: Adam Smith, the famous philosopher and political economist who
wrote such books as *The Theory of Modern Settlements* and *The Wealth of
Nations*; Sanford Fleming, a famous engineer and inventor, who
introduced Universal Standard Time to the world and the Threepenny
Beaver, Canada's first postage stamp; missionary John Philip, who
travelled to South Africa in 1818 and fought for the indigenous and
coloured people's rights. In addition, David Steel, the former leader of
the Liberal party and Gordon Brown, the current Prime Minister, both
hail from Kirkcaldy.

In 1985 the town adopted Willie Johnston as one of its famous sons.
The Port Brae is situated near the town's waterfront and directly opposite
the old harbour. When Willie and Margaret took over the pub it was very

much a male-orientated establishment and because of Willie's footballing background it would remain so. Certainly, the main topic of discussion would mainly revolve around football. In the first few weeks Willie dedicated himself to learning more about the bar trade (today, in 2008, there are a few customers who still believe he'll never make a barman). Then came a phone call from Hong Kong. Willie's former Glasgow Rangers colleague Alex Miller was manager of Hong Kong Rangers and wanted Willie to join him for a few months to help in the development of the team. Football was still very much in Willie's blood, so he packed a bag and caught a flight to the Orient, leaving Margaret to run the bar.

He assisted Alex in the coaching of the Hong Kong players and even played two games for the club before the monsoons came. Willie found the monsoons quite frightening, a far cry from a wet and windy day back in Scotland. Eventually, he decided: "To hell with this" and returned to the relative safety of Kirkcaldy.

A few weeks later Willie was working behind the bar when Davie Clarke, the manager of East Fife, whose home ground is only a matter of five miles from Kirkcaldy, walked through the door. He wanted Willie to join his struggling First Division side but Willie was reluctant to do so. They had a few drinks together and Davie continued to persuade Willie to join the club. "Look Willie, why not come along and help us out?" said Davie. "We need all the help we can get to avoid relegation."

Eventually Willie agreed and played in three games. With his assistance East Fife successfully avoided the drop, finishing tenth. Willie was 39 years old.

Two seasons later, when Davie Clarke was manager of Falkirk, again he contacted Willie. This time he wanted him to help with coaching the reserve team. Again Willie agreed. He stayed almost a season training and coaching the youngsters, a role he enjoyed immensely. Willie recalls returning to Ibrox, where the Falkirk reserve team were to play Rangers reserves. Davie Clarke also travelled, to run his eye over his most promising youngsters. The Rangers team that night was a who's who of first-teamers, most of whom were returning from injury. In the dressing room prior to the game Davie knew he was struggling to put out a team of 11 fully fit players. He glanced at Willie. Willie shook his head and said: "Oh no … I'm not going out there!"

But again Clarke was persuasive and Willie put on a Falkirk strip for the first and only time. It was March 1988, Willie was 42 years old and perhaps it was fitting that he would play his last ever game on the ground where his career began all those years ago.

After the match Willie was lying in the bath, a cigarette clenched between his teeth, when his old Rangers boss Willie Waddell entered. "Willie, you played well tonight," he said. "I'll offer you the same terms as I did in 1973."

They laughed about it and parted on better terms than they had so many years earlier. At this point Willie turned full-time behind the bar at the Port Brae.

In 1992 Willie and Margaret purchased the pub from the brewery and set about turning it into a successful little bar. Throughout the years many famous footballers have visited and enjoyed a night with Willie and his fo)tball-daft clientele. Football fans from all over Scotland, from Birmingham and even from Vancouver have made the pilgrimage (and still do) to the Port Brae just to meet with Willie Johnston. Such is the legend of t ie man.

> Willie: I always saw myself running a bar when my retirement from the game came along and time in the Port Brae seems to have passed so quickly. The bar is very much a football establishment and I always set out to make all fans welcome in the pub irrespective of which team they support. From behind the bar (as with my football career) I have met a lot of nice people. Many of them have been regulars for a great number of years and I'd like to take this opportunity to thank them for their loyal custom; it has been greatly appreciated.

Now, in 2008, the bar is under the ownership of his son Dean and his daughter-in-law Melanie. Willie can still be found serving for a few hours most days of the week or standing in his favourite spot at the end of the bar. Invariably the conversation is football. When not discussing football he can be found playing cribbage (in which his counting of points is suspect and often called into question) or pool (in which his ability bears no comparison to his football) for his usual stake of a half-pint of lager. Willie also plays for the Port Brae 'B' team in the local quiz league. Each team can play a maximum of four players from six during a match, with substitutes allowed on at half-time. Willie, more often than not, makes his appearance from the bench and regularly throws his team into confusion by supplying three or four answers to the same question.

One evening when we were having a social drink at the bar, I asked Willie to select a team of Xl players whom he would rate as the best he has ever played with. This proved to be more difficult than I'd first imagined and took a great deal of time as players were crossed off (not unlike his quiz answers) and replaced by others. The final Xl: (In brackets- where they played together)

Bruce Grobbelaar
(Vancouver Whitecaps)

Sandy Jardine   John Greig   Ronnie McKinnon   Eric Caldow
(Rangers/Hearts)   *(Rangers)*   *(Rangers)*   *(Rangers)*

George Best   Bryan Robson   Jim Baxter   Charlie Cooke
(Benefit match)   *(West Brom)*   *(Rangers)*   *(Scotland)*

Colin Stein   Denis Law
(Rangers)   *(Scotland)*

Subs: Alan Rough (Scotland), Danny McGrain (Scotland), Kenny Dalglish (Scotland), Tony Brown (West Brom) and Willie Henderson (Rangers) .

Willie believed that this team, under the guidance of Sir Alex Ferguson, could take on the world. He then smiled at me and said: "I can't pick a team without picking another one that would be full of rascals!"

Willie's team of rascals (some of which he never played alongside, but has certainly played against):

Alan Rough
(Scotland)

Tommy Gemmell   Kenny Burns   Mick Martin   Derek Statham
(Celtic)   *(Scotland)*   *(West Brom)*   *(West Brom)*

Jimmy Johnstone   Stan Bowles   Jim Baxter   George Best
(Scotland)   *(QPR)*   *(Rangers)*   *(Man Utd)*

Maurice Johnston   Frank McAvennie
(Celtic)   *(Celtic)*

Subs: Alfie Conn (Rangers), Duncan McKenzie (Everton), Tommy Hutchison (Coventry), John Osborne (West Brom) and Asa Hartford (West Brom).

Coach – Tommy Docherty.

Social Conveners: Himself and Len Cantello (West Brom).
Kit man: Peter Marinello (Arsenal).
Coach driver: Andy Gray (Aston Villa).
Dieticians: Joe Harper (Scotland) and Alan Rough (also the goalkeeper).

This team could also take on the world but would probably drink the planet dry first.

As we approached the end of work on this book we discussed any regrets that Willie may have had in his long career. Only two came to his mind – Argentina, and the incident with John McMaster during the Rangers v Aberdeen game in 1980. The rest of his career he would not change in the slightest. Football has been good to him. He's met a lot of nice people and made some excellent friends. He is left with myriad wonderful memories. However, even today he still has anger in his heart towards the SFA and certain factions within the media. His anger, in both cases, concerns the events of Argentina in 1978. The treatment he received from the SFA prior, during and after being sent home from the World Cup was despicable – and for that, he will never forgive them. Equally, he can offer no forgiveness to the media. He feels they should be completely ashamed of how they reported those events to the public in a cynical attempt to destroy his career. Meanwhile they hounded his wife and family relentlessly and turned their lives into a nightmare.

Willie: The gutter press of my time (is it any different now?) were beyond a shadow of a doubt the lowest of the low. They would twist an ordinary story and make it sensational. Where they couldn't find a story they would make it up. They have the power to destroy people's lives and, following Argentina, they certainly tried that with me. Yet there were reporters among them who did have a sense of decency and would report things as they really were. Three such reporters spring to mind: Kenny Gallacher, Roger Baillie and Dougie Baillie. The majority of the rest deserve to be where they really belong – in the gutter!

Since his retirement from the game, the media still can't bring up the name of Willie Johnston without referring to the failed drugs test of 1978. Willie recalls an incident in 1988 when he received a call from a reporter with the *Scottish Sun*. The subject – the Olympics and, in particular, Ben Johnson, recently exposed as a drugs cheat. Johnson had beaten Carl Lewis in the 100m final in Seoul and had subsequently been stripped of the title after failing a test. Willie was well aware of this and asked the reporter: "And what do you want from me?"

The reporter's answer resulted in a stunned silence from Willie that lasted a number of seconds.

"Is Ben a relation of yours?"

Eventually, when the power of speech returned, Willie replied: "Apart from the fact that my surname has the letter 'T' in it and his doesn't, there's the small matter of me being a white Scotsman from Fife and Ben Johnson being a black man, who was born in Jamaica!"

"I know all that," said the reporter. "But are you related?"

Willie: It is now 30 years since I was sent home from Argentina and I am well aware that I will never be free from the stigma surrounding the whole affair. Even to this day, if drugs hit the headlines in any form of sport the phone at the Port Brae is sure to get hot. The Ben Johnson story was utterly ridiculous. The reporter offered me money to quote on the affair. Then his questions started getting ludicrous: "Obviously Ben is related to you? Is he a cousin? When was the last time you had a family get-together?"

Even when I pointed out the subtle little differences between the two of us – our nationality, the different spelling of the surname, the slight difference in the colour of our skin – the reporter was still adamant there was a story to be found. I still shake my head and smile about the whole affair and the tale gets a fair few tellings in the Port Brae!

It is now 2008. Willie is 61 years old and is a happy and contented person. He has four grandchildren: Christopher and Alix from his daughter Stephanie and son-in-law Kevin; Matt and Ellie from his son Dean and daughter-in-law Melanie. Matt, at ten years of age, is already a keen footballer and showing promise.

Just as we reached the conclusion of writing this book in May 2008, Dean and Melanie became the proud parents of another son – Jay Johnston. What better place to end the tale. Young Jay, allegedly, retaliated when the midwife smacked his bottom – perhaps another legend has arrived?

35

MEMORIES OF FORMER PLAYING COLLEAGUES

LEN CANTELLO

(Len was a skilful and clever midfield player who joined West Brom in 1968 as a 17-year-old. He remained at the club until June 1979, when he was transferred to Bolton Wanderers).

I remember Willie's arrival at the club in 1973 when he was transferred from Glasgow Rangers. At the time I didn't know a great deal about him – although I was aware that he'd scored two goals in a European final. I recall that he hadn't played for a long while following a heavy suspension up in Scotland and it showed during training. After each training session we would do 20 laps of the pitch and Willie could never get his head around this. He hated it. Willie was an explosive flying machine and couldn't see the purpose of running 20 times round the pitch. He definitely didn't come in first on any of those excursions.

Willie was quite a character in the dressing room and everybody loved him. He was a good athlete and was so fast that it was scary. Once he settled at the club a ritual developed after training, between four of the fastest players at the club – Laurie Cunningham, Alistair Brown, Cyrille Regis and Willie. They would all go out with their spikes on and run a 100-yard dash. After 20 yards, when Willie was in front – and he was always in front – he would stop and declare himself the winner. The others would continue till the end. Willie's reason and theory for stopping was simple – you don't do a hundred-yard sprint in a football match, so what's the point?

I recall his first game for the club against Liverpool. Don Howe, our manager at the time, was giving his team-talk in the dressing room. He was hammering home to us that we should beware of their English international full-back, Phil Neal. He pointed out that Phil was a very clever and fast player, he would be a real danger when coming forward. Willie piped up: "Don't worry about him, Boss. He'll never be in our box – he'll be too bloody busy chasing me!"

Willie was right. Phil had a torrid time against him.

It would have to be said that Willie was a very nice guy and a great character, and perhaps the only people within the game who would say a bad word about him would be referees. Willie was undoubtedly one of the best Scottish wingers of all time, alongside Jimmy Johnstone and Willie Henderson.

Very few players from my time would be able to adapt to the modern game, but most certainly Willie would be one who could. His skill and pace would see him shine, and I would have no hesitation in putting him in the same category as the Manchester United pair of Giggs and Ronaldo.

ALEX SMITH

(A former midfielder who played with Dunfermline, Rangers and Aberdeen. He joined Rangers in 1966 for a record transfer fee of £55,000. Alex was a member of the 1967 team that played in the Cup Winners' Cup final, and in that season he finished as the club's top goal scorer, with 23 goals).

Willie was only a lad when I came to Ibrox, but even then his ability and speed were very much apparent to all at the club. When Willie broke into the first team, Rangers suddenly found themselves with two of the fastest wingers in the country – Henderson and Johnston. Yet we struggled to win trophies. I'm convinced much of the reason for this failure was the fact that myself and the other players coming through the middle of the park were much too slow to keep up with the two Willies.

As a youngster Willie was a modest, unassuming lad, qualities that he still has to this day. He has no airs and graces. I watched his career develop with great interest and am proud to say I had the privilege to have played alongside him. Willie was a great entertainer and a real top-class winger.

Willie remembers Alex as a classy player who could score goals for fun. He also recalls a story relating to Alex and his lack of speed. A sprint coach had arrived at Ibrox and his object was to make the players fitter and faster. On his first day he had said to Alex: "Don't worry, son. I'll take several seconds off your time over a 100-yard sprint."

According to Willie, Alex smiled at the coach and replied: "No you won't ... I'm the slowest thing on two legs!" Every training day the sprint coach would appear, put the lads through their paces and then time each one with a stopwatch. After four or five days he approached Alex and announced: "Today Alex I'm not going to use the stopwatch on you." The coach then pulled a calendar from his pocket and continued: "I'll time you with this!"

ALFIE CONN

(Alfie was the first post-war footballer to play for both Rangers and Celtic. He made his senior debut for Rangers in 1968 as a 16-year-old. He was part of the Rangers team that won the European Cup Winners' Cup in 1972. In 1974 he joined Tottenham Hotspur and became a huge favourite with their fans. They dubbed him 'The King of White Hart Lane.' Then in 1977 he crossed that famous Glasgow divide and joined Celtic. Alfie won two Scottish Caps and in 2007 was inducted into the Rangers Hall of Fame).

I was only a boy when I joined Rangers and Willie was already an established player in the first team. I used to travel through to Glasgow by train with all the Fife boys, including Bud. Off the park he was quiet and unassuming. He'd like a cup of tea and a fag ... but buying cigarettes was not his forte.

It was when I'd broken into the first team that it became evident to me just how good a player Willie was. As a midfielder, all you had to do was get the ball to him and he would create something out of nothing. He was absolutely superb.

I recall a European game where the manager had identified the weakness of our opponents as being their right-back. The instructions to the team were simple – get the ball to Bud at every opportunity. We did this for more than 65 minutes of the game; Willie kept destroying the full-back and created chance after chance for our strikers. On one occasion the attack broke down and the opposition counter-attacked. I won the ball in midfield and made the pass to Bud, who was still running back from their 18-yard box. Willie turned and blasted the ball into the stand, then turned and screamed at all his team-mates: "Give the ball to somebody else. I'm knackered!"

I have so many memories of Willie on the park that it's difficult to pick out one to highlight. Certainly I'll never forget the day when we played Celtic and he sat on the ball to take the tension out of the game. The match had been really physical, and was played at 100 miles an hour. Willie had been giving the Celtic defence a torrid time and decided to give them (and his colleagues) a breather by inviting anybody to come and get it. He was a showman.

Off the park Willie liked a beer or two. I remember an occasion when the two of us went for a drink following a game. I went up to the bar and bought two pints of lager and placed them on the table. Willie looked at the two pints, looked at me and said: "I can't drink a pint!"

I had to go back to the bar and buy him a half-pint. Twenty half-pints later the original pint was still sitting on the table. It always confused me that he couldn't drink a pint, but he could drink 20 half-pints.

Although Bud was relatively quiet off the park, he was completely different on it. As soon as he pulled on that jersey, be it for Rangers, West Brom or Hearts, his personality changed. He became as brave as a lion and at times turned into Hannibal Lecter – he could eat defenders for breakfast! Willie was greased lightning, could tackle, shoot with both feet and was great with his head. He also had fantastic vision and could read a game so well. If he were playing today defences would be unable to cope with him. He would be a revelation!

Bud was a true character of the game and I am proud to call him a great friend.

COLIN STEIN

(Colin became the first £100,000 transfer between Scottish clubs when he joined Rangers from Hibernian in 1968. He scored in the famous Cup Winners' Cup final of 1972, in which Willie contributed the other two goals. He played a total of 202 times for Rangers and was a prolific goal-scorer and a great favourite with the fans. In 1973 he was transferred to Coventry. Colin played 21 times for Scotland, scoring four goals on his debut against Cyprus).

I made my debut for Rangers against Arbroath, I rarely got a kick of the ball and Willie had scored two goals before half-time – I think he was trying to show me how it was done. The next game we played was a European tie. Again, Willie had scored two goals before half-time. In the second half I scored a hat-trick; it was my turn to show him. After the match I knew a partnership had been born. He was the perfect foil for me, drawing defenders away and creating lots of space for me to work in. He was a tremendous player. He was so fast it was unbelievable. I remember during training he would wear pit boots, even in the sprints. That was the only time I could beat him for speed – when he was wearing those damned pit Boots.

The Argentina affair aggrieves me. Willie was the complete player and had no reason to take a stimulant of any kind. I do not believe for one minute that the urine sample was Willie's. No one will convince me otherwise. On top of this, the SFA's handling of the affair was diabolical and they should be ashamed of themselves. They treated him like a piece of dirt and tried to destroy the career of one of Scotland's greatest players of all time. With a lesser man they would have succeeded, but Willie rose above it and continued to entertain fans throughout his long and illustrious career.

Since we retired from football Willie and I have travelled around the world together, attending functions and talking about our playing days. We have had great times together and our friendship has spanned 40 years – may it continue for another 40.

GARY MACKAY

(No one has made more appearances for Hearts than Gary Mackay. The midfielder wore the famous maroon shirt 640 times between 1980 and 1994, creating a record that is unlikely to be broken).

When Willie arrived at Hearts the club was going through a transitional period. A lot of young players were breaking into the team, including myself.

We were slightly in awe of him when he joined us. His name was synonymous with big clubs like Rangers and West Brom, and with international football. From his first day in the dressing room he quickly made us feel at ease. He was a normal down-to-earth guy who didn't think he was above us in any way, which sums up the humility of the man.

He was brilliant with all the young players and helped us strive to become the best we could be on the football park, while he continued with his own career. Sandy Jardine and Alex McDonald knew they had to turn the club around but they couldn't always be in the dressing room giving us their opinions and guiding us. This task was left to the older heads like Willie and Jimmy Bone, and they were good at it. Willie also instilled a level of pride amongst the younger players and he would always turn up for training wearing a collar and tie. He was the ultimate professional and played a huge part in us winning promotion back to the Premier Division in his first season.

I remember Willie's last day at the club. As I said, he always turned up wearing a collar and tie. In addition to this he would wear an expensive *Parka*, which was his pride and joy. That day after training, all the young players decided to wear an item of Willie's clothing in the bath – this was our way of saying goodbye to an exceptional player. Willie didn't object but he made it perfectly clear to us that "no bugger was to touch the *Parka*!" Willie travelled back to Fife that day dressed in a tracksuit and, naturally, sporting his *Parka*.

Willie didn't suffer fools gladly and if he became your friend you were a friend for life. I am proud to say that all these years later Willie Johnston is still my friend.

BOBBY LENARDUZZI

(Bobby Lenarduzzi, although born in Vancouver, began his professional career in 1970 as a 15 year-old at Reading. He would make 67 appearances for the club before being transferred to Vancouver Whitecaps in 1974. Lenarduzzi holds the record for the most games played in the NASL, with 312 appearances. He was capped on 42 occasions for Canada between 1973 and 1987. In 2001 Bobby was inducted as a player into the Canadian Soccer Hall of Fame. He is currently president of soccer operations for Vancouver Whitecaps).

Having played in England with Reading, I was familiar with the name of Willie Johnston. I had watched his exploits on TV when he was with Rangers and even more of them when he joined West Brom. I heard of his transfer to Vancouver and was really excited at the prospect of playing alongside such a high-profile footballer. When he arrived I was surprised that he didn't talk a lot – I soon realised this only applied off the football park. I was still a youngster when Willie made his debut for the Whitecaps and as we were both left-sided players (I played left-back) I would take instructions from him prior to every game. The instructions were invariably the same: "Pass the ball to me." The only one thing I knew for certain was that he would rarely pass it back.

Willie always seemed to be most comfortable when surrounded by the opposition's defenders and he would still shout: "Give it to me." I normally would, and at times it would look as though Willie was trapped in a pinball machine. Yet, somehow, he would consistently emerge with the ball. He was amazing. He had a knack for taking players on. In my career I never played against Willie – and thank God I didn't. He was a defender's nightmare. I remember a game against New York Cosmos when their Iranian defender, Eskandarian, tried to intimidate Willie – big mistake! He may be small but you don't mess with Willie Johnston. The two of them ended up rolling on the ground and Willie was far from being the loser. Eventually Pele, then the ambassador for the Cosmos, came on the park to calm matters and normality resumed … although minus Willie and a few others.

Yes, Willie was a character, a football genius, and an all-round good guy. With Willie what you see is what you get – it was my privilege to have played alongside such a talented footballer.

ASA HARTFORD

(Asa Hartford joined West Bromwich Albion in 1967 and made his debut the following season as a 16-year-old. Asa was a classy left-sided midfield player who made 214 appearances for the club, scoring 18 goals, before being sold in 1974 to Manchester City. He also had spells at Nottingham Forest, Everton, Fort Lauderdale (US), Norwich and Bolton Wanderers. He had stints in management with Stockport County, Shrewsbury and at Stoke City, where he was assistant to fellow Scot Joe Jordan. Hartford won 50 caps for Scotland (35 while at Manchester City) and scored four international goals).

When Willie arrived at the Hawthorns I was already an established player in the first team. Naturally, as a fellow Scot, I knew Willie's background and the calibre of player he was. However, on our first meeting I found him to be a quiet, almost nervous man – both these characteristics disappeared as soon as he went on the football park. He had a reputation at Rangers of being a classy free-scoring winger, but I think he went something like 39 games at West Brom before hitting the back of the net. When finally he did score it was worth waiting for. I think it was against Exeter in the League Cup and it was a goal in the same category as Archie Gemmill's in the 1978 World Cup.

Being a left-sided midfielder I would play directly alongside Willie and it wasn't long before a good partnership developed. At throw-ins Willie would ask me to throw the ball long, beyond him and his marker. They would both turn and give chase – a race that Willie would nearly always win comfortably. Defenders who got wise to this would stand well off him, so I would throw the ball short to Willie and he would turn and run at the defender and choose the right moment to sent it past him. The result was invariably the same – Willie would win. He was as quick as lightning. Willie was a smoker and I could never understand how someone could smoke and be so fast. He also had great ball control and vision, but pace was his real weapon. In the modern game there is nobody as fast as Willie was and he would be a sensation if he played today. I'm only glad I had the opportunity to play alongside such a skilful, talented player.

36

GLASGOW RANGERS FANS – MEMORIES OF WILLIE

I was fortunate enough to be at the Cup Winners' Cup final in Barcelona when we won the trophy. Bud scored two goals – but that apart, he was immense during the game and, indeed, throughout the campaign. Along with Jim Baxter he was one of the truly world-class players ever to wear a Rangers jersey. I feel privileged to have seen him at his best.

John Bremner, Glasgow

I have great memories of Wee Bud – he was quick, brave, comfortable with the ball on either foot, good in the air for a wee guy and he could score goals. In today's terms that would add up to a hefty transfer value. Add to that his love for the club and there's no doubt he is a Rangers great. I think John Greig has said he was the best young Scottish player of that era and that's some compliment.

Andy Kerr – Rangers fan in England

Having lived for a while in Fife I can actually understand what Bud says. He usually lets his football do the talking anyway. When I asked him what he would have been doing if he hadn't played football, Bud told me that he'd probably have been relieving roofs in Fife of excess lead. The metal dealer's loss was Rangers' gain as he delighted legions of Rangers fans with memories of great goals and outrageous skills.

Bud could have entered a greyhound race and won. He was that quick and as a winger he could score goals. He would be a £15 million player in today's terms. I remember Bud playing against Hibs and beating the same player four times before leaving him on his backside. I think he only did it because he spotted some money on the pitch – you know what Fifers are like.

He timed his runs into the box with precision, he got a yard on every defender he played against and he found space where none looked possible. For a wee guy he could out-jump defenders six inches taller than himself. I think Bud made 75 per cent of Colin Stein's goals – or 99 per cent as Bud would have you believe. When Bud got the ball you always knew he could make something happen and he very rarely disappointed. He sometimes got to the bath before the rest of the players, but it was all due his commitment to the cause.

We've had the pleasure of Bud's company in Dubai for a pro/celebrity golf tournament and it has to be said he was better footballer than a golfer! A true Rangers legend.

Norrie MacDonald – Rangers fan in Middle East

Willie Johnston was one of the fastest footballers I have ever seen. I can remember when he first came into the great Rangers team of the 1960s and he looked like he'd been part of the team for years. I loved to see Bud play at inside-left. For me that was his best position and if he was played there more often I am sure he would not have been sent off so many times.

He was a natural who could score with his head or either foot. He could out-jump most centre-halves, even though they were over six feet tall and good in the air. I remember thinking when he left Rangers the first time that we had lost a legend. It was great when John Greig brought him back to the club. I have also spoken to fans of West Brom, Vancouver Whitecaps and Hearts, and they all said the same – that he was a hero of theirs. That in itself speaks volumes.

I have been lucky enough to have travelled all over the world with Bud during my time here at Rangers. He is a really nice guy off the field and has some fascinating stories to tell about his time in football. I can't wait to read his book.

Jim Hannah – Fans Liaison Officer, Rangers FC

I saw Willie playing for Rangers during the 1970s and was in Barcelona for the European Cup Winners' Cup final. Wee Willie helped us lift the cup courtesy of two fine goals. Later I watched, and got to know him, when he played for the Vancouver Whitecaps. Just recently (in 2008) I spent time with him in Calgary for the NARSA convention. He was, as ever, the consummate diplomat, always with a ready smile and willing to talk to people. He remains a true gentleman and ambassador for Rangers Football Club.

David Fletcher – Rangers fan in Vancouver

I have many happy memories of Willie 'Bud' Johnston, none more so than the two goals scored in Barcelona (sadly I was not at the game). Then there was the pinpoint accuracy of his cross for big Derek Johnstone to score in the 1970/71 League Cup final against Celtic. That brought a much-needed and welcome trophy to Ibrox.

Willie, to me, was a football fan's dream, such was his pace, skill and scoring ability. You were always on your toes when he was in possession of the ball. There were other occasions when he would give the ref his opinion on matters which thereby led to a sending off. During my time as a Rangers fan I have been blessed to have seen entertainers such as Cooper, Gascoigne, Baxter and Laudrup. Willie Johnston deserves to be mentioned in the same sentence.

Richard Porter – Rangers fan in Northern Ireland

We first saw Willie Johnston in European games in the 1968/69 season against Newcastle United. He immediately became a favourite through his gallus* style of play. Cheekily taking the ball to an opponent and baiting him to tackle, Willie was off down the wing as soon as the defender lunged in, leaving the poor fellow in his wake. We remember seeing Willie sit on the ball a few times. No memory is more vivid than one from the 1970 League Cup final, when he was up against Lisbon Lion Jim Craig. It was late in the game and Rangers were 1-0 up. Jim came flying in, but such was the speed of Willie that he accelerated down the wing, leaving Craig very embarrassed. Willie also provided the cross for the 16-year-old Derek Johnstone to score the only goal that day.

Bud could play anywhere; up front, on the right, through the middle, but mainly on the left. No one could catch him and he's the only player we've ever seen who could run flat out to the byline and cross a ball with such precision. We saw him play his last game for Rangers (in his first stint) around 1972/73, when he was sent off against Partick Thistle. I (George Hughes) was a young boy at the time and I cried. Even I knew that Willie would have to leave Scotland. The SFA banned him for six weeks and his Rangers career was effectively over.

Willie and Colin Stein were our heroes. We don't think Stein would have scored half the amount of goals he did without Willie's service. Willie had the George Best looks with his long hair and equally brilliant skills. When he moved to West Brom he helped make Cyrille Regis a household name at club and international level.

*Scottish word meaning bold.

George Hughes and Dougie Chisholm – Rangers fans from Melbourne

37

WEST BROM FANS –
MEMORIES OF WILLIE

Willie was the type of player who could always do something special. However a game was going – good, bad or indifferent – there was *always* the chance that his love for providing entertainment could come to the fore. A dazzling run, a great goal, and the fans would be on their feet. A great run followed by a wayward cross into the Brummie Road End, and there'd be curses. But it would soon be forgotten because *that* was Wee Willie Johnston.

A cheeky rascal was Willie. Resembling a naughty schoolboy, who needed to be watched closely in case he bunked off lessons, he demonstrated his character when wearing a Baggies shirt. When he was seemingly out of the game, his marker would pay less and less attention to him, only to find suddenly that he had disappeared. "Where's he gone? Hell, he was there a minute ago, what have I done?"

The answer was simple! Willie had received a pass, decided it was time to spark the game into life, and left a trail of unbelieving opponents on their backsides. Then he'd either put the ball into the back of the net himself or lay on a pinpoint cross for Bomber Brown, Big Cyrille Regis or any other grateful Baggie to slot home .

Mission accomplished, he'd turn away with that trademark grin lighting up his face. Yes, he'd done it again. "Nice one Willie, Nice one Son, Nice one Willie, Let's have another one"!

Terry Wills, Birmingham

Willie was such a fantastic player – he would make my heart flutter with excitement and expectation every time he got the ball. He was a joy to behold. Oh, how I wish we had a player of his talent and pace at the Hawthorns today.

Dave Bristow, Birmingham

38

HEARTS FANS – MEMORIES OF WILLIE

I remember being at a game at Tyncastle standing/sitting in the covered Wheatfield Road stand. We were 0-2 down when Willie came on very late as substitute, I think it was versus Rangers. Fans were making to the exits, but as soon as Willie took up his position on the left wing I can clearly remember him facing the fans and pointing to his wrist, gesturing to the leaving fans that there was still time to get a result. He was correct because we scored two goals in the dying minutes and he was instrumental in both. I think this shows his fighting spirit and never-say-die attitude. He had a lot of setbacks in his career but he kept coming back. As this example shows he didn't give up easily.

Colin Laidlaw, Lytham St Annes

My most vivid memory of Willie was during a game at Ibrox. Hearts were comfortably leading Rangers and Willie sat on the ball and invited the Rangers defence to come and try to get it off him. He was a showman through and through.

John Hinchcliffe, Manchester Hearts Supporters Club

Willie was such a clever, inspiring player to watch, artful, cheeky and undoubtedly a rascal. It's such a pity that players of his calibre seem to have disappeared from the game, making football very much the loser because of it.

Bob Simmons, Edinburgh

39

WILLIE JOHNSTON CAREER STATISTICS

Rangers
1964 –1972 & 1980 – 1982
Willie played 393 times and scored 125 goals
Honours: Scottish Cup 1966, Scottish League Cup 1964 & 1971, European
Cup Winners' Cup 1972

West Bromwich Albion
December 1972 – March 1979
Willie played 261 times and scored 28 goals
Honours: Promotion to Division One 1976

Vancouver Whitecaps
Two spells, summer 1979 and summer 1980
Willie played 48 times and scored 5 goals
Honours: Soccer Bowl Champions 1979

Birmingham City
Willie played from October 1979 – February 1980 and made 15 appearances, scoring 1 goal.

Heart of Midlothian
September 1982 – February 1985
Willie played 94 times, scoring 12 goals

East Fife
April 1985
Willie played 3 games

Scotland
In his first period at Rangers Willie won 9 Scottish caps. While at West
Brom he played a further 13 times for his country, making 22 caps in all

1965
13 Oct   Poland, Hampden Park (lost 1-2)
24 Nov   Wales, Hampden Park (won 4-1)

1966
2 April   England, Hampden Park (lost 3-4)
11 May   Holland, Hampden Park (lost 0-3)

1967
22 Nov   Wales, Hampden Park (won 3-2)

1968
24 Feb   England, Hampden Park (drew 1-1)

1969
6 May   Northern Ireland, Hampden Park (drew 1-1)
                (as sub for Charlie Cooke)

1970
18 April   Northern Ireland, Windsor Park, Belfast (won 1-0)
11 Nov   Denmark, Hampden Park (won 1-0)

1977
27 Apr   Sweden, Hampden Park (won 3-1)
28 May   Wales, The Racecourse Ground, Wrexham (drew 0-0)
                (as sub for Bruce Rioch)
1 June   Northern Ireland, Hampden Park (won 3-0)
4 June   England, Wembley (won 2-1)

15 June	Chile, Santiago (won 4-2)
18 June	Argentina, Buenos Aires (drew 1-1).
	Willie sent off, but later rescinded
23 June	Brazil, Rio de Janeiro (lost 0-2)
7 Sep	East Germany, East Berlin (lost 0-1)
21 Sep	Czechoslovakia, Hampden Park (won 3-1)
12 Oct	Wales, Anfield (won 2-0)

1978

17 May	Wales, Hampden Park (drew 1-1)
20 May	England, Hampden Park (lost 0-1)
3 June	Peru, Cordoba (lost 1-3)